# The Containment of Soccer in Australia

Soccer has become the most popular organised team sport for Australian children. It far outstrips the popularity of the three other football codes that are played in Australia – rugby league, rugby union and Australian Rules football.

Yet the soccer participation phenomenon in Australia is matched neither by the media coverage of the game, nor by the academic interest in the game. With a few notable exceptions in academic sports history, the game of soccer remains understudied in comparison with the other football codes. And, apart from interest that is generated by World Cup campaigns, the media coverage of soccer is largely marginalised, and becomes most emphasised when reporting on aspects of 'hooligan' crowd behaviour. Issues associated with national identity and citizenship are far more likely to be raised around soccer than the three other football codes.

This book investigates some of the ways that soccer has been maintained as marginal to Australian identity, and why the sport remains vitally important to some marginalised groups within these communities.

This book was previously published as a special issue of *Soccer and Society.*

**Chris Hallinan** is Associate Professor with the Centre for Australian Indigenous Studies at Monash University in Melbourne, Australia. His research interests are within the politics of ethnic, racial and national identities, youth studies, and ethnographic research methods.

**John Hughson** is a Professor of Sport and Cultural Studies with the University of Central Lancashire. He was educated in Australia. His research interests are broadly within the social and historical study of culture with an emphasis on sport, particularly the connections between sport and other areas of culture including the arts.

I0084468

# The Containment of Soccer in Australia

## Fencing Off the World Game

Edited by Chris Hallinan and John Hughson

Routledge
Taylor & Francis Group

LONDON AND NEW YORK

First published 2010 by Routledge
2 Park Square, Milton Park, Abingdon, Oxfordshire OX14 4RN

Simultaneously published in the USA and Canada
by Routledge
711 Third Avenue, New York, NY 10017, USA

*Routledge is an imprint of the Taylor & Francis Group, an informa business*

First issued in paperback 2014

This book is a reproduction of *Soccer and Society*, vol. 10, issue 1. The Publisher
requests to those authors who may be citing this book to state, also, the bibliographical
details of the special issue on which the book was based

Typeset in Times New Roman by Value Chain, India

*British Library Cataloguing in Publication Data*
A catalogue record for this book is available from the British Library

ISBN 13: 978-1-138-88058-0 (pbk)
ISBN 13: 978-0-415-57562-1 (hbk)

# CONTENTS

Sport in the Global Society – Contemporary Perspectives

Series Editor: Boria Majumdar

# The Containment of Soccer in Australia
Fencing Off the World Game

# Sport in the Global Society – Contemporary Perspectives

Series Editor: Boria Majumdar

The social, cultural (including media) and political study of sport is an expanding area of scholarship and related research. While this area has been well served by the Sport in the Global Society Series, the surge in quality scholarship over the last few years has necessitated the creation of *Sport in the Global Society: Contemporary Perspectives*. The series will publish the work of leading scholars in fields as diverse as sociology, cultural studies, media studies, gender studies, cultural geography and history, political science and political economy. If the social and cultural study of sport is to receive the scholarly attention and readership it warrants, a cross-disciplinary series dedicated to taking sport beyond the narrow confines of physical education and sport science academic domains is necessary. Sport in the Global Society: Contemporary Perspectives will answer this need.

*Other Titles in the Series*

**Australian Sport**
Antipodean Waves of Change
*Edited by Kristine Toohey and Tracy Taylor*

**Australia's Asian Sporting Context**
1920s and 19330s
*Edited by Sean Brawley and Nick Guoth*

**'Critical Support' for Sport**
*Bruce Kidd*

**Disability in the Global Sport Arena**
A Sporting Chance
*Edited by Jill M. Clair*

**Diversity and Division – Race, Ethnicity and Sport in Australia**
*Edited by Christopher J. Hallinan*

**Documenting the Beijing Olympics**
*Edited by D. P. Martinez*

**Football in Brazil**
*Edited by Martin Curi*

**Forty Years of Sport and Social Change, 1968-2008**
"To Remember is to Resist"
*Edited by Russell Field and Bruce Kidd*

**Global Perspectives on Football in Africa**
Visualising the Game
*Edited by Susann Baller, Giorgio Miescher* and *Raffaele Poli*

**Global Sport Business**
Community Impacts of Commercial Sport
*Edited by Hans Westerbeek*

**Governance, Citizenship and the New European Football Championships**
The European Spectacle
*Edited by Wolfram Manzenreiter and Georg Spitaler*

**Reviewing UK Football Cultures**
Continuing with Gender Analyses
*Edited by Jayne Caudwell*

**South Africa and the Global Game**
Football, Apartheid and Beyond
*Edited by Peter Alegi* and *Chris Bolsmann*

**Sport – Race, Ethnicity and Identity**
Building Global Understanding
*Edited by Daryl Adair*

# Abstracts

*Getting a ticket to the world party: televising soccer in Australia*

DAVID ROWE AND CALLUM GILMOUR

Australia currently has the world's most restrictive legislation designed to protect sports content of national and cultural significance from subscription television exclusivity. Despite this powerful 'anti-siphoning' regime, association football (soccer) has been systematically removed from Australian free-to-air television screens through a combination of regulatory neglect and influence peddling; a lingering ethnocentric disdain for the sport; an increasingly under-funded public broadcasting sector, and the encroachment of a global media conglomerate promoting an internationally ascendant model of 'user-pays' audience aggregation. In addressing the position of televised soccer in Australia, we analyse the country's peculiar ensemble of social, cultural, political and economic influences that is retarding the long-term development of the sport within a highly competitive national 'landscape'. We argue that, for it to become a full player in the 'world game' and even in its 'own backyard', soccer in Australia requires proper representation within the still powerful sphere of free-to-air television.

*Soccer and the politics of identity for young Muslim refugee women in South Australia*

CATHERINE PALMER

This study explores the ways in which a group of young Muslim refugee women in Adelaide, South Australia, draw upon their experiences of playing in a soccer team as a way of establishing and embellishing a particular cultural identity that both affirms and challenges many of the traditions of Islam. Based primarily on qualitative interviews with the players, this study examines some of the ways in which they construct notions of self, sameness and difference as young Muslim women growing up in Australia's fifth largest capital city. The study is centrally concerned with the ways in which these young refugee women articulate their social identities through the traditions Islam and the resources of western popular culture. As is argued in the following pages, the soccer team provides a unique site through which to explore the politics of identity for young refugee women in contemporary Australia.

*Football barriers – Aboriginal under-representation and disconnection from the 'world game'*

JOHN MAYNARD

Indigenous Australians have had some great successes in Australian football and rugby. However, this success has not been mirrored in the 'world game', soccer. This study examines the reasons for such under-representation in Australia. The barriers to access to soccer were a combination of racist government policy which restricted the movement of Aboriginal people, and thus their opportunities to engage with a game that was not located near the isolated reserves in which they were held. The most successful Aboriginal players were fortunate that their circumstances placed them in close proximity to locales that were soccer strongholds. Moreover, the multicultural environment of post-Second World War Australian soccer provided these players a haven from the prejudice and racism of wider Australian society. The fact that soccer itself faced obstacles of acceptance in mainstream Australian sporting culture also impeded an Aboriginal presence. However, in recent years, several players have broken through to play in the national league and gain national representative honours.

### 'Holding their own': Australian football, British culture and globalization

STEPHEN WAGG AND TIM CRABBE

This study looks historically at the Australian presence in English football culture. In essence, it describes a transition from Aussie-footballer-as-rarity to the contemporary situation in which Australians line up as simply one unremarkable nationality among the many represented in British football's contingent of migrant workers. To illustrate this transition there is a discussion of the case study of Craig Johnston, who, by definition, was an extraordinary presence in the English First Division between 1978 and 1988. The study then analyses the representation of Australian football in the British sports press and of the British- (and Europe- ) based 'Socceroos' in the Australian media. These representations are considered alongside the testimony of Aaron Downes, who, at the time of writing, captains Chesterfield in the English Coca Cola Football League Two representing one of hundreds of non-elite migrant Australian football workers contracted to clubs across Europe.

### Sheilas, wogs and metrosexuals: masculinity, ethnicity and Australian soccer

JESSICA CARNIEL

This study utilizes metrosexuality and soccer as two important and interconnected texts to illuminate how new forms of consumption have altered understandings of ethnicity and masculinity. It argues that soccer's recent rise in popularity in Australia and the rise of the metrosexual are both related to new forms of postmodern consumerism that are significantly influenced by the shift from multiculturalism to cosmopolitanism. This argument is applied to the Australian context in order to explore the complex processes of the de-ethnicization of soccer in the 1990s and its lingering effects as Australia moves to become recognized as a major player on the world scene, both on and off the pitch.

### Soccer in the west: the world game in Australia's western periphery

PHILIP MOORE

This study examines aspects of the history of soccer (Association Football) in Perth, Western Australia. The game was introduced in the late nineteenth century but it did not become central in the local sporting calendar. The game was reborn with the arrival of the 'new Australians' after the Second World War yet it remained marginal. Soccer's place in Perth has often been represented as being due to the overwhelming ethnic involvement in the sport, as in other parts of Australia, but there is more to the story than such a reductionist explanation. Adopting a figurational approach this study examines established and outsider relations in the development of the game in Western Australian society. The account that emerges is of a complex organizational struggle over control of the sport. The focus on established and outsider relationships in a figurational context provides a useful way of accounting for this history.

### *You have the right to remain violent: power and resistance in the club*

BILY BOSEVSKI AND CHRIS HALLINAN

This study examines the aggressive commodification and corporatisation strategies experienced by a Macedonian-based club in the north-western suburbs of Melbourne. The administrative acquisition of the club by a quasi-corporate consortium colloquially referred to as the 'Silver Lining' emphasized an abated model of its cultural heritage in favour of a newly fashioned corporate identity. Further evidence obtained via fieldwork observations and interviews documents the evolution of the power relationship between the club's supporters and its administrators over a five-year period. We draw on Bhabha's construct of cultural identity and internal differentiation to analyse the expressive forms of social resistance appropriated by football (soccer) spectators/supporters as agency toward preservation of a particular socio-cultural identity.

### *Fan perspectives of change in the A-League*

DANIEL LOCK

Football in Australia has undergone pronounced changes since 2003. Significant changes to national league competition structure have been made in an attempt to separate the sport from its socio-historical links with expressive ethnicity. This study employs a qualitative methodology to analyse members of foundation ALeague club Sydney FC to examine two specific research interests. Firstly, the study examines the extent fans perceive the A-League to represent a change from the NSL. Secondly, in a league that appears to have shed ethnic linkages, how do individuals identify as fans with a specific A-League club?

### *'Fencing them in': the A-League, policing and the dilemma of public order*

IAN WARREN AND ROY HAY

The establishment of an elite national Australian soccer league has been accompanied by an unprecedented growth in popularity for the world game in several Australian cities. Such growth presents numerous challenges for public order maintenance, particularly in light of the widespread concern over the relationship between soccer, disasters in major closed venues and violence. After outlining the emerging issues, and the extant Australian research into the phenomena of policing and sports crowd disorder, this study offers a knowledgebased approach to foster informed, reflective and collaborative policing in elite and sub-elite soccer venues. Rather than advocating a fundamental shift in the current public order policing paradigm, we suggest drawing on elements of best practice that are currently adopted in other Australian sporting and public order settings and appropriate overseas experience to facilitate a better understanding of the dynamics of Australian soccer fandom. The result should be the promotion of safer yet exciting events at which interactive crowd management based on harm minimization principles are key features.

# The beautiful game in Howard's 'Brutopia': football, ethnicity and citizenship in Australia

Chris Hallinan[a] and John Hughson[b]

[a]School of Sport and Exercise Science and Centre for Ageing, Rehabilitation, Exercise and Sport, Victoria University; [b]Sport and Cultural Studies, and International Football Institute, University of Central Lancashire

Writing in the British newspaper *The Observer* in 2006, Kevin Mitchell commented on the centrality of sport to the Australian way of life: 'sport defines their culture … It is their proud, shouting declaration of statehood to a world that is literally and notionally far away'.[1] Whether or not Mitchell was peddling a well-worn stereotype of sport-mad Australia he was certainly correct in suggesting that sport has long been and continues to be a core symbol of Australian identity. National teams are often portrayed as the ultimate bearers of Australia's collective pride. Major sporting occasions such as the Olympic and Commonwealth Games and World Cups and championships provide occasion for the display of national unity and sometimes celebration.

Such was the case with the coming together of soccer players to represent Australia in the 2006 FIFA World Cup. Indeed, the World Cup provided soccer with occasion to slip its usual marking as 'other than Australian', i.e. the marking of soccer as being from elsewhere, as a foreign game, and for this reason existing on the margins of the Australian Anglophone sporting mainstream. Soccer's perceived un-Australianness reflects its post-war history of association with ethnic communities of non-English-speaking background. Relatedly, the familiar representation of soccer is one of fragmentation, even confrontation. In the latter regard it is not overstating the point to suggest that a *moral panic* has long existed whereby ethnic groups stand accused within media reportage of using the soccer terrace as a forum for violence, as the stock standard phrase goes, 'for the settling of age old ethnic grievances'.[2] Admittedly, crowd disturbances associated with tensions between certain ethnic groups have spasmodically occurred at soccer matches in Australia, but of greater interest to the cultural analyst is the readiness of the media to amplify such occurrences and routinely typify them as un-Australian.

In his paper 'The Battle of Ideas in Australian Politics,' published in late 2006, Kevin Rudd argued: 'For Howard and the political project for which he stands, there is a twist: *There is nothing to fear but the end of fear itself.*'[3] Rudd is now Prime Minister and Leader of the Labor Party at the national government level in Australia. Rudd's paper claimed that a hallmark of the preceding Prime Minister John Howard and his ousted Liberal (Conservative) government was the marking of events and activities as 'un-Australian' and the associated threats posed to national security by the intrusion of 'foreign' otherness. During his 11 years as Prime Minister, Howard was overt in his public support for the Australian men's cricket team and the Australian men's rugby team – teams that are representative of the most Anglocentric sports in Australia. He was quoted as saying the pinnacle of success is captaining the Australian (men's) cricket team.

Kevin Rudd appropriated the term 'Brutopia' to draw attention to the collective effect of a set of Howard government policies and practices that borrowed heavily from the exclusionary populist politics of the now discredited right-wing One Nation Party. The nationalism espoused by the earlier Australian governments of Keating, Hawke, Fraser and Whitlam resulted in characterizations of a contemporary multicultural society. Writing in the 1990s Graeme Turner contended:

> Australia will never again be a culturally homogenous nation. As multiculturalism moves into its third decade, we have a society which must accept that it is made up of radical and exciting differences – of culture, of heritage, of ethnicity. Nevertheless, it is a society which is bound together by what it shares: the multiple experiences of living in Australia.[4]

However, by the late 1990s Howard's brand of nationalism railed against a multicultural society based on pluralistic values. He argued for a return to a simplistic monocultural way of life steeped in nostalgic longing for the Anglo place that Australia supposedly once was. Soccer as an 'ethnic' sport cannot be at home in this imagined Australia. The marginalization of soccer, which had even continued in the Australian press and commercial television throughout the heyday of multiculturalism, became more pronounced during the Howard government's tenure. During this time 'non Anglo' soccer clubs were subject to sustained pressure to relinquish any 'foreign' allegiance, and when the national league was scrapped and replaced by the Hyundai A-League in 2005, teams tendering for inclusion in the new league were forbidden from having any so-called 'political' association. The interestingly named Hyundai A-League presented a symbolic return to the pre-1970s immigration policy of assimilation where people (or soccer clubs in this case) are expected to fit into a cultural grid. No allowance is made for the differences that others might bring to the cultural landscape – assimilation places the onus of compliance on the outsider coming in.

As indicated above, the mass media in Australia has long maintained disdain for 'ethnic' soccer clubs, at least at the premier competition level. Since the establishment of the first national league in 1977, media critics have called for the severing of linkages between ethnic communities and soccer teams – the 'de-ethnicizing' of soccer, is the term commonly used within Australian academe.[5] The demand has hinged on the presumption of two imperatives, one cultural, the other economic. The economic imperative holds quite simply that the domestic soccer competition cannot enjoy widespread popularity as long as the ethnic affiliations of clubs are maintained. The economic imperative is underpinned by a morally asserted cultural imperative that divesting the sport of foreign allegiances is the Australian thing to do. The ongoing agenda from the time of the 1970s to 'de-ethnicize' the national soccer league has rested on these twin imperatives.

Multiculturalism has only occasionally been mentioned within media discussion of soccer but it has undoubtedly remained, even when unspoken, at the core of debate. The most interesting evocations of multiculturalism tend to come from soccer fans, and from diametrically opposed viewpoints. Take, for example, these two letters sent to the *Australian and British Soccer Weekly* regarding the banning of so-called foreign flags from soccer stadiums. They typify the polarization over the 'de-ethnicizing' of soccer issue.

> Australia is no doubt a multicultural nation but I don't want to see Greek, Italian or Croatian flags at our games ... these should be substituted for icons or colours which appeal to the non traditional supporters.

> The clubs in Australia were established by ethnic groups with a lot of hard work and sheer determination, and for the ASF to ban ethnic flags is an insult. This is our way of expressing who we are and how far the game has gone in Australia. After all, isn't Australia a multicultural society?[6]

The former viewpoint sees multiculturalism as acceptable only through an assimilationist lens. It suggests that migrant Australians should conform to a singular expression of national identity and that allegiances contrary to being Australian have no *right* to be displayed in support of soccer teams, especially in a domestic league. The latter view suggests that the former view misconstrues the idea of multiculturalism. More importantly, it disputes the failure to give recognition to multiculturalism in practice. Those who derisively mark soccer as un-Australian, deny the special meanings that this marking gives to the game. In other words, soccer has developed historically within Australia as a genuinely multicultural practice, and, in this respect, is *uniquely* Australian.

When we first started writing on Australian soccer in the early 1990s, although this was some years subsequent to the historian Geoffrey's Blainey's well-publicized alarmism about multiculturalism being out of step with public sentiment, we thought we were on a secure intellectual terrain defending the retention of links between ethnic communities and soccer clubs via reference to multiculturalism. This view may have been naive at the time; it would certainly be so now. We are drawn to Peter Beilharz's observation that through the 1990s a dominant frame of discourse emerged with 'fear and loathing' of ethnic otherness at its core.[7] Soccer might appear to some removed from the Tampa Affair, the Border Protection Bill and the Cronulla Beach Riots on the scale of public alarm,[8] but we would argue that the unwillingness of Anglo-Australian sports fans to embrace domestic soccer over the years is a reflection of the widespread cultural xenophobia now at the surface of public debate. While previously bi-partisan political support for multiculturalism in policy helped to ensure some reasonable level of public debate, the former Howard government abandoned the decency of its predecessors in favour of what Beilharz refers to as a 'masterful politics of populism'. According to Beilharz:

> Populism works as a kind of ventriloquism, claiming often to represent ethnos as demos, to present the spirit of a people against their enemies or others. It is an invisible politics of representation, especially when its leaders ... claim to stand for their people and against a putative enemy of the people ... outsiders, radicals, others, are blamed for global disorder that washes over into the south land, and its insiders are the intimate enemy.[9]

The enemy within has never been more feared than at present as the Cronulla riots of December 2005 and the subsequent moral panic testify. Cronulla is located within the Sutherland Shire – a municipality which has among the lowest proportions of non-English-speaking-background residents in Australia. According to journalist Sharon Verghis:

> Live long enough in Sutherland Shire and you soon become familiar with the codes and rules, unwritten but understood, that govern the area's most famous attraction, Cronulla Beach. If you're a white local, it's your beach. If you're wog/Leb in any way 'ethnic', you go to nearby Brighton-le-Sands, or try your luck elsewhere.[10]

The outbreak of racialized violence at Cronulla specifically targeted young non-Anglo males. According to Poynting,[11] the violence was the inevitable outcome of a sustained campaign of vilification directed at the 'Middle Eastern/Muslim enemy' instigated by both the populist media outlets and the Howard government.

Although fear of Middle-Eastern background male youth is nothing new, the Cronulla Beach episode and its aftermath serve to highlight the threat of cultural others who seemingly refuse to integrate into the Australian way of life. Such has long been the case with soccer. The so-called rioting soccer supporter of, for example, Sydney Croatia, was a harbinger of the ethnic youth on the rampage through Sydney suburbs after the initial day of attacks on Cronulla beach and surrounds – for the xenophobe it is all part of the same tendency. And even without the occurrence of crowd disorder at soccer matches, the very existence of clubs whose supporters chant Croatia, Hellas, Serbia or some other national affiliation is perceived as a threat to Australian cultural unity.

The post-Cronulla panic emphasized where the foreign threat resides – in the suburbs. Specifically, in the case of Sydney, in the unsafe western suburbs – media reportage has left the impression that Bankstown is something of a headquarters for gangs of Middle Eastern youth. The reported confrontations between Serbian and Croatian youth supporters of rival soccer teams in early 2005 in and around Bossley Park and Edensor Park also highlighted the south-western suburbs of Sydney as dangerous places. The suburbs, in Australia as elsewhere, have long existed as a maligned place for cultural commentators, not so much in fear of violence but boredom. The reference to the 'emptiness and meaninglessness' of the suburbs has been echoed by critics of both left and right sympathies. However, while the term 'suburban sprawl' still denotes derision, the suburb is the preferred terrain of the populist politician. As Beilharz observes in regard to John Howard, 'the dominant narrative is the regional ideology of the old, rural Australia reconfigured and located now in between, in the suburbs'.[12] John Howard's desired suburban inhabitants were featured on the cover of the policy document *Future Directions* released during the first term of his Liberal party leadership in the late 1980s – an Anglo-looking nuclear family were shown standing in front of a white picket fence.[13] Howard would not permit the foreign threat from within to unsettle this image of quiet domesticity in the suburbs. He did not accept that there are any underlying and embedded problems, for example, racism. He thus interpreted the Cronulla riots as a 'law and order issue', not a result of racism. However, the former Prime Minister remained vigilant to the suburban infiltration of unacceptable displays of ethnic otherness. Accordingly, the burqa should not be worn because it is 'confronting' to the core set of values upon which social cohesion depends.[14] From this perspective, Australia can only afford one culture, yet multiculturalism has given the erroneous view that Australia is a 'federation of cultures'.

Howard's mono-culturalism was supported – and possibly upstaged – by his deputy party leader Peter Costello. Costello's speech to the Sydney Institute in February 2006, titled, 'Worth Promoting, Worth Defending: Australian Citizenship, What it Means and How to Nurture It', surely stands as the most explicit attack on multiculturalism by a senior politician since Al Grassby (former Immigration Minister in the Whitlam Labor Government) introduced the term to Australian politics in the 1970s. Costello believes that taking on Australian citizenship changes a person's identity to the extent that previous cultural attachments must be relinquished if they in any way hinder embracing the new country and 'what it stands for'. Costello nominates supporting the

Socceroos as an indication of good citizenship and cites a relevant example in connection to the 2006 World Cup campaign:

> I was reminded of this recently when watching the Socceroos play in the World Cup Qualifier against Uruguay. A television commentator was moving amongst the crowd that was lining up to come into the ground. He came across an elderly woman with a heavy accent. He asked her where she came from, and she replied, 'I come from Uruguay to Australia twenty years ago.' The reporter said, 'So you're barracking for Uruguay.' The woman was outraged. 'No!' she yelled back at him. 'I go for Australia!' and looked incensed that he would think otherwise. Whether she went on to say 'Australia is my country' I can't be sure but that is what she meant. If you loved Uruguay, wanted to speak Spanish, loved Uruguayan food, culture and political institutions you would not mark out Australia as the place to pursue these passions. The fact that you have moved to Australia says that there is something about Australia that you want to embrace that you do not find in your country of birth.[15]

Costello went on to lambaste politicians and those in the public arena who encourage maintenance of cultural allegiance to a former homeland. According to Costello, this form of encouragement facilitates an interpretation of multiculturalism that is 'confused, mushy, and misguided'. Soccer offers to the incomer a telling means of declaring the new and undivided cultural identity. For Costello it can be used as a test of national loyalty, much as cricket supporting was proposed as a test of loyalty to England by the former Conservative politician Norman Tebbit.

Yet, while such possibilities for the expression of Australianness arise with the improved standing of the Australian men's soccer team, the domestic national league presents a different situation altogether. As indicated, it is in relation to the national league that the contours of multiculturalism have been most contentiously debated over time. However, the supporters of an ethnically cleansed national league – and this would surely include the former Prime Minister and his party deputy – can take comfort in the relatively new Hyundai A-league. In 1992 the premier national league consisted of the following teams: Apia Leichhardt, Marconi Fairfield, Parramatta Melita, Sydney Croatia, Sydney Olympic, Heidleberg Alexandria, Melbourne Croatia, Preston Macedonia, South Melbourne Hellas, Brisbane United, Adelaide City Juventus, West Adelaide Hellas, Newcastle Breakers and Wollongong City. The Hyundai A-League is currently made up of the following teams: Adelaide United, Central Coast Mariners, Wellington (NZ) Phoenix, Sydney FC, Queensland Roar, Newcastle United Jets, Perth Glory and Melbourne Victory. After more than a decade of various attempts to restructure the national soccer league, always with an administrative view to severing the connection between competing teams and ethnic groups, the very idea of restructuring was abandoned for a scorched earth policy whereby the existing league was decommissioned and tenders called for admission by clubs to a new league, that which became the Hyundai A-League. Subsequently, the Hyundai A-League was established with a 'constitution' setting strict terms to which bidding consortiums needed to comply. Although ethnicity was not mentioned, competing clubs were forbidden from having a 'political' identity.[16] The old supporter base in ethnicity has thus been gutted from the new league, and team names signifying cultural identity have been replaced by nebulous sobriquets.

Nevertheless, the Hyundai A-League has undoubtedly been popular with many soccer fans and those commentators opposed to the former arrangements. Match attendance rates for early seasons have well exceeded those for previous national league competitions. Field-work conducted by the authors in Melbourne shows that some fans subscribe to the A-League promotion of a 'family friendly' match environment and welcome the removal of clubs associated with particular ethnic groups.[17] This association of a safe spectator environment with non-ethnic-based soccer support is worth probing. Is it really about a concern with exposure to physical violence or is the fear more routine and less alarmist, a fear of not wanting to be confronted in the sporting domain by cultural unfamiliarity?

At the core of Australian soccer's rejection has been its gritty cosmopolitanism. Remove the grit and we can perhaps accept ethnic diversity. A sanitized cosmopolitanism allows A-league teams to include players from a range of ethnic backgrounds, yet the same teams cannot be seen to represent the cultural difference residing in Australian suburbs. In the words of Paul Gilroy: 'we are all sealed up inside our frozen cultural habits, and there seems to be no workable precedent for adopting a more generous and creative view of how human beings might communicate or act in concert across ... ethnic ... divisions.[18]

The lived experience of multicultural relations in Australian soccer has undoubtedly been problematic, messy and uneasy, but as such has reflected the inevitable tensions of a cosmopolitan reality and served as a collectively created arena of cultural negotiation. Accordingly, we would argue, the erasure of the mark of un-Australian from soccer, so gleefully greeted by some, should be lamented by Australians concerned that cultural differences be played out naturally rather than quashed by political, commercial and administrative fiat.

It needs to be said that this is our view, a view that has influenced the title of this collection. However, we do not expect all contributors to the issue to subscribe to our view – Australian soccer as *Fenced Off* – and some will be less critical of the developments within Australian soccer than we are in this brief opening piece. The concern of the collection is with soccer in contemporary Australia at a time of significant political change and each of the essays offer some reflection as to where soccer might be headed as the first decade of the new millennium draws to a close. The essays raise new points of enquiry about the continuing importance of soccer to discussions of Australian national consciousness and cultural diversity and we hope they gain a readership not only within sport studies but across broader fields such as sociology, cultural studies and political science. We close with a very brief summary of each essay.

David Rowe and Callum Gilmour discuss how the television broadcasting regulations and policies have resulted in the continued marginalisation of soccer football. The exclusive rights held by the Foxtel network is beneficial to the co-owners including the Murdoch and the Packer families. The policy was developed by the Howard coalition government and fences in the viewing opportunities to cable television subscribers. Rowe and Gilmour claim that a substantial revision of broadcast policy is necessary to facilitate growth in the sport and to broaden audience access.

If the critical analysis of soccer and identity has been limited, then studies including female participation have been non existent. Catherine Palmer not only investigates the experiential reality of females in soccer but also enters the world of those girls whose families came to Australia as refugees. Further, these girls are Muslim and, as with Muslim Australians in general, have been the object of public demonisation at a political level and through the mass media.[19] Against this backdrop, Palmer analyses how these girls are able to negotiate their sense of identity through playing football.

Aboriginal Australians have long experienced a generalized exclusion from key arenas of Australian society. With the exception of a few examples, including Australian Rules football and Rugby League, the same holds for access and opportunity in sport. John Maynard traces the history of exclusion and discrimination in soccer but concludes optimistically with the view that the emergence of Aboriginal players such as Jade North provides reason to be optimistic about a substantial increase in Aboriginal players in future seasons.

Almost the entire Australian national men's team (known as the Socceroos) for the 2006 World Cup plied their trade in Europe. The most celebrated players, Cahill, Emerton, Kewell, Neil and Viduka, were key members of various English Premier League teams. England has long been a destination for ambitious Australian players. Steven Wagg and Tim Crabbe analyse the British response to matches between England and Australia, the English-based Socceroos, and draw upon a case analysis for player insight. They conclude that the potential of the sport in Australia to 'hold its own' is somewhat connected to continuing contradictions and to global television – that is, the ability of Australian players in the English Premier League and the team at the World Cup to 'hold their own'.

Drawing upon the recent attention directed at David Beckham and the success of the 2006 World Cup campaign for the Australian team, Jessica Carniel argues that metrosexualism and cosmopolitanism have changed understandings about ethnic identity and masculinity. Furthermore, Carniel maintains that these interconnected complex developments, provide a new basis for understanding developments within Australian soccer beyond the pro- and anti-ethnicity binary.

While most academic research has focussed on soccer in the east of Australia, Philip Moore has written, over a number of years, about soccer in the west. In the present essay, Moore takes issue with the common assumption that soccer in Perth and Western Australian can be readily attributed to the volume of involvement from post-war migrant groups. Moore insists that is an oversimplification to view the growth of the sport in this light. Indeed, the promise of government funding support in the last decade was conditional upon the sport being managed 'in the national interest'. To this end, Moore argues, the new outsiders in control and in the development of soccer in the distant west have been those embracing the anti-ethnicity agenda.

Much of the published research on soccer and identity has understandably focussed upon relationships about Australianness and tensions between rival groups. The study of a suburban Melbourne club takes a different approach. In addition to the external challenges of maintaining a preferred Macedonian identity, the Preston Lions contend with internal tensions. Bily Bosevski and Chris Hallinan use a fieldwork-based approach to describe and analyse the power struggles between a hooligan-influenced group known as the Preston Boys and a group known as The Silver Lining which takes up a corporate managerial approach to club affairs.

Daniel Lock's fieldwork study of the Sydney FC supporters in the Hyundai A-League competition provides a valuable insight into the fan response to the game's dramatic re-organization. Lock finds a highly positive response from the Sydney FC fans as they enthusiastically embrace the new competition. Lock thus implies criticism of those who protest loudly about the A-League by giving voice to the 'silent majority' – those who deem the venture an outstanding success. However, Lock also suggests that it is rather early to tell whether or not the A-League will develop a fan base into future years by extending into the broader ranks of Australian sport followers.

The mass media has routinely made much of security and safety factors at soccer matches in Australia. Managing crowd behaviour has long been considered a centrepiece of the development of soccer's appeal. Indeed, part of the constitutional basis for participation focussed directly on conditions for entry into the grounds and as well as a limitation of expressive behaviour once inside. The volume concludes with Ian Warren and Roy Hay's discussion on how authorities might better manage policing and crowd control at events. They maintain Australian police have often struggled with managing the behaviour in a range of situations. This is particularly the case with younger people. To better cope with what is deemed to be a hostile site by many, Warren and Hay contend that authorities would benefit from the innovative practices used elsewhere in the world.

## Notes

1. Mitchell, 'Faraway World where Sport is a Shouting Declaration of Statehood'.
2. Hughson, 'Football, Folk Dancing and Fascism'.
3. Rudd, 'The Battle of Ideas'.
4. Turner, 'After Hybridity', 411–18.
5. For discussion of some of this material see Hughson, 'Football, Folk Dancing and Fascism'.
6. Ibid., 169.
7. Beilharz, 'Rewriting Australia', 437.
8. The 'Tampa Affair', the Border Protection Bill, and the Cronulla Beach Riots refer to key incidents in Australian politics that were used by the Howard Federal Government to generate fear and loathing amongst the electorate in the lead up to the Federal Election.
9. Ibid., 439–40.
10. Sharon Verghis, 'Welcome to Cronulla'. *Sydney Morning Herald*, December 13, 2005.
11. Poynting, 'What Caused the Cronulla Riot?'
12. Beilharz, 'Rewriting Australia', 441.
13. Brett, *Australian Liberals*, 185.
14. David Humphries, *Sydney Morning Herald*, February 25, 2006.
15. Peter Costello, 'Worth Promoting, Worth Defending: Australian Citizenship, What It Means and How to Nurture It'. Address to the Sydney Institute, delivered February 23, 2006.
16. Report of Independent Soccer Review Committee into the Structure, Governance and Management of Soccer in Australia, April 2003, 28.
17. Hallinan, Hughson and Burke, 'Supporting the "World Game"'.
18. Gilroy, P. *After Empire*, 70.
19. Turner, 'After Hybridity'.

## References

Beilharz, P. 'Rewriting Australia: the Way We Talk About Fears and Hopes'. *Journal of Sociology* 40, no. 4 (2004): 432–45.
Brett, J. *Australian Liberals and the Moral Middle Class: From Alfred Deakin to John Howard.* Cambridge: Cambridge University Press, 2003.
Gilroy, P. *After Empire: Melancholia or Convivial Culture.* London: Routledge, 2004.
Hallinan, C., J. Hughson, and M. Burke. 'Supporting the "World Game" in Australia: a Case Study of Fandom at National and Club Level'. *Soccer in Society* 8, no. 2 (2007): 283–97.
Hughson, J. 'Football, Folk Dancing and Fascism: Diversity and Difference in Multicultural Australia'. *The Australian and New Zealand Journal of Sociology* 33, no. 2 (1997): 40–55.
Mitchell, K. 'Faraway World where Sport is a Shouting Declaration of Statehood' *The Observer,* 10 December 2006. http://www.guardian.co.uk/sport/2006/dec/10/ashes2006.cricket1/print.
Poynting. S. 'What Caused the Cronulla Riot?' *Race & Class,* 48, no. 1 (2006): 85–92.
Rudd, K. 'The Battle of Ideas in Australian Politics' *The Monthly,* November 2006. http://www.themonthly.com/au/tm/node/312.
Turner, G. 'After Hybridity: Muslim-Australians and the Imagined Community'. *Continuum* 17, no. 4 (2003): 411–18.

# Getting a ticket to the world party: televising soccer in Australia

David Rowe and Callum Gilmour

*Centre for Cultural Research, University of Western Sydney, New South Wales, Australia*

## Introduction: television sport in transition

The relationship between professional sport and television is deeply symbiotic[1] and the historically fluctuating fortunes of association football in Australia, as elsewhere, are closely linked to regulatory, industrial and economic shifts within the television industry on both local and global levels.[2] Over the past two decades, professional football (and sport in general) has come to rely upon the sale of television rights as its primary source of direct and indirect revenue[3] and new forms of media delivery, such as subscription television, have sought to capitalize on the passions of sports fans to draw in paying subscribers for sport content and related products.[4] This intensified commodification is a particular feature of the emergence of the 'media sports cultural complex',[5] wherein the exploitation of 'the affective (often profoundly romantic) investment that "sportslovers" display is contrasted with the continuous process, intensive production and sales technique of the sportsbiz'.[6]

The trajectory of Australian professional soccer's journey from its former status as a marginalized second-tier sport[7] to its emergence as a significant commercial component of the Australian media sports cultural complex, then, is a journey informed and shaped by developments within the national television industry. In particular, Australian soccer's current position is explored here in relation to the role of national regulatory bodies and governments in balancing public and private expectations that, in turn, directly affect access to televised sports content for Australian citizens. The shift in televised sport to commercial and subscription-based television platforms, the rise of the media sports cultural complex, and the increasing emphasis on private corporate interests and marketization within public policy formation, are understood here as symptomatic of a wider relationship to the processes of late capitalism.

Both the increasing commercialization of broadcast systems and the transition to multi-channel distribution are indicative of larger global shifts that have seen a reduction in the public provision of services and an increase in private control and ownership.[8] These are prominent features of neo-liberalism and late capitalism, which are the defining political economic conditions of the late twentieth and early twenty-first centuries, of which 'a decrease in the centrality of the state as a provider of goods and services' is a prominent feature.[9] National and regional television systems have undergone processes of internationalization, commercialization and privatization[10] that have significantly altered not only the manner in which audiences can access televisual texts, but also the ways in which the television and associated media industries attract revenue – with audiences increasingly targeted as subscribers rather than as viewers, and customers as opposed to citizens.[11]

As television audiences have fragmented, broadcast television has experienced a decline in its overall audience share,[12] while the medium's confidence in live sports content, as an economically viable aggregator of mass audiences, has waned. The deregulated and commercialized television environment is characterized by a shift towards user-pays economic models like subscription (pay) television, which target audiences based on specific demographic qualities and viewer tastes with a precision that the free-to-air broadcast model cannot – and is not designed to – match. As the effects of deregulation and marketization have seen sports content increasingly split across free-to-air and subscription platforms, the declining audiences of free-to-air television no longer routinely support the widespread broadcast of sport during prime time. The US networks, for instance, now attract less than 50% of all viewing, as the niche-oriented audience address mode of multi-channel television attracts an ever expanding (albeit diluted) audience share.[13]

Televised sports content has itself become increasingly marketized and commodified over the past two decades as global and national television systems have expanded, integrated, privatized and commercialized, so that 'Major changes in the television cultures of many nations (such) as technological innovation, industrial realignments, and modifications in regulatory philosophy have begun to produce a new audiovisual landscape'.[14] The proliferation of audiovisual delivery modes, including digital, satellite, cable, microwave and broadband, is challenging the long-entrenched mass broadcast model that pioneered the delivery of televised sports content. In Australia, which followed the dominant British, continental European and Asian pattern of development of sport television – commencing with public service broadcasting, then supplemented by commercial free-to-air television, and then both strongly challenged by subscription television – the threatened migration of premium sport to restricted television platforms has been highly controversial.[15]

Patterns of television consumption are altering as technological changes and media deregulation has enabled a multi-channel transmission system, stimulating audience fragmentation, and encouraging niche-oriented programming streams. In this increasingly competitive national, regional and metropolitan television marketplace a premium is placed upon broadcast content with a proven record of 'driving' both platform subscription and audience aggregation, with sports content emerging as pivotal to the economics of multi-channel television. Soccer in Australia, therefore, has been caught up in the contest for sport content rights between the major media corporations – the Packer Organization's Nine Network (with the family's ownership share now considerably diluted by a private equity sale); the Seven Network (whose Chairman, Kerry Stokes, has also reduced his stake through a private equity arrangement); Telstra, the country's largest telecommunications company; and the most prominent of all in global terms, Rupert Murdoch and News Corporation. Australian sport television, therefore, has been clearly caught up in global media sport developments that are interacting with the specific conditions of its national context.

**Australian televised sport in demand: free-to-air versus subscription**

In the recent history of television in many countries, the most significant content migration in the subscription television era has been sports programming, which has proven extremely effective in drawing subscribers to new television services. 'Sport has been the vehicle for bringing dramatic attention to new media forms.'[16] A significant proportion of live televised professional sport over the last two decades has migrated to subscription television platforms across the world, with only limited resistance or protection from national governments and regulatory bodies by means of so-called 'anti-siphoning' measures.[17] A particular feature of late capitalism and neo-liberal economic organization is both the appropriation of public culture by commercial interests and the collusive willingness of governments to facilitate its privatization and deregulation. The most powerful figure in this television sport content migration has been Rupert Murdoch, who has famously described 'sport as the battering ram' for his global pay television and interactive services ambitions.[18]

Murdoch's News Corporation (News Corp) conglomerate has utilized the purchase of sports rights to add instant prestige and to induce subscribers to nascent satellite and cable television platforms across the globe. News Corp's international annexure of subscription television sports rights began in 1992 when the company's fledgling British satellite television platform BSkyB (British Sky Broadcasting) was integral to the creation, promotion and exclusive subscription television broadcasting of a new 'breakaway' league involving the previous members of the Football League's First Division competition. Murdoch's retooled Premier League became an international broadcasting phenomenon, attracting viewers around the globe and cultivating new audiences and revenue streams in emerging markets across the Asian continent. The financial success of the Premier League, achieved despite the smaller audiences available on subscription platforms, was the catalyst for a radical shift in the manner in which the sport was packaged, delivered and received. For the first time, British consumers were required to pay in order to access the national game on television – albeit in greater supply and with various technical and stylistic innovations, and with a competition that was so rich that it could attract football stars from all over the world.[19]

Murdoch's purchase of the Premier League rights initiated a domino effect amongst the British sporting industry – with other major sports such as rugby union, rugby league, cricket and boxing selling their television rights to BSkyB. Before long the majority of live major league sport on British television was broadcast on subscription television platforms.[20] Adapting this model to an international market, News Corp's global pay television platforms have secured the most popular sports content in each of the regions in which they operate. In Italy, Sky Italia broadcasts Serie A football, Fox Sports in the US has rights to a number of major league sports competitions, Sky TV in NZ dominates local broadcasting of rugby union, league and cricket, and Star TV in Asia is the chief broadcaster of the region's most popular sports league, the English Premier League. News Corp has also recently bought a stake in pay TV sport in Germany and in several other European and Middle Eastern countries.

However, to a certain extent, Australia has been the notable exception to the global trend of sport's migration to subscription-based delivery platforms, in no small part due to the significance of sporting competition to Australian social and cultural identity. As Richard Cashman argues, sport occupies a pivotal position within Australia:

> Social commentators … have long declared that the country is a paradise of sport. They have argued that many Australians have an obsession with sport and that sporting culture is central to Australian life. Some have said that the Australian passion for sport is distinctive and even unique.[21]

Nowhere on earth has sport been more central both to the national psyche and *Zeitgeist* as Australia, which, as a relatively new nation, utilizes sporting competition as the principal outlet for the performance of many national identity rituals.[22] For this reason, and because of the historical political influence of its free-to-air networks, Australians have enjoyed the most vigorous regulatory defence of their right to watch sport on free-to-air television in the world. The now symbiotic relationship between sport and the media within the media sports cultural complex is accentuated in Australia, where the right to more-or-less free access to popular televised sport has been defended by successive governments as a public good with inherent cultural value to the Australian population, as well as a major source of advertising revenue for, in particular, Packer's Nine Network.

In Australia, then, News Corp has been denied the relatively unregulated access to exclusive live sports rights that it has encountered in other national media markets. Indeed, the introduction of subscription television services into the Australian market in 1995 was one of the latest in the Western world.[23] Previously, repeated attempts to introduce pay television services into the Australian mediascape were thwarted, despite the then Australian media regulatory body, the Australian Broadcasting Tribunal (ABT), recommending in 1982 that pay television services be introduced as soon as possible.[24] Australia's incumbent free-to-air lobby, led by then Nine Network owner Kerry Packer and his Publishing and Broadcasting Limited conglomerate, successfully influenced governmental broadcasting policy regarding the introduction of pay television services throughout the 1980s. The relationship between the Packers and, especially, the Labor government of the time (1983–96) was often regarded as that between 'mates'.[25] The resistance of the commercial free-to-air broadcasters to pay TV only subsided when they themselves became involved in subscription television – PBL via the now defunct Optus Vision platform and later Foxtel; and the Seven network via the C7 sport channels.

Despite the introduction of subscription television in 1995, media policy and regulation have continued to favour the interests of the Australian commercial free-to-air television sector. Changes to broadcast legislation announced by (then) Australian Communications Minister Helen Coonan in 2006 continued largely to reinforce incumbency in the free-to-air industry. Chief amongst these initiatives were the maintenance of free-to-air broadcasters' first option on most major sports rights; a refusal to grant a fourth commercial television broadcast licence; exclusive access to the digital television broadcasting spectrum for existing free-to-air broadcasters; relaxation of cross-media ownership laws allowing incumbents to own both television stations and newspapers in the same regional and city markets; and relaxation of foreign owner-ship laws enabling large share deals with overseas companies, private equity arrange-ments or lucrative whole company sales to foreign buyers.[26]

One of the key sites of contestation for the incumbent free-to-air broadcasters and their lobby group, *FreeTV*, and the still fledgling subscription television sector (repre-sented by the Australian Subscription Television & Radio Association – ASTRA), is in the area of sports rights legislation. Resistance to the privatization of sports content is legitimized in Australia through the administration of anti-siphoning legislation by a government agency, the Australian Communications and Media Authority (ACMA). These provisions list, on the advice of the Minister, a series of sports events required to be offered initially to Australia's free-to-air broadcasters before any subscription television operators may bid for the rights. In turn, the legislation has performed a significant role in maintaining the presence of most 'major league' professional sport on Australian free-to-air television.

However, as is discussed later, soccer in Australia appears to be an exception to the rule, with the 2006 sale of its television rights to News Corp's 50% owned and operated subscription television channel platform Fox Sports, granted regulatory approval via the omission of most soccer-related events and competitions from the anti-siphoning list. This is the latest in a lengthy history of setbacks and impediments that have retarded the growth and potential of soccer within both the Australian mediascape and in its wider socio-cultural context. Indeed, circumstances have conspired to foster the unlikely 'fencing off' of Australian televised soccer from mass television audiences, including: regulatory neglect or ignorance within the otherwise rigorous anti-siphoning regime; an historical antipathy or ambivalence towards the sport within Australian society where it has been marginalized through a dismissive discourse that situates soccer as 'alien' to Anglo Australian socio-cultural norms;[27] intensive competition for media space within a saturated Australian professional sports calendar that uniquely supports 'four dynamic football codes';[28] and the declin-ing presence of prime time sport on Australian commercial television. It is appropriate here to examine something of the cultural history of soccer in Australia.

## Soccer in the Australian media sports cultural complex

The mainstream media in Australia have traditionally been indifferent, if not hostile to soccer, often portraying the sport as 'un-Australian' and invoking discourses of 'deviancy' (especially of a violent, sectarian kind) and 'otherness'.[29] The promotion of sport as an intrinsic site of Australian national cultural affinity has tended to rest on outmoded and anachronistic Anglo-Celtic, colonialist discursive formations that are frequently reproduced within the mainstream media coverage of sports such as rugby league, rugby union and cricket.[30] This distorted Anglo-Celtic rendering of Australian identity is reflected to some degree by ACMA's acceptance of all one-day and test cricket matches played by the Australian national cricket team overseas as available to pay television broadcasters – except those matches played in England, the former colonial power.[31] Media sport coverage is largely focused on sports closely identified with Australia's British colonial and imperial history, subse-quently linking sporting contests in Australia with an Anglo-Celtic perception of national identity that dismisses the profound demographic changes wrought by post-war immigration and, of course, the history of indigenous peoples in the country.[32]

For example, in announcing his network's securing of the television rights to broadcast the 2012 London Olympic Games, Nine Network chief executive David Gyngell reinforced this articulation of Australian national identity in a public statement: 'London is a solid cultural fit with our viewing audiences and will achieve strong ratings particularly with the historical links in sporting and cultural terms between Australia and the United Kingdom.'[33]

Importantly, these 'colonial' sports also have the advantage of their restriction to a limited range of competitive nations, which has allowed Australians various opportunities to bask in the reflected glory of 'World Cup' victories in 'Empire sports' such as rugby league, rugby union, netball and cricket. As one commentator has acerbically observed:

> The painful truth is Australians only really care about sports we know we're a very good chance of winning. That's why we care about 'world cups' where only a handful of countries participate. The kind of World Cups where we're a very good chance, even on a bad day, of taking home a trophy.[34]

Soccer, on the other hand, while English in origin, was widely celebrated by the large numbers of southern European immigrants who settled in Australia after the Second World War, and who tended to be branded as 'ethnic' or 'alien' by an ethnocentric, Anglo-dominated Australian media.[35] As Hay has put it, 'Soccer is characterized as a migrants' game, even though many of the migrants playing or watching the game are of second or later generations.'[36] In addition, the commercial media, especially commercial current affairs television and tabloid newspapers, tended to portray football fandom in Australia as violent and socially divisive,[37] reporting on any outbreaks of ethnically-related violence at Australian soccer matches as instances of the unwarranted importation of 'ancient' conflicts (ignoring, in the process, Aboriginal dispossession and the history of English-Irish conflict). Within a classical 'moral panic' framework of exaggeration, distortion, prediction and symbolization,[38] and utilizing local soccer violence to promote a thinly veiled anti-immigration ideological position connecting Australian soccer to social disunity and disorder:[39] 'The establishment media, that is the branch of the media which is really controlled by fans of other sports saw football as a threat so they ... proactively cultivated this image that it's not our game, it's "un-Australian", it's something foreigners do'.[40]

Soccer in Australia has long had deep roots within those ethnic diasporas that have utilized it both as a locus of identity performance, and as a significant focal point of social organization within migrant communities.[41] Many clubs, such as Melbourne Croatia, Sydney Hakoah and Sydney Olympic, emanated from ethnic community associations, and it was this support that maintained the sport during its leanest years:

> Critics contend that soccer at the club level has failed the test of 'Australian-ness'. It has been generally derided as un-Australian – or less Australian than other sports – because many teams and clubs were founded by, and remain linked organizationally, to non-Anglo ethnic communities.[42]

In terms of participation at a 'grass roots' level, soccer has, in fact, been highly successful across the social spectrum, both Anglo-Celtic and otherwise, but, like some other sports – such as the female-dominated sport of netball – its local community prominence has had considerable difficulty in making the transition to established, well-remunerated and media-visible professional sport. Hallinan, Hughson and Burke attribute this problem to the above described issue of non-Anglo ethnic connotation:

> While soccer football is the most popular participation team sport in Australia, it lags in the media and (as a) spectator sport – with media commentators long suggesting that the 'world' game is un-or less-Australian because many teams and clubs are founded/organized around 'ethnic' non-Anglo derivatives.[43]

Yet, what they are also describing is a deep gulf between community/semi-professional sport, and its fully professional form that demands an increasingly corporatized organizational discipline and ethic of capital accumulation. Australian soccer under 'ethnic regimes' has often been accused – and often not unreasonably – of financial mismanagement, uninspired leadership, factional infighting, and a continued failure to market and package the local game to advertisers, mass spectators and media interests alike. Thus, when Hay notes, as quoted below, Australian soccer's difficulties with securing free-to-air television coverage, he is also registering the necessity of the kind of organizational transformation that turns a relatively local, community-oriented, loosely organized cultural practice into a rationalized enterprise:

> It is often argued that soccer has shown a persistent failure to obtain and hold media coverage, particularly free-to-air commercial television. Often the code has not been able to provide an attractive product for hard-headed commercial realists in the media industries. It is a chicken and egg problem however: if soccer can produce the continuing audience then it will attract free-to-air commercial television, but television exposure is seen as necessary to achieve a broader audience for the game.[44]

Soccer in Australia does clearly have considerable commercial and professional potential, and the capacity to draw the large television audience that must take the 'high end' of the game well beyond the ethnically-based clubs that once dominated it. The one-club-per-city structure of the A-League, in particular, was designed to loosen its historical connection to ethnic groups. This socio-demographic limitation, though, was exchanged for another – that of the subscription television audience.

### Subscribing to sport in Australian television

The availability of free-to-air soccer in Australia is not just threatened by subscription television, impotent regulatory resistance and institutionalized historical bias, but also by the shifting economics of the commercial broadcasting industry itself, which, faced with a declining audience share, less 'specialized' and ageing demographics, and the increasingly high prices paid for sport by pay television operators, is finding that live prime time sport no longer delivers the equivalent audiences and revenues as its regular scripted entertainment, reality and variety programming.[45] Subsequently, prime time sport has fallen out of favour, to a certain extent, with broadcast television networks in Australia and also around the world.

Subscription television consumption has increased rapidly on a global scale over the past decade – with mature markets such as the US recording as high as 82% penetration.[46] Increasing viewers, demographic-specific audience aggregation and multiple revenue streams have given the subscription television industry increased legitimacy and an ability to compete with traditional broadcasters for pivotal content such as sports rights. The combination of professional sport's relatively recent dependence on television revenue, the shifting delivery modes and economic models now utilized by a rapidly fragmenting television industry, and the common reduction worldwide (with exceptions such as Britain) of public broadcast funding – has left many professional sports, Australian soccer amongst them, facing a significant dilemma. Premium sports receive the ever increasing sums of television rights reve-nue that the burgeoning global subscription television sector provides, albeit with the understanding that their product will in most cases be exposed to smaller, fragmented paying audiences.[47] In Australian television industry terms: 'A football product will attract on free-to-air roughly five times the audience it will bring on pay TV. So if a game brings in 20,000 viewers on Pay, the same game will attract 100,000 on free to air.'[48] For emerging sports like soccer in Australia, then, pay television exclusivity runs the risk of limiting its audience reach and, therefore, of retarding its develop-ment. While subscription television engenders a 'motivated' audience, it is also very much a 'converted' or 'pre-existing' one. 'Casual', 'part time' or 'non-initiated', viewers – whose access to the game provides the greatest opportunity for the sport's expansion – will have little opportunity to be exposed to a sport that is broadcast almost exclusively on pay television. This development poses serious long-term threats to sports and professional sports leagues in Australia that rely on television exposure to promote and expand their product's appeal to new audiences, and to interact and 'bond' with their primary target markets. This trend is particularly evident in the United States, where declining free-to-air ratings have seen much major league sport siphoned to cable television – as described in US industry blog *Sports Media Watch*:

> On January 22, 2002, the NBA announced a new six-year television deal with Disney and Time Warner that would put the NBA All Star Game and Conference Finals on cable. It was a date that should be remembered as the start of the disappearance of sports on network television. With a dwindling TV audience, professional hoops risks permanently becoming a niche attraction on cable. Cable subscriber (revenue) may wow league owners, but it dilutes the appeal of the game and would likely stifle the long-term financial growth of the league. In the NFL, ESPN bought the rights to network television staple *Monday Night Football*. The move of MNF, one of the NFL's crown jewels, to cable, turned the NBA's move from an isolated deal into the start of a trend – with Major League Baseball making a similar move. By 2007, the idea of airing marquee events on cable was no longer considered dangerous, but instead part of a new sports/television landscape with a massive decline in the amount of sports on free TV.[49]

This example became increasingly relevant to Australia in 2005 when the Ashes cricket series, played in England, was ignored by free-to-air commercial broadcasters. This was because of the series' clash with the year-round programme schedule. It was left to minority public broadcaster, the Special Broadcasting Service (SBS), ironically a channel established to provide specialist television services for Australia's migrant communities,[50] to broadcast this most 'Anglo' of sporting contests. SBS's unlikely and unexpected acquisition of the Ashes rights prevented one of the blue ribbon events on the Australian sporting calendar being voluntarily surrendered by the free-to-air industry to subscription television, as SBS Director Nigel Milan remarked:

> We've been very strong supporters of the anti-siphoning legislation and it struck us, with free-to-air television unable or unwilling to actually do it … and the ABC [Australian Broadcasting Corporation, the major national broadcaster] having scheduling problems, it was time for us to step up to the table. Normally these sorts of things are a very serious auction, and you expect it to be a bit out of the league for SBS, but with the commercials walking away from it, and the ABC obviously having one or two problems coming to the table, we were able to pull the rights out of the bag, and basically give this wonderful competition coverage to all Australians.[51]

It is somewhat ironic, then, that the recent elevation of soccer in the Australian public consciousness (after a long period of marginality, not least through its association with the 'minority' broadcaster SBS) coincides with significant changes in the relationship between free-to-air broadcast television and sports content that threaten its widespread visibility and profile in Australia. It is doubly ironic that in Australia, where sport's position on broadcast television is defended by stringent government legislation, soccer is largely televised to the minority of viewers (approximately 24 per cent) currently with access to domestic pay television services, even fewer of whom subscribe to the now tiered Fox Sports channels that televise football.[52] Soccer may, therefore, be seen as something of a victim of its own recent success – its 'record' (for the sport in Australia) television rights deal with pay television network Fox Sports providing rare financial security but with minimal exposure.

The story so far, then, of soccer in Australia, is in some ways a microcosm of the wider changes within the global television system discussed above. It has a long history of struggling for acceptance and mainstream popularity,[53] and so it is curious that soccer's most tangible example of its newfound economic and public popularity in Australia – a television rights deal worth AU$120 million[54] – serves to obscure it from the wider public domain. This incongruous situation has arisen out of the aforementioned period of uncertainty in broadcast free-to-air television, and also as a result of the lack of protection afforded by the anti-siphoning legislation explicitly designed to counter such circumstances. At this point, therefore, it is useful to revisit more closely the sometimes bizarre television history of soccer in Australia.

**Soccer and multicultural television in Australia**

Traditionally, the major television broadcaster of soccer in Australia has been the public broadcaster SBS,[55] established in 1980 in order to provide a media platform of engagement and recognition for Australia's migrant populations and ethnic diasporas.[56] SBS has long been seen as the 'home' of soccer on Australian television screens, with a history of broadcasting Australian national team matches, and the defunct National Soccer League, as well as a wide variety of international matches and tournaments, including World Cups and the European Champions League. While SBS's exemplary coverage did much to maintain soccer's visibility amid mainstream television apathy, its minority audiences and multi-ethnic remit inadvertently served to further marginalize the sport within the media and wider society. As SBS 'pundit' and author of the book, *15 Days in June: How Australia Became a Football Nation*, Jesse Fink has remarked, 'there are a lot of people around Australia who still regard that fine broadcaster as an ethnic enclave or, to borrow a line from the great Johnny Warren, a home for "sheilas, wogs and poofters"'.[57] The use of this Australian vernacular language by the late soccer player and television presenter Warren as the title of his autobiography, was intended to reflect what he saw as an entrenched cultural bias against soccer in Australia through a denigratory association with women, non-Anglo immigrants, and male homosexuals.

By the 1990s, SBS was subjected to the aforementioned global downturn in the funding of public broadcasting. In particular, it faced pressures to monetize and capitalize on its audience through the introduction of advertising to supplement its inadequate public funding, and by 'mainstreaming' its content and demographic address, while simultaneously facing competition for some of its niche-oriented content (like soccer) from the nascent subscription television sector.

Allegations have flown about SBS's diminishing commitment to LOTE (languages other than English) programmes. In October 2003, FECCA (Federation of Ethnic Communities' Councils of Australia) accused SBS Television of 'running the risk of losing the audience it was established to serve'. There is also a fear that the search for a broader audience is leading to the acquisition and commissioning of programmes that are 'safer and blander', that SBS will become 'a poor man's version of a commercial network rather than providing a challenging alternative'. The harshest critics fear that SBS will end up looking like a second-rate cable-TV station, running reality TV shows and English-language drama series that the free-to-air channels have rejected as either being too limited in their appeal or too provocative.[58]

SBS's soccer viewership had continued to expand as the network sought more mainstream audiences in the face of extensive budgetary reductions under the Howard Coalition government (1996–2007). Soccer, it was increasingly appreciated, also had a strong, largely male Anglo following, with especially strong interest in English football, especially the Premier League – and a corresponding increase in the cost of broadcast rights. A shift towards an increasingly advertiser-funded revenue model, including an expanding array of English-language programming, was reflected in the diversifying and indeed 'mainstreaming' of the network's sport portfolio. Subsequently, sports with a long history of mass audience appeal in Australia, like the aforementioned Ashes cricket series and the Olympic Games, appeared on SBS and placed significant pressure on the channel's soccer budget, which was already under threat from subscription television services and rising rights fees. SBS's expanding sports remit, the rising popularity of soccer, and the (then) Department of Communications, Information Technology and the Arts's (DCITA's) failure to place most key soccer events on the anti-siphoning list, all contributed to Australian soccer's progressive transfer to subscription television platforms (now including ESPN).

Beyond SBS and pay TV, Australian commercial television has flirted intermittently with soccer over the years. In 1977 Channel Seven was the chief television broadcaster for the Philips League, Australia's first national sporting league of any kind, and a bold attempt by soccer authorities to shift the peripheral status of the game. Later (in 1998) Channel Seven paid AU$25 million for the rights to the local game for a ten-year period. However, the contract negotiated by the then governing body Soccer Australia contained few, if any, stipulations on how or where the sport should be broadcast, with Seven ignoring the sport on its flagship free-to-air network, and relegating matches to its struggling (and now defunct) pay television channel C7, which had failed to obtain carriage on Australia's most popular subscription television platform, Foxtel. Channel Nine had also become interested in soccer when it believed that the Australian national team would reach the 1998 World Cup Finals – an interest that waned when it failed to do so.

Australian soccer's current exclusive pay television rights deal with Fox Sports arrived in the same year that the sport attained its most notable impact on the Australian public consciousness. While the signing of the sport's first significant television rights deal was heralded as a key milestone in the 'mainstreaming' of Australian association football, its exclusivity separated it from the other football codes and cricket, which enjoy legislative protection and significant free-to-air coverage. In 2005 the sport's profile, marketability, revenue capacity and competitiveness within the Australian media sport market greatly increased with the Australian national team's qualification for the 2006 FIFA World Cup; the launch of a heavily promoted and financed national professional league (the A-League), and Australia's transition from the small Oceania Confederation to the vast Asian Football Confederation (AFC). Record soccer attendances were recorded at both national team and club levels across Australia between 2005 and 2006, as Australians began to embrace a 'mainstream' soccer culture heavily promoted across multiple media platforms:

> Qualifying for the first time since its World Cup debut in 1974, this international soccer tournament generated an unprecedented level of excitement amongst Australians. Games were screened in large outdoor spaces, such as Federation Square in Melbourne. People braved cold winter nights and rearranged their sleeping patterns in order to be part of the tournament as it happened. In short, Australia went soccer mad.[59]

However, unlike the other established 'major league' sports in Australia, whose league competitions and national teams' free-to-air television status are protected from siphoning, the televising of Australian soccer at all levels (excluding the World Cup finals) is now restricted to subscription television platforms, especially the Fox Sports Channel on Foxtel.

### Australian soccer's new deal

The current subscription television contract, signed in 2006, was the best on offer in a direct financial sense, but hampers Australian soccer's capacity to sustain its newfound appeal, and to further expand its brand awareness to a wider community. So, while public interest in the game may be at an all-time high, a lack of visibility on the majority of Australian television screens poses potentially hazardous roadblocks for the wider development of the game within the Australian media sports market. Media coverage of soccer in Australia has never matched its participation, which 'by 2005 numbered over 600,000' people, making it the nation's most popular team-based participation sport.[60]

However, while Australian soccer now enjoys its richest ever television contract, it is experiencing the same lack of mainstream exposure that it suffered during its ill-fated relationship with the Seven Network. The vast majority of domestic football and Australian international football is on subscription television platforms. The sport's hard-won, nascent mainstream status is threatened by the blanking out of most free-to-air football coverage in Australia, with the anti-siphoning regime, ironically, protecting the English Football Association (FA) Cup Final for free-to-air television, but not the A-League Final.

Fox Sports has been slowly eroding SBS's football coverage over the past decade and a half, first securing an exclusivity agreement for the Australian rights to the English Premier League competition, then the European Nations Cup (UEFA Euro 2004), and even some of SBS's on-air presenters. But it is the current deal for rights to competitions involving Australian sides that is most threatening to the sport. The current seven-year Foxtel deal involves exclusive live coverage and highlights packages of the national A-league competition, all matches involving Australian club sides in the Asian Champions League, all matches involving Australian sides at the FIFA-endorsed World Club Championship, all Australian national team (the Socceroos) friendly fixtures, Socceroo World Cup Qualifying Fixtures, Socceroo Asian Cup qualifying matches, Socceroo Asian Cup matches, and Socceroo Confederations Cup fixtures and Olympic qualifying games. With the Disney-owned ESPN channel broadcasting Italian and Spanish league football, the FA Cup (the final of which is simulcast on both free-to-air and pay), and UEFA

Champions League, SBS has faced an unremitting erosion of its free-to-air television football coverage.

However, the shifting economics of broadcast television and the saturation coverage already afforded the long established mainstream sports of rugby, rugby league, cricket and Australian Rules football on free-to-air television, alongside the increased cost of soccer's broadcast rights, means that there is little available space for the sport on the existing free-to-air platform. In this light, the Fox Sports-A-League arrangement can be viewed as symptomatic of the aforementioned transformations in the global television system, where increased privatization, marketization and fragmentation have shaped an increasingly competitive, mutating television environment. As former SBS Head of Sport and Australia's leading football commentator, Les Murray, comments:

> What has allowed the pay operators such easy access to this content is that the richer commercial free-to-air networks, Seven, Nine and Ten, were not sufficiently interested to compete for football. Given that TV money provides the riches needed to sustain the game, it would be hard to fathom how the bleeding A-League may have survived had it not been for the Fox deal.[61]

Yet there remains a sense of indignation that this has occurred in Australia at the expense of terrestrial television viewers and their access to sports that are of 'national significance'.[62] However, it appears that Australia's long serving Coalition Government (voted out of office after 11 years in November 2007) had been caught off guard by football's emergence in the Australian sportscape. Former Communications Minister Coonan had reportedly remarked that World Cup soccer 'probably attracts the same level of audience interest as the Tour de France'.[63] However the mass engagement displayed by the Australian television audience with the 2006 World Cup[64] suggested otherwise, with 3.4 million viewers watching the final qualifying match against Uruguay,[65] and 2.3 million viewers watching the Australia versus Italy quarter-final game, a record Australian early hours television audience (the match commencing at 1.00 a.m. Australian Eastern Standard Time).[66] Indeed, one media research company argued that official ratings seriously underestimated 2006 World Cup viewership in Australia, claiming that 'Nearly seven million Australians (40% of Australians aged 14 and over – 48% of men and 32% of women) watched the SBS's live broadcast of Australia's heartbreaking last-minute loss against Italy early Tuesday morning, according to a special Roy Morgan telephone survey', with an estimated 7.115 million watching a match against Japan that commenced at 11.00 a.m.[67]

Soccer in Australia has continued its rise in popularity since the 2006 World Cup, with significant print coverage and record ratings on pay television,[68] but its reach is nonetheless seriously reduced by a free-to-air presence confined to brief highlights in news and sports magazine programmes. The manifest result is reflected in a letter to the editor of the Sydney paper, *MX*, in which a young football fan describes his difficulty gaining access to televised soccer coverage:

> The fact that all the Socceroos games are broadcast exclusively on Foxtel is appalling. The FFA wants to make football the No. 1 sport, and yet not everyone is able to see the national team play. I had to sit outside a corner shop in Harris Park in the freezing cold to watch their game vs. Argentina. I couldn't go to a pub because I'm underage. In my opinion, the Socceroos belong to us, so all of their games should be made available to the general public, not just those privileged enough to have Foxtel. Also the fact that

none of the A-league games is broadcast on free-to-air TV is depressing. How are we supposed to support the league if not all of us are able to see it?[69]

Australian anti-siphoning legislation at present attaches more significance to the quarter finals of the French Open Tennis Tournament than to the World Cup qualifying matches involving the Australian national soccer team. Under the current provisions, which last until December 2010, all internationals played by the Australian Rugby League, Rugby Union, Cricket and Netball teams are protected from pay TV exclusivity. As Murray notes:

> [This] deal that [sees] the television rights to our national football team, and our elite football league, signed away to pay until 2013 was all done within the law and with commercial realities in play. Nobody can be blamed, not the FFA, which was desperate for the money, not SBS, which is playing with tax-payer dollars, and certainly not Fox, which is in the business of being in business. The only party that remains muddled in all this is the Federal Government which, for whatever mysterious reason, has chosen not to protect the Socceroos and the A-League for free TV.[70]

The world game, it seems, is still having difficulty overcoming its long-term disadvantage in the Australian context, with most of its major events not judged to be of sufficient national cultural significance to be preserved for the over 95% of homes that receive free-to-air television.


### Conclusion: events of national significance?

It is clear that, unlike the mature and genuinely platform-plural media markets like the US and UK,[71] where multi-channel viewership rivals and in some cases surpasses broadcast television, the Australian pay television market is still in a developmental stage. The concept of the 'post broadcast' era[72] then – certainly as it applies to the demise of 'mass', free television – has clearly different implications and consequences in different regions or nations. The development of national media markets is dependent on more than global influences, but also uniquely 'local' factors, such as cultural patterns, histories, social structures, economic conditions, ideological emphases, regulatory regimes, technological adoption rates and population size. In Australia, the socio-cultural factors that have played a significant role in the shaping of the local mediasportscape have tended, it has been argued here, to place soccer at the margins of public life.

The policy of successive Australian governments to restrict the flow of televised sport content from free-to-air television to subscription television has retarded the growth of pay television in Australia. In the process, though, it has recognized and maintained the centrality of selected forms of sports representation as markers of cultural citizenship.[73] In opposition, the Australian Labor Party opposed the Fox Sports television deal for soccer,[74] and following its election to government in late 2007, was under pressure both to place more soccer matches on the anti-siphoning list (a Ministerial prerogative under the legislation) and to allow the contract to stand. Minister Stephen Conroy chose the latter, citing heavy contract-breaking penalties for Football Federation Australia.

While the current (post-) broadcast era has witnessed an uneven, but detectable international trend towards a decline in free-to-air television consumption, in Australia, as elsewhere, the medium maintains its ability to reach the largest single audience within the domestic mediasphere, especially during mega sports events such as the Olympics and the World Cup.[75] Broadcast television, then, remains a vital venue for the advancement of public discourse and the performance of national identity politics. Australian soccer's large-scale absence from free-to-air platforms reduces the sport's ability to insinuate itself into its national culture, so placing serious limitations on its growth potential and standing within the Australian media sports cultural complex. This 'fenced off' position implicitly reproduces prejudices that the game is somehow 'un-Australian'.

Given that no contemporary sport can thrive without a major media presence, and the continuing power of the small screen and still prominent place of sport as its content (in both free-to-air and pay television), soccer in Australia can legitimately claim that it, too, merits a place in the programme schedule across television platforms. Until the reach and penetration of subscription television approaches that of free-to-air, and a multiplicity of media platforms enables the delivery of premium sports content at a comparably low cost to that of the 'box in the corner', it is for the Australian state to intervene in the widespread distribution of the mediated, 'live', vibrant and popular texts that constitute Australian soccer in motion.

## Notes

1. Boyle and Haynes, *Power Play*; Brookes, *Representing Sport*.
2. Miller *et al.*, *Globalization and Sport*.
3. Bolotny and Bourg, 'The Demand for Media Coverage'.
4. Booth and Doyle, 'UK Television Warms Up.'
5. Rowe, *Sport, Culture and the Media*.
6. Rowe, *Popular Cultures*, 120.
7. Hughson, 'Football, Folk Dancing and Fascism', 168.
8. Bolotny and Bourg, 'The Demand for Media Coverage'; Jacka, 'Public Service TV'; Van Zoonen, 'Popular Qualities in Public Broadcasting'.
9. Sinclair, Jacka and Cunningham, *New Patterns in Global Television*, 1.
10. Yong Jin, 'Transformation of the World Television System'.
11. Miller, *Cultural Citizenship*.
12. Flew and Gilmour, 'Television and Pay TV'.
13. Croteau and Hoynes, *The Business of Media*.
14. Sinclair, Jacka and Cunningham, *New Patterns in Global Television*, 1.
15. Rowe, 'Watching Brief: Cultural Citizenship and Viewing Rights'
16. Leever and Wheeler, 'Mass Media and the Experience of Sport', 141.
17. Rowe, *Sport, Culture and the Media*
18. R. Milliken, 'Sport is Murdoch's Battering Ram for Pay TV'. *The Independent*, October 16, 1996. http://findstudys.com/p/studys/mi_qn4158/is_19961016/ai_n14086559.
19. Brookes, *Representing Sport*
20. Redhead, *Post Fandom*.
21. Cashman, *Paradise of Sport*, vi.
22. Cashman, 'The Australian Sporting Obsession'; McKay, *No Pain, No Gain?*; Parker, 'An Investigation'; Stoddart, *Saturday Afternoon Fever*.
23. Flew and Gilmour, 'Television and Pay TV'.
24. Cook, 'Steering Between Private and State Power'; Dwyer, 'Emerging Policies for Pay-TV'.
25. Chadwick, *Media Mates*.
26. Australian Associated Press (AAP), 'Mixed Response to Planned Media Reforms'. *Yahoo News*, July 13, 2006. http://au.news.yahoo.com/060713/2/zrkz.html.
27. Miller, 'The Unmarking of Soccer'.
28. M. Cockerill, 'Talkin 'Bout a Soccer Revolution'. Interview with John O'Neill. *The Sydney Morning Herald*, July 24, 2004. http://www.smh.com.au/studys/2004/07/23/1090464862506.html?oneclick=true.

29. Hay, 'Our Wicked Foreign Game'; Hughson, 'Australian Soccer'.
30. Stoddart, *Saturday Afternoon Fever*; Cashman, *Paradise of Sport*.
31. Australian Communications and Media Authority (ACMA), 'Anti-Siphoning List Commencing 2006'. *ACMA* website, 2006. http://www.acma.gov.au/WEB/STANDARD/pc=PC_91822.
32. Jupp, *The Australian People*.
33. Australian Associated Press, 'Nine, Foxtel Secure London 2012'. *The Sydney Morning Herald*, October 13, 2007. http://www.smh.com.au/news/tv--radion/nine- foxtel-secure-london-2012/2007/10/13/1191696217431.html.
34. J. Fink, 'Wake Up, Australia'. *Fox Sports* website, May 23, 2007. http://blogs.foxsports.com.au/football/index.php/foxsports/comments/wake_up_austr alia1.
35. Mosley, 'Soccer'; Miller, 'The Unmarking of Soccer'.
36. Hay, 'Our Wicked Foreign Game', 165; Mosley, 'Balkan Politics in Australian Soccer'.
37. Vamplew, 'Violence in Australian Soccer'.
38. Cohen, *Folk Devils and Moral Panic*.
39. Hallinan and Krotee, 'Conceptions of Nationalism'.
40. Les Murray, interview, June 1, 2006, transcript, The Fifth Estate – RMIT Journalism, http://fifth.estate.rmit.edu.au/transcript-les-murray-interview.php.
41. Hay, 'British Football'; Cashman, *Paradise of Sport*.
42. Hughson, 'Australian Soccer', 14–15.
43. Hallinan, Hughson and Burke, 'Supporting the "World Game" in Australia', 283.
44. Hay, 'Our Wicked Foreign Game', 172.
45. R. Masters, 'You'll Have to Pay if You Want to Watch the Ashes'. *The Sydney Morning Herald*, August 15, 2003. http://www.smh.com.au/studys/2003/08/15/1060588534898.html.
46. Gartner Inc, 'Saturation of U.S. Pay-TV Market Creates Challenges for Emerging IPTV Services, Says Gartner'. *Tekrati* website, October 1, 2007. http://telecom.tekrati.com/research/9414/.
47. R. Clarke, 'The Future of Sports Broadcasting Rights'. *SportBusiness* website, 2002. http://www.sportbusinessassociates.com/sports_reports/BroadcastingRightsExecSummary.doc.
48. L. Murray, 'Football's New TV Realities'. *The World Game* website, April 15, 2007. http://www.theworldgame.com.au/opinions/index.php?pid=st&cid=86558&ct=22.
49. Sports Media Watch, 'Trend to Oblivion'. *Sports Media Watch* website, January 9, 2007. http://sportsmediawatch.blogspot.com/2007_01_09_archive.html.
50. O'Regan and Kolar-Panov, 'SBS-TV: A Television Service'; Lawe Davies, 'SBS- TV and its Amazing World'.
51. Australian Associated Press (AAP), 'SBS Secures Free-to-Air Ashes Rights'. *The Sydney Morning Herald*, March 1, 2005. http://www.smh.com.au/news/Cricket/SBS- secures-free-toair-Ashes-rights/2005/03/01/1109546807204.html.
52. Australian Subscription Television and Radio Association (ASTRA), 'Industry Overview: Subscription Television'. *ASTRA* website, 2007. http://www.astra.org.au/study.asp?section=2&option=1&content=1.
53. Hughson, 'Australian Soccer'.
54. D. Rowe, 'Australian Soccer: A Pay TV Exclusive'. *Online Opinion* website, April 28, 2006. http://www.onlineopinion.com.au/view.asp?study=4406.
55. Jones and Moore, 'He Only Has Eyes for Poms', 16.
56. Smaill, 'Narrating Community'.
57. J. Fink, 'Wake Up, Australia'. *Fox Sports* website, May 23, 2007. http://blogs.foxsports.com.au/football/index.php/foxsports/comments/wake_up_austr alia1.
58. D. Enker, 'Where to now SBS?' *The Age*, May 27, 2004. http://www.theage.com.au/studys/2004/05/26/1085461820488.html.
59. Carmiel, 'Bipolar (Un)patriots', 1
60. Australian Sports Commission (ASC), 'Exercise, Recreation and Sport Survey (ERASS)'. *ASC* website, 2006. http://www.ausport.gov.au/scorsresearch/erass2005.asp.
61. L. Murray, 'Football's New TV Realities'. *The World Game* website, April 15, 2007. http://www.theworldgame.com.au/opinions/index.php?pid=st&cid=86558&ct=22.
62. Australian Communications and Media Authority (ACMA), 'Anti-Siphoning List Commencing 2006'. *ACMA* website, 2006. http://www.acma.gov.au/WEB/STANDARD/pc=PC_91822.

63. S. Conroy, 'Coonan Should Amend Anti-Siphoning List to Include Socceroos World Cup Qualifying Matches'. June 13, 2006. http://www.senatorconroy.com/quest43.html.
64. M. Hirons, 'Soccer Continuing to Challenge other Football Codes'. *Sweeney Sports Research Consultants* media release, August 6, 2006. http://www.sweeneyresearch. com.au/newsPDF/news_pdf_11.pdf.
65. Agence France-Presse (AFP), 'Socceroos Score Record Television Audience'. *ABC News* website, November 17, 2005. http://www.abc.net.au/news/stories/2005/11/17/1509305. htm.
66. Special Broadcasting Service (SBS), 'Record Year for SBS'. *SBS* website, media release, November 8, 2006. http://www20.sbs.com.au/sbscorporate/media/documents/76262006__ annual_report 0506.doc.
67. Roy Morgan Research, 'Nearly 7 Million Australians Watched Socceroos Last- Minute Loss Against Italy'. June 29, 2006. http://www.roymorgan.com/news/polls/2006/4043/.
68. Four Four Two, 'Japan Game a TV Record'. *Four Four Two* website, July 23, 2007. http://au.fourfourtwo.com/news/56973,japan-game-a-tv-record.aspx.
69. Aaron, letter to the editor. *MX*, September 13, 2007.
70. L. Murray, 'Football's New TV Realities'. *The World Game* website, April 15, 2007. http://www.theworldgame.com.au/opinions/index.php?pid=st&cid=86558&ct=22.
71. J. Robinson, '21st Century Sport: Screen Grab'. *The Observer*, November 4, 2007. http:// sport.guardian.co.uk/news/story/0,,2205107,00.html.
72. Given, *Turning off the Television*.
73. Rowe, *Sport, Culture and the Media*; Miller, *Cultural Citizenship*.
74. Australian Labor Party, 'Socceroos Fans Pay The Price For Howard's Inaction'. April 25, 2006. http://www.alp.org.au/media/0406/mscomit260.php.
75. Roche, *Mega-Events and Modernity*.

## References

Bolotny, F., and J-F. Bourg. 'The Demand for Media Coverage'. In *Handbook on the Economics of Sport,* ed. W. Andreff and S. Symanski, 112–36. Cheltenham: Edward Elgar Publishing, 2006.

Booth, D., and G. Doyle. 'UK Television Warms Up for the Biggest Game Yet: Pay-per-View'. *Media, Culture & Society* 19, no. 2 (1997): 277–84.

Boyle, R., and R. Haynes. *Power Play: Sport, the Media and Popular Culture.* Harlow, UK: Pearson Education, 2000.

Brookes, R. *Representing Sport.* London: Arnold, 2002.

Carmiel, J. 'Bipolar (Un)patriots: National Identity, Ethnic Identity and the 2006 FIFA World Cup'. Paper presented at the annual conference of the Cultural Studies Association of Australasia, December 6–8, 2006. http://www.unaustralia.com/electronicpdf/Uncarniel. pdf.

Cashman, R. 'The Australian Sporting Obsession'. *Sporting Traditions* 4, no. 1 (1987): 47–55.

Cashman, R. *Paradise of Sport: The Rise of Organized Sport in Australia.* Melbourne: Oxford University Press, 1995.

Chadwick, P. *Media Mates: Carving up Australia's Media.* Melbourne: Macmillan, 1989.

Cohen, S. *Folk Devils and Moral Panics: The Creation of the Mods and Rockers.* St Albans, Herts: Paladin, 1972.

Cook, P.G. 'Steering Between Private and State Power: The Upheavals in Australian Broadcasting and Rationales for Regulation'. *Continuum: The Australian Journal of Media & Culture* 4, no. 1 (1990). http://wwwmcc.murdoch.edu.au/ReadingRoom/4.1/Cook.html.

Croteau, D., and W. Hoynes. *The Business of Media: Corporate Media and the Public Interest.* New York: Pine Forge Press, 2001.

Dwyer, T. 'Emerging Policies for Pay-TV: Official Conceptions of Audience in Transition'. *Continuum: The Australian Journal of Media & Culture* 4, no. 1 (1990). http:// wwwmcc.murdoch.edu.au/ReadingRoom/4.1/Dwyer.html.

Flew, T., and C. Gilmour. 'Television and Pay TV'. In *The Media and Communications in Australia,* ed. S. Cunningham and G. Turner, 175–92. Sydney: Allen and Unwin, 2005.

Given, J. *Turning off the Television: Broadcasting's Uncertain Future.* Sydney: University of New South Wales Press, 2003.

Hallinan, J., and M.L. Krotee. 'Conceptions of Nationalism and Citizenship Among Non-Anglo-Celtic Soccer Clubs in an Australian City'. *Journal of Sport and Social Issues* 17, no. 2 (1993): 125–33.

Hallinan, J., J.E. Hughson, and M. Burke. 'Supporting the "World Game" in Australia: A Case Study of Fandom at National and Club Level'. *Soccer in Society* 8, no. 2/3 (2007): 283–97.

Hay, R. 'British Football, Wogball or the World Game? Towards a Social History of Victorian Soccer'. *Australian Society for Sports History (ASSH) Studies in Sports History 10: Ethnicity and Soccer in Australia,* (1994): 44–78.

Hay, R. 'Our Wicked Foreign Game: Why has Association Football (Soccer) not Become the Main Code of Football in Australia?' *Soccer in Society* 7, no. 2/3 (2006): 165–86.

Hughson, J. 'Australian Soccer: "Ethnic" or "Aussie"?: The Search for an Image'. *Current Affairs Bulletin* 68, no. 10 (1992): 12–16.

Hughson, J. 'Football, Folk Dancing and Fascism: Diversity and Difference in Multicultural Australia'. *Journal of Sociology* 33, no. 2 (1997): 167–86.

Jacka, E. 'Public Service TV: An Endangered Species'. In *Television: Critical Concepts in Media and Cultural Studies,* ed. T. Miller, 249–67. London: Routledge, 2003.

Jones, R., and P. Moore. 'He Only Has Eyes for Poms: Soccer, Ethnicity and Locality in Perth'. *ASSH Studies in Sports History: Ethnicity and Soccer in Australia,* no. 10 (1994): 16–32.

Jupp, J. *The Australian People: An Encyclopaedia of the Nation, its People and their Origins.* North Ryde, NSW: Angus & Robertson, 1988.

Lawe Davies, C. 'SBS-TV and its Amazing World'. *Media Information Australia. Incorporating Culture and Policy,* no. 89 (1998): 87–108.

Leever, J., and S. Wheeler. 'Mass Media and the Experience of Sport'. *Communications Research* 20, no.1 (1993): 125–43.

McKay, J. *No Pain, No Gain?: Sport and Australian Culture.* New York: Prentice Hall, 1991.

Miller, T. 'The Unmarking of Soccer: Making a Brand New Subject'. In *Celebrating the Nation: A Critical Study of Australia's Bicentenary,* ed. T. Bennett., P. Buckridge, D. Carter, and C. Mercer, 104–20. Sydney: Allen and Unwin, 1992.

Miller, T. *Cultural Citizenship: Cosmopolitanism, Consumerism and Television in a Neoliberal Age.* Philadelphia, PA: Temple University Press, 2006.

Miller, T., G. Lawrence., J. McKay, and D. Rowe. *Globalization and Sport: Playing the World.* London: Sage, 2001.

Mosley, P. 'Soccer'. In *The Oxford Companion to Australian Sport,* ed. W. Vamplew, K. Moore, J. O'Hara, R. Cashman, and I.F. Jobling, 316–23. Melbourne: Oxford University Press, 1992.

Moore, J. 'Balkan Politics in Australian Soccer'. *ASSH Studies in Sports History: Ethnicity and Soccer in Australia,* no. 10 (1994): 33–43.

O'Regan, T., and D. Kolar-Panov. 'SBS-TV: A Television Service'. In *Australian Television Culture,* ed. T. O'Regan. Sydney: Allen & Unwin, 1993.

Parker, C. 'An Investigation of the Australian Passion for Sport'. *Australian Studies,* November 28, 1996. http://people.hws.edu/mitchell/oz/papers/ParkerOz.html.

Redhead, S. *Post Fandom and the Millennial Blues: The Transformation of Soccer Culture.* London: Routledge, 1997.

Roche, M. *Mega-Events and Modernity: Olympics and Expos in the Growth of Global Culture.* London: Routledge, 2000.

Rowe, D. *Popular Cultures: Rock Music, Sport and the Politics of Pleasure.* London: Sage, 1995.

Rowe, D. *Sport, Culture and the Media.* Maidenhead and New York: Open University Press, 2004.

Rowe, D. 'Watching Brief: Cultural Citizenship and Viewing Rights'. *Sport in Society* 7, no. 3 (2004): 385–402.

Sinclair, J., E. Jacka, and S. Cunningham, eds. *New Patterns in Global Television: Peripheral Visions.* New York: Oxford University Press, 1996.

Smaill, B. 'Narrating Community: Multiculturalism and Australia's SBS Television'. *Journal of Communication Inquiry* 26, no. 4 (2002): 391–407.

Stoddart, B. *Saturday Afternoon Fever: Sport in the Australian Culture.* Sydney: Angus and Robertson, 1986.

Vamplew, W. 'Violence in Australian Soccer: The Ethnic Contribution'. *ASSH Studies in Sports History: Ethnicity and Soccer in Australia,* no. 10 (1994): 1–15.

Van Zoonen, E., ed. 'Special Issue: Popular Qualities in Public Broadcasting'. *European Journal of Cultural Studies* 7, no. 3 (2004).

Yong Jin, D. 'Transformation of the World Television System Under Neoliberal Globalization'. *Television and New Media* 8, no. 3 (2007): 179–96.

# Soccer and the politics of identity for young Muslim refugee women in South Australia

Catherine Palmer

*School of Applied Social Sciences, Durham University, Durham, UK*

## Introduction

The embodied politics of identity that surround Muslim women's participation in sport and physical activity is an increasing part of our social and sociological landscape. Strandbrau has explored the ways in which 'a sense of doing something that does not fit with what one believes to be moral'[1] may explain the under-representation of Muslim girls taking part in physical activity in Norway. Dagkas and Benn have examined the restrictions posed by religious factors such as Ramadan or veiling on Muslim women's experiences of playing sport in Great Britain and Greece.[2] Palmer has noted some of the practical issues such as transport and cost that frequently act as barriers to participation in sport for refugee communities in Australia, which increasingly include groups from Muslim countries who have re-settled in the West.[3] While Islam as a barrier to participation in sport in primarily Western countries has been a focus for these and other scholars, others have sought to document the nature of participation of sport for Muslim women in Muslim countries, noting the different conditions that women participate under, when compared to the West.[4] While the different positions espoused in these accounts usefully highlight the heterogeneity and fluidity of Muslim women vis-à-vis sport, indeed, 'the bodies of Muslim women in sport are experienced and mediated through different ideological interpretations of Islam [and] within the particular political arrangements of specific countries',[5] they nonetheless emphasize that, for Muslim women, their experience of sport involves a number of decisions and statements about their bodies and selves that are both personal and political at one and the same time.

With this as background, this study explores the ways in which a group of young, Muslim, refugee women in Adelaide, South Australia, use their shared experiences of playing in a soccer team as a way of establishing and embellishing a particular cultural identity that both affirms and challenges many of the traditions of Islam. Drawing on a series of qualitative interviews with, and many hours of field observations of, the players at training, competition and in other social settings, this study is particularly concerned to tease out some of the ways in which these young women negotiate what are, at times, quite complex cultural politics for young Muslim women growing up in Australia's fifth largest capital city. The study is primarily concerned with the ways in which these young refugee women articulate their social identities through the traditions of Islam and the resources of western popular culture. As is made clear in the following pages, the soccer team in which these young women play provides a unique site through which to explore the politics of identity for young refugee women in contemporary Australia.

## Context

The fieldwork which informs this study was carried out between June 2003 and March 2006 in a public housing estate in metropolitan Adelaide that is known as The Parks.[6] As is the case elsewhere, public housing estates in Australia have increasingly become 'problem places' that are home to 'problem people'.[7] The shift over the past two decades from public housing for families and working tenants to public housing as welfare housing has meant that estates like The Parks now feature amongst some of the most impoverished urban areas in Australia.

As well as providing accommodation for those who are disadvantaged through poverty, unemployment or mental illness (among other things), a significant proportion of public housing in The Parks is given over to accommodating newly arrived refugees. Many of the residents in The Parks come from Somalia and Ethiopia, and more recently from countries such as Uganda and Sudan. There are inevitably conflicts along race lines in these communities. Young Anglo Australian men, who struggle to find employment and who bemoan their lack of a 'lucky break', routinely retaliate against the new arrivals in their communities. The broader political discourse of 'queue jumpers', 'illegals' and indeed 'the war on terror' doesn't help to promote congenial relationships within these communities where incidences of violence and conflict are already quite high.

Such stark social realities have drawn recognition from community development workers and others that there is a need to provide 'diversionary activities' for disenfranchised local residents as a way of averting them from drugs, crime and other anti-social behaviours.[8] For many years, young men have been seen as a vulnerable population group, and have been given opportunities to abseil, bushwalk, rock climb and to experience the adrenaline of risk in ways that don't involve substance abuse or violence between themselves or against the women of their communities.[9] Increasingly however, the young women of these communities have recognized that they have been left out of this recreational framework, and while they do not necessarily wish to sky dive or bungee jump, they nonetheless want the same opportunities for recreation that are afforded to the men folk of their communities. It was in this context that the soccer team came to fruition.[10]

In 2003, a group of young Muslim women from The Parks were lobbied for their local community health service to provide opportunities for them to take part in sport.

The women approached the youth worker from the health service who had been working most closely with them on re-settlement issues such as language, employment and education, and they argued, quite convincingly, that there was a need to provide culturally appropriate sporting opportunities, namely soccer, for women from the predominantly Muslim Somali and Ethiopian communities now living in The Parks. Soccer was chosen as it was a sport that many of the girls had expressed a desire to play. They had seen their brothers, cousins and other male relatives playing soccer, both in their country of origin and on re-settlement in Australia and, in a moment reminiscent of the film *Bend It Like Beckham*, these young women wanted a similar opportunity to take part in team sport. Following this request, the local health service allocated a community development worker to work closely with the local Somali community (in the first instance) to develop a programme whereby young women could train for and compete in a soccer carnival that is held as part of Refugee Week in Adelaide each October. The first year of the programme (2003) involved roughly 16 young Muslim women, mainly of Somali background, aged between 12 and 20, who took part in weekly training sessions and then in the final competition itself. The numbers have since grown and, in 2006, there were about 40 young women from various backgrounds who competed at the Refugee Week soccer carnival.

**Methodology**

The data reported in this study is part of a broader study of participation in sport for young refugee women in Adelaide. The focus of this study is on ameliorating the barriers to participation in sport that many refugees face on resettlement in the West. While the broader study has a number of additional research foci and adopts a range of methodological approaches (analysis of secondary data sources, in-depth qualitative interviews with young refugee women and their families, interviews with policy makers and local agencies, a photo-voice component, field observations and interviews with the community development workers in The Parks and other areas), this study reports primarily on the interviews with, and field observations of, the young women who play in the soccer team.

The methods reported in this study include two reflective discussion groups, each involving 13 members of the soccer team; ad-hoc discussions with the players during training; field notes of researcher observations during training and competition and four face-to-face interviews with the parents (three mothers, one father) of participating young women. These were conducted through an interpreter to facilitate discussion from Somali to English and vice versa. All of the interviews were digitally recorded and transcribed verbatim. Each of the interviews lasted approximately 40 minutes, with the exception of the discussion groups, which took about one and a half hours each time.

**Header in a *hijab*?**

The interview and field observation data suggested that there was great diversity in the ways in which the Muslim women in the soccer team interpreted Islam, and this manifested itself as a constantly shifting tension in which the young women parleyed their multiple, often conflicting, cultural identities as members of a sporting team, as members of the Somali community and as young women growing up in contemporary Australian society.

Some of the players, for example, were relatively unconcerned about the religious import of engaging in sport and physical activity. Others, by contrast, who adhered to a more traditional interpretation of Islam, followed much more closely the religious requirements of concealing their bodies from male view, particularly when engaging in exercise or physical movement. As such, there was a need to accommodate flexible uniform requirements which could both respect these religious beliefs and also preserve the collective identity of the soccer team which wearing a uniform affords. Some of the team elected to wear the shorts and short-sleeved tops of the customary soccer strip, while others chose to wear long sleeved T-shirts and tracksuit pants under their uniform. Some young women wore a bandana in place of their *hijab* (headscarf which covers the hair and neck area). Others wore the *krimar* (which covers the hair and front of the body) during training and competition, while a small number who normally wore the *niqab* (face veil, often worn with the *krimar*), removed it when in the female-only training environment. Still others elected to play entirely bare headed.

The different veils that the women wore clearly signalled different interpretations of Islam, and this had consequences for how the players negotiated their involvement in the soccer team with their families in particular. In the cases of the women who wore the *krimar* or the *niqab*, it was crucial that they could play and train in settings that were entirely away from the male gaze. One mother notes that:

> Traditionally, there is a strong sense of gender roles, and women's roles are in the home, and we have the idea of protecting our young women. So, the idea of the veil is about covering their bodies and not having men who aren't their family seeing their intimate identity as a woman. So, the idea of girls playing sport and having their legs showing was a big issue for me when Aaliyah and Sabah[11] said they wanted to join the team.

This issue of concealing the body from the male gaze proved particularly problematic at the final Refugee Week competition itself, when the men from the Somali and other communities came to watch the young women compete. Several of the families were happy for their daughters to train in a female-only environment, but they were reluctant to let their daughters then compete in the soccer carnival, where men would be watching.[12] For some of the young women, however, the fact that they would be 'on show' and in the company of the young men from their community was a huge motivation for them to play at the carnival. It was a chance, in the words of one of them, to 'meet lots of hot guys'; these are, after all young women at an age when sexual exploration is an inevitable part of establishing one's own identity. Of central concern for this study however, this conflict between being 'a good Muslim girl' (as one of the players described herself) and the open flirtation of teenage romance captures the world of negotiated identity or 'identity work', to coin Walseth's term,[13] within which these young women continually operate.

The importance of the need to conceal the body from male view was recognized by the players, albeit grudgingly in some cases. For many of the players, this was often voiced in terms of parental disapproval, rather than their own religious beliefs. Habiba, for example, recalls that 'my dad didn't like us wearing the shorts. They're thinking we're trying to be masculine, more like a guy than a girl with the shorts and the soccer. For me, I don't care.' Such comments suggest that, while for players like Habiba, religion played a relatively minor role in their lives, honouring such religious modesty was nonetheless a central concern for her parents. This was a theme that consistently emerged throughout my research. When I asked one of the players how her parents felt about her playing soccer, she replied: 'at first, dad said "you're a girl, you're a

Muslim girl, you shouldn't be doing that. You shouldn't be wearing the shorts and showing guys your body". And later when we wore the pants at the carnival he was like "oh, ok".' This father's belated acceptance of his daughter's participation in sport, and indeed, the need for the players to be mindful of the religious modesty which underpins their faith, certainly suggests that, for the Muslim women at the centre of this study, taking part in sport must always be done in culturally prescribed ways. As Hargreaves writes, 'the issue of [Muslim women's] participation in sport is tied to strongly held beliefs about the female body that is embraced by culture, tradition, religion and politics'.[14]

While such flexible uniform arrangements were part and parcel of the Muslim women's soccer team, they nonetheless brought into sharp relief many of the issues that Muslim women encounter in Australian (and other) society more broadly. On the one hand, some of the players expressed frustration and resentment at having to play and train in clothes that were oppressively hot and restricted their movement. On the other, those who wore the *krimar* and the *niqab* relished the opportunity of being in a female-only environment, for it allowed them to remove their clothing without fear of patriarchal reprisal. Irrespective of their degree of adherence to the traditions of Islam, the players were all mindful of the ways in which their dress limited their performance as soccer players. For some of the better players, this was a source of great frustration. Nadeen, the goal keeper for the team, recalls that:

> There are things like the girls who wear *hijab*, … initially when we started playing, the girls would take their *hijabs* off to header the ball and then they'd put it back on after. It was good that they felt comfortable to do that and didn't feel as through they [the coaches] were disrespecting our culture, but it made it hard to pass the ball, as the girls weren't where they should be in position but were putting their veils back on, or whatever.

Such tensions between the perceived oppression of women and the respect for the tradition of veiling are a common feature in debates about Muslim women in the West.[15] While the veil promotes modesty by protecting the female body from view, it nonetheless restricts movement and symbolizes a traditional Islamic culture that is seen (predominantly by Western scholars) as being at odds with the secular West. As Nakamura summarizes, 'many Westerners consider the practice of covering one's body to be oppressive, however, for many Muslim women, the *hijab* does not hide but protects their bodies and their "moral safety". These contrasting views of the female body and its role in self-expression have great implications for immigrant Muslim women'.[16] That said, however, the added layer of patriarchal dominance – that men frequently dictate the terms of the veiling – continues to make the veiled woman a symbol of an ideological tug-of-war between Islamic and secular ideologies.[17]

Such competing tensions were evidenced in the need for the players to display 'non-sexualized' movements in training and competition. Soccer drills such as learning how to 'chest' the ball [block a chest-high pass with the front of the body] were directly at odds with the beliefs of some of the players (and their parents) that the body was essentially 'unphysical' and not to be used to display overt muscularity, power or sexuality. For the more conservative players, a manoeuvre like 'chesting' represented not only an explicit display of physicality but also an intrusion on their intimate selves. For these women, 'chesting' was an explicit display of sexuality and, accordingly, they were reluctant to use this technique in training or in competition. Such reluctance created some tensions within the team, with the less conservative players feeling that their more modest team mates were not pulling their weight and using the full range of skills they had at their disposal. As was the case with much of the interactions between the players, these competing tensions around modesty and physicality served to highlight the fluid and contested nature of sport – and identity – for these young Muslim women. Such competing perspectives served to accentuate the diversity of beliefs within the Muslim families involved in the soccer team, underscoring the need to recognize the multiple, negotiated interpretations of Islam, and how this is then brought to bear on a range of cultural practices and processes.

### Islam or The OC?

While the diversity of attitudes towards the need to conceal the body at training and competition highlighted most visibly the heterogeneity within the Muslim women in the team, the interview data, in particular, suggested that participation in the soccer team also allowed for the expression and negotiation of some fine-grained identity politics that both affirmed and *challenged* many of the traditions of Islam. For some, religion played a relatively minor role in their lives, and these women embraced a range of western cultural practices like clothing styles, popular music, television programmes and new technologies such as mobile phones, social networking websites and MP3 players. For others, these were regarded as the pursuit of Western excess which represented a threat to traditional Islamic culture and beliefs.

In many ways, the women in the soccer team embraced aspects of popular culture that may sit at odds with wider perceptions of Muslim women, both within Islamic cultures and in the secular West as well. These young women were highly typical of other girls growing up in a hugely mediated, Western consumer society. They were conscious of their body shape (they spoke of their uniforms 'making them look fat'), mindful of the latest fashions and obsessed with boys, movie stars and the latest 'spunks' of popular music. Indeed, the version of femininity that these young women acted out shared many of the mannerisms and attributes of adolescent girls in Australia more broadly in terms of sexual exploration, their testing of boundaries and their romantic 'crushes' on the stars of popular film and music.[18]

By way of illustration, the girls in the soccer team would often 'play' at femininity. That is, they would often act out several of the more stereotypical roles made available for women in popular culture, such as the 'sexy' back up singer in a music clip; the love interest of Brad Pitt or 'Summer' from 'The OC', a beautiful but doomed character in a popular American television import. On one occasion, for example, one of the young women brought a blonde wig along to training and the girls all took it in turns wearing the wig and pretending to be the 'girl in the film clip with Nelly', an R&B artist who was popular at the time of fieldwork. Much attention was given over to head canting, 'mincing' and acting out the highly stylized poses featured in many popular music film clips.

The analytical point to note from this is two fold: first, the girls, in taking on these sorts of female roles, were content to just be in the background. They were happy to be the love interest or the back up singer rather than the leading role. Such positionings make sense when viewed through the lens of the intermeshing and often contradictory domains that the players constantly negotiate. Despite their exposure to a range of other media images that may have provided more powerful role models for young women, these young women nonetheless all fell back on their own culturally mediated conceptions of their own gender roles in which their subservience to men is re-enforced, even within the female-only training environment. In other words, the players could have chosen to be Avril Lavine or Amy Winehouse. Instead they opted to play the backing singer.

Second, in such accounts, the traditions of Islam and the (post-)modernity of popular culture occupy an uneasy relationship. As Ahmed and Donnan point out: 'whereas the post-modern Western world promotes a culture of change, youth and consumerism, embracing noise, movement and speed, traditional Islam discourages change and emphasises calmness and stability'.[19] Yet, for many of the young women, communication – with their parents, siblings, friends and class mates – was done in a split second via blue tooth and text messaging. While there is no place for film stars, music clips or MP3 downloads in the Muslim ideal, the parameters of Islamic thinking cannot be seen as outside of broader cultural processes which increasingly emphasize the commodification and secularization of social life. It is sport, as a very particular cultural site, that brings these tensions to the foreground in highly compelling ways. As Hargreaves writes: 'for Muslims across the world there is a conflict in the way in which they live their lives between the Islamic tradition and the pervasive influence of western culture. Since sport insinuates Westernisation, it presents women with particular bodily and cultural uncertainties.'[20]

In many ways, these Muslim refugee women acted out a version of femininity that many women in the West would no doubt be familiar with, for it traces a common trajectory through adolescence. Nonetheless, there were stark differences that were undeniable. These women brought to their enactment of femininity a very particular cultural history that few of us can perhaps appreciate. The young women all spoke of truly traumatic experiences common to other refugee women[21] which they had endured. These included rape and violence, torture and persecution, the loss of family members and other loved ones, as well as periods of time spent in refugee camps prior to settling in Australia and in detention centres on arrival. On re-settlement, these young women then take on additional responsibilities that underscore the gendered hierarchy of Islamic life. With their cultural roles very much defined by their domestic responsibilities as carers and nurturers,[22] these women, some as young as 12 or 13, are expected to take on the tasks of English translation for their parents or older relatives, cooking, cleaning and the minding of younger siblings, often in addition to attending school and in some cases holding down part-time jobs as well. These young women are positioned in their own communities in very particular ways that impose definitions and limitations which many in the West find difficult to reconcile.[23]

In this context, the existence of an all-Muslim women's soccer team may appear something of a paradox, yet it serves to underscore the complexity of the politics of identity for young Muslim women who have resettled in countries like Australia. In their on-going presentation of self as young women, their worlds are constituted by not one but many intermeshing domains or, in Bourdieu's terms. 'fields'.[24] Being a young Muslim refugee woman in a country like Australia involves an endless series of strategies and readjustments as these women continually negotiate and reposition themselves in a world of fine difference where the similarities are often more revealing of difference than the differences themselves.

Such observations share parallels with those of Kay who notes that 'minority ethnic youth have been described as skilled cross-cultural navigators, who draw, not only on their own and the majority culture, but also other minority cultures in the population'.[25] While Kay cautions against the assumption that such navigational processes are unidirectional – that Muslim youths are presumed to move only towards the more progressive elements of other cultures – the findings from this study suggest that the young women do not jettison their Muslim culture, but incorporate it as an 'adjustment strategy'[26] into their evolving identity as Muslim women in Australia.

## Performing identity

This negotiation of 'fields' was made maximally visible in the final soccer carnival that the young women had been training for. When talking to the players, it was evident just how important the performative space of the final carnival was to them.[27] As Jamira notes: 'I liked competition because people were showing more effort than they did at practice.' In addition to demonstrating their skills on the soccer pitch, the players could showcase themselves as young women, and most importantly, they could showcase themselves as Somali in an environment where a number of other cultural identities were on display through the various teams competing in the carnival. As the community development worker involved in the programme put it: 'the thing about a multicultural carnival is the whole community comes to watch. You've got teams representing their country, and that's a big deal for them.' On the day of the Refugee Week Soccer Carnival, this celebration of culture and homeland was displayed in a sensory feast of colour, sound, movement and language. Proud family members held Somali flags high, many of the parents who had come to watch the team were adorned in traditional African clothing, drum beats rang out from the side lines and an unfamiliar language was carried through the air as the players called out to their parents from their positions on the pitch. The community development worker continues: 'what we saw on the day was that the girls played a game of soccer … and the communities could see that this was a positive experience for them, and from that, there was a sense of pride in the young people from their communities.'

The crucial point to note about the soccer carnival was that, in performing in front of other members of their community, many of the more traditional elements of their identity as Muslim women were reinforced. While training had provided a mechanism through which the players could explore the more 'western' aspects of their identity (such as music and mobile phones), the carnival brought to the foreground many of the long-held traditions of Islam, particularly the need to cover the female body. While there had been considerable flexibility as to what the players wore at training, at the carnival, *all* of the women wore long sleeves and tracksuit pants under their strip as recognition of their Islamic backgrounds. While Walseth[28] reports that when young Muslim women in Norway took part in sport they experienced sanctions and harassment from their community, this does not appear to be the case in the Australian context. If anything, soccer became a means through which the women could present a visible, narrative of achievement on behalf of the broader Somali community. These young women, in other words, became important ambassadors for their community is a broader political and racial environment which seeks to marginalize and 'Other' those resettled in Australia on humanitarian grounds.

## Discussion: Muslim women, identity and sport

This study has been concerned with exploring how a group of mainly Somali, young Muslim refugee women construct their individual and collective identities through sport. To do this, it has outlined the ways in which these women draw on the traditions

Islam and the resources of western popular culture in, at times, quite contradictory ways. While adolescence is rarely straightforward for anyone, these young women must contend with an additional set of tensions and complexities. As refugee women, resettled in a new country, the players in the soccer team are 'out-of-place' in a number of ways.[29] Displaced geographically, they are also 'out-of-place' culturally in terms of the uneasy fit between the traditions of Islam and the excesses of popular culture which they now encounter. As described in this study, social and sporting identities for these young women are constructed relationally; through their team-mates, their parents and the broader community alike. In other words, the women in the soccer team are culturally constituted within competing social worlds, as well as through a broader political discourse that positions them as 'Other'.

This ethnographic study of a Muslim refugee women's soccer team has served to highlight the complex set of relations which underscore the formation of one's identity as a social being. For these women, as indeed for other diasporic communities, identity is not fixed, but fluid, affected by changing political, social and cultural conditions. As Hall writes:

> identities are never unified and, in late modern times, increasingly fragmented and fractured; never singular but multiply constructed across different, often intersecting and antagonistic discourses, practices and positions. They are subject to a radical historicisation and are constantly in the process of change and transformation.[30]

Through the actions and interactions of the players as they geared up for the Refugee Week Soccer Carnival, we get some sense of how these multiple, intermeshing and contradictory identities are both produced and then *performed*.

While this study has been centrally concerned with the fluid and competing practices and positions through which identities are socially constituted in contemporary times, the political implications of this are never far away. All of the players whose lives inform this study also face the burden of *poverty* as well. All of the players live in one of Adelaide's poorest communities, and there is a need to consider this axis of inequality as well. As Hargeaves writes: 'these women come from historically marginalised groups who have had to struggle against particularly harsh forms of discrimination and have constructed their own sporting identities in changing and difficult conditions'.[31]

As this study has endeavoured to tease out, there is not a 'one size fits all' interpretation of what it means to be a young Muslim woman: indeed, there is great fluidity and difference within this particular cultural category, and this has implications for how Muslim women are perceived and regarded in the West, for 'the bodies of Muslim women are regulated within the broader context of local-global relations and in relation to Western femininities and sexual politics'.[32]

There is also a great similarity between the version of adolescent femininity enacted by the young Muslim refugee women whose lives inform this study and that embraced by other young women from Anglo-Australian backgrounds. It is these fine distinctions rather than the obvious differences of culture or religion as embodied in language or dress, for example, that may ultimately prove more instructive about the ways in which we come to understand how young Muslim (and other) women construct their identities through social and sporting behaviours. It is this accommodation and negotiation of 'sameness' and 'difference' that is particularly intriguing, for it hits on one of the most enduring themes in sociological and other inquiries: how is identity defined and created; where is it located and how is it communicated? The question of 'how do you know who you are' is at the centre of much critical inquiry, and as presented here, the soccer team provides a unique site through which to explore such questions of identity for young Muslim refugee women in contemporary Australia.

## Notes

1. Strandbrau, 'Identity, Embodied Culture', 28.
2. Dagkas and Benn, 'Young Muslim Women's Experiences'.
3. Palmer, 'A World of Fine Difference'; Palmer, *Evaluation of the New Arrival*.
4. For example, Balboul, 'Sporting Females in Egypt'; Morgan, 'Hassiba Boulmerka and Islamic Green'; Walseth and Fasting, 'Islam's View on Physical Activity', Hargreaves, 'The Muslim Sports Heroic'; Hargreaves, 'Sport, Exercise'.
5. Hargreaves, 'Sport, Exercise', 74.
6. The Parks' takes its name from the five suburbs in Adelaide's north-west which comprise the estate. It was constructed by the SA Housing Trust between 1945 and 1964, as part of an overall economic development strategy that sought to provide low-cost rental housing for workers and their families which was close to the manufacturing and automotive factories in the area at the time. Economic changes in The Parks and other public housing estates, coupled with shifts in family structures and progressively tighter restrictions governing access to public housing have 'resulted in tenants who increasingly experience problems of unemployment, low-income and poverty and, in some instances, increasing incidences of crime and violence' (Palmer *et al.*, 'Challenging the Stigma', 412).
7. Arthurson and Jacobs, 'A Critique of the Concept of Social Exclusion'.
8. For example, Drummond, *The Young Males*; Crabbe, 'A Sporting Chance', Morris, Sallybanks and Willis, *Sport, Physical Activity*.
9. Much research has documented the positive impacts of recreation programmes for 'at-risk' youth (see Wilson and White, 'Tolerance Rules', for a summary). However this has tended to focus on the experiences of men. In a related vein, many of the classic sociological and cultural studies of 'youth', such as those undertaken in the mid 1970s by the Centre for Contemporary Cultural Studies (e.g. Hall and Jefferson, *Resistance through Rituals*; Hebdidge, *Subculture*; Willis, *Learning to Labour*) have been critiqued because the experiences of female youth were largely absent from the empirical research.
10. It has been noted elsewhere that women from culturally diverse backgrounds are less likely to participate in sports activities, engage in physical activity or be sports spectators (Acosta, 'The Minority Experience in Sport'; Armstrong, Bauman and Davies, *Physical Activity Patterns*; Collins, 'Social Exclusion and Sport'; Taylor, 'The Rhetoric of Exclusion').
11. All names have been changed to protect the identities of the players involved.
12. While it is beyond the scope of this study, it is worth noting that this created some conflicts between the families within the Somali community.
13. Walseth, 'Young Muslim Women', 75.
14. Hargreaves, 'The Muslim Sports Heroic', 47.
15. Pfister, 'Doing Sport in a Headscarf?'.
16. Nakamura, 'Beyond the *Hijab*', 22.
17. Hargreaves, 'Sport, Exercise', 74.
18. Driscoll, *Girls*; Bloustien, *Girl-Making*.
19. Ahmed and Donnan, *Islam, Globalisation and Postmodernity*, 12–13.
20. Hargreaves, 'The Muslim Sports Heroic', 49.
21. Sideris, 'War, Gender and Culture'.
22. Beishon, Modood and Virdee, *Ethnic Minority Families*; Menski, 'South Asian Women in Britain'.
23. See Ahmed, *Women and Gender in Islam*; Hargreaves, 'The Muslim Sports Heroic'.
24. Bourdieu, *The Fields of Cultural Production*.
25. Kay, 'Daughters of Islam', 370.
26. Markovic and Manderson, 'Nowhere is as at Home'.
27. A number of feminist scholars have discussed the importance of these sorts of 'physical moments' as a means of empowering women through physical activity. See Bell,

"'Knowing What My Body Can Do"'; Brace-Govan, 'Looking at Body Work'; Gilroy, 'The EmBody-ment of Power'; McDermott, 'Towards a Feminist Understanding of Physicality'.
28. Walseth, 'Young Muslim Women and Sport'.
29. Douglas, *Purity and Danger.*
30. Hall, 'Introduction: Who Needs "Identity"?', 4.
31. Hargreaves, 'Introduction', 1.
32. Hargreaves, 'Sport, Exercise', 74.

## References

Acosta, R. 'The Minority Experience in Sport: Monochromatic or Technicolor?' In *Women in Sport: Issues and Controversies,* ed. G. Cohen and J. Joyner-Kersee, 204–13. Newbury Park, CA: Sage, 1993.

Ahmed, A., and H. Donnan, eds. *Islam, Globalisation and Postmodernity.* London: Routledge, 1994.

Ahmed, L. *Women and Gender in Islam.* London: Yale University Press, 1992.

Armstrong, T., A. Bauman, and J. Davies. *Physical Activity Patterns of Australian Adults: Results of the 1999 National Physical Activity Survey.* Canberra: Australian Institute of Health and Welfare, 2000.

Arthurson, K., and K. Jacobs. 'A Critique of the Concept of Social Exclusion and its Utility for Australian Social Housing Policy'. *Australian Journal of Social Issues* special edition on Social Exclusion and Social Inclusion, 39, no. 1 (2004): 25–40.

Balboul, L. 'Sporting Females in Egypt: Veiling or Unveiling – an Analysis of the Debate'. In *Sport, Leisure Identities and Gendered Spaces,* Vol. 67, ed. S. Scraton and B. Watson, 74–85. Eastbourne: LSA Publication, 2000.

Beishon, S., T. Modood, and S. Virdee. *Ethnic Minority Families.* London: Policy Studies Institute, 1998.

Bell, M. '"Knowing What My Body Can Do": Physical Moments in the Social Production of Physicality'. *Waikato Journal of Education* 10 (2004): 155–67.

Bloustien, G. *Girl-Making: A Cross-Cultural Ethnography on the Processes of Growing Up Female.* New York: Berghan Press, 2003.

Bourdieu, P. *The Fields of Cultural Production.* Cambridge: Polity Press, 1993.

Brace-Govan, J. 'Looking at Body Work: Women and Three Physical Activities'. *Journal of Sport and Social Issues* 26, no. 4 (2002): 403–20.

Collins, M., with T. Kay. 'Social Exclusion and Sport in a Multicultural Society'. In *Sport and Social Exclusion,* ed. M. Collins, 123–40. London: Routledge, 2003.

Crabbe, T. 'A Sporting Chance: Using Sport to Tackle Drug Use and Crime'. *Drugs: Education Prevention & Policy,* 7, no. 4 (2000): 381–91.

Dagkas, S. and T. Benn. 'Young Muslim Women's Experiences of Islam and Physical Education in Greece and Britain: A Comparative Study'. *Sport, Education and Society* 11, no. 1 (2006): 21–38.

Douglas, M. *Purity and Danger: An Analysis of Concepts of Pollution and Taboo.* London: Routledge & Kegan Paul, 1996.

Driscoll, C. *Girls: Feminine Adolescence in Popular Culture and Cultural Theory.* New York: Columbia University Press, 2002.

Drummond, M. *The Young Males and Socialisation Project: Evaluation Report.* South Australia: The Crime Prevention Unit, Attorney General's Department, 1999.

Gilroy, S. 'The EmBody-ment of Power: Gender and Physical Activity'. *Leisure Studies* 8, no. 2 (1989): 163–71.

Hall, S. 'Introduction: Who Needs "Identity"?' In *Questions of Cultural Identity,* ed. S. Hall and P. Du Gay, 1–17. London: Sage, 1996.

Hall, S., and T. Jefferson. *Resistance Through Rituals: Youth Subcultures in Post-War Britain.* London: Hutchinson, 1976.

Hargreaves, J. 'Introduction'. *Heroines of Sport: The Politics of Difference and Identity.* London: Routledge, 2000.

Hargreaves, J. 'The Muslim Sports Heroic'. In *Heroines of Sport: The Politics of Difference and Identity.* London, Routledge, 2000.

Hargreaves, J. 'Sport, Exercise and the Female Muslim Body: Negotiating Islam, Politics and Male Power'. In *Physical Culture, Power and the Body,* ed. Jennifer Hargreaves and Patricia Vertinsky, 74–100. London: Routledge, 2007.

Hebdidge, D. *Subculture: the Meaning of Style.* London: Methuen, 1979.

Kay, T. 'Daughters of Islam: Family Influences on Muslim Young Women's Participation in Sport'. *International Review for the Sociology of Sport* 41, no. 3–4 (2007): 357–75.

Markovic, M., and L. Manderson. 'Nowhere is As At Home: Adjustment Strategies of Recent Immigrant Women from the Former Yugoslav Republics in Southeast Queensland'. *Journal of Sociology* 36, no. 3 (2000): 315–28.

McDermott, L. 'Towards a Feminist Understanding of Physicality Within the Context of Women's Physically Active and Sporting Lives'. *Sociology of Sport Journal* 13, no. 1 (1996): 12–30.

Menski, W. 'South Asian Women in Britain, Family Integrity and the Primary Purpose'. In *Ethnicity, Gender and Social Change,* ed. R. Barot, H. Bradley, and S. Fenton, 81–98. London: Macmillan, 1999.

Morgan, W.J. 'Hassiba Boulmerka and Islamic Green: International Sports, Cultural Differences and their Post-modern Interpretation'. In *Sport and Post-modern Times,* ed. Genevieve Rail, 333–44. New York: SUNY, 1998.

Morris, L., J. Sallybanks, and K. Willis. *Sport, Physical Activity and Antisocial Behaviour in Youth.* Canberra: Australian Institute of Criminology, Trends & Issues in Criminal Justice, No. 249, 2003.

Nakamura, Y. 'Beyond the *Hijab*: Female Muslims and Physical Activity'. *Women in Sport & Physical Activity,* 11, no. 1 (2002): 21–48.

Palmer C. 'A World of Fine Difference: Sport and Newly Arrived Young Refugee Women in Adelaide, South Australia'. Study presented to Department of Gender Studies, University of Otago, Dunedin, New Zealand, September 2005.

Palmer C. *Evaluation of the New Arrival Young Women's Soccer Program.* South Australia: Department of Health, Adelaide Central Community Health Service, 2005.

Palmer, C., A. Ziersch, K. Arthurson, and F. Baum. 'Challenging the Stigma of Public Housing: Preliminary Findings from a Qualitative Study in South Australia'. *Urban Policy & Research* 22, no. 4 (2004): 411–26.

Pfister, G. 'Doing Sport in a Headscarf? German Sport and Turkish Females'. *Journal of Sport History* 27, no. 3 (2000): 497–524.

Sideris, T. 'War, Gender and Culture: Mozambican Women Refugees'. *Social Science and Medicine* 56, no. 4 (2003): 713–24.

Strandbrau, A. 'Identity, Embodied Culture and Physical Exercise: Stories from Muslim Girls in Oslo with Immigrant Backgrounds'. *Young* 13, no. 1 (2005): 27–45.

Taylor, T. 'The Rhetoric of Exclusion: Perspectives of Cultural Diversity in Australian Netball'. *Journal of Sport and Social Issues* 28, no. 4 (2004): 453–76.

Walseth, K. 'Young Muslim Women and Sport: the Impact of Identity Work'. *Leisure Studies* 25, no. 1 (2006): 75–94.

Walseth, K., and K. Fasting. 'Islam's View on Physical Activity and Sport'. *International Review for the Sociology of Sport.* 38, no. 1 (2003): 45–60.

Willis, P.E. *Learning to Labour: How Working Class Kids Get Working Class Jobs.* New York: Columbia University Press, 1977.

Wilson, B., and P. White. 'Tolerance Rules: Identity, Resistance and Negotiation in an Inner City Recreation/drop-in Centre: An Ethnographic Study'. *Journal of Sport and Social Issues* 25, no. 1 (2001): 73–103.

# Football barriers – Aboriginal under-representation and disconnection from the 'world game'

John Maynard

*Wollotuka School of Aboriginal Studies, University of Newcastle, New South Wales, Australia*

## Introduction

Australian Aboriginal achievement in football – Australian Football (AFL), Rugby League and Rugby Union – is well documented, but achievement in the 'world game', soccer, has been largely missed. However, Aboriginal players like Charles Perkins, John Moriarty, Gordon Briscoe and Harry Williams did scale heady heights in Australian soccer. The multicultural environment of post-Second World War Australian soccer may have offered these players a haven from the prejudice and racism of wider Australian society. Nevertheless, an Aboriginal presence in the 'world game' has been one of great under-representation. More than 30 years ago, noted soccer historian the late Sid Grant was able to express with some authority that Aboriginal players had 'excelled in the junior ranks especially in the Northern Territory, but the instinctively fast reflexes and speed of our native people has been largely unexploited in soccer'.[1]

The question needs to be raised: why have Aboriginal players not taken a greater role in Australian soccer? Unquestionably, Aboriginal players historically were ignored by the soccer authorities. But prior to the 1960s they suffered a similar fate with the other codes and sports as well.

Racial factors were undoubtedly reasons why so few Aborigines played in any of the major football codes before World War II. Although Australian football and rugby were immensely popular by the turn of the century, and rugby league grew rapidly after 1907,

(Sir) Doug Nicholls (1906–88) was one of the few to play in top ranks of football. After he was initially rejected on racial grounds at Carlton in the VFL – they said he smelled.[2]

Regarding soccer, it is important to realize that most Aboriginal people lived in areas where the sport was largely unknown. The fact that soccer has faced obstacles of acceptance in mainstream Australian sporting culture may also have impeded an Indigenous presence. Soccer in Australia in the later nineteenth century through to the mid-twentieth century gained a foothold primarily in areas where there were large numbers of British miners. From the 1950s, its bases of support were located in centres with significant European migrant communities. In both instances, these were typically urban locations. In contrast Aboriginal people had no access to these soccer strongholds, as from the latter stages of the nineteenth century they had been segregated away from wider Australian society and placed under tight government control.

Certainly the other football codes, Australian Football League (AFL), Rugby League and Rugby Union, have since the 1960s recognized and lifted barriers that prevented the potential of indigenous players breaking through. These other codes established connections with and within indigenous communities. The AFL in particular has established training and coaching programmes targeting indigenous communities, with profitable returns. In the past three decades some of the greatest AFL players of all-time have been indigenous players. Some commentators feel similar results could be achieved in the round-ball code. 'Judging by the way they play Aussie rules, indigenous footballers might be capable of similar miracles on the soccer pitch.'[3] Certainly the late great 'Socceroo' captain Johnny Warren had no hesitation in stating that, in the past, 'the authorities including the Australian Soccer Federation were negligent in seeing the potential that lies within Aboriginal communities not addressed'.[4]

## Traditional culture and sport

In the wake of the horrific impact of British occupation in 1788, Aboriginal people and culture suffered decimation of catastrophic proportions. Some social commentators with a conscience noted the terror inflicted upon the Indigenous population:

> We have not only taken possession of the lands of the aboriginal tribes of this colony, and driven them from their territories, but we have also kept up unrelenting hostility towards them, as if they were not worthy of being classed with human beings, but simply regarded as inferior to some of the lower animals of creation.[5]

The injustice of these actions prompted some to recommend action to absolve guilt: 'Their doom is sealed, and all that the civilised man can do … is to take care that the closing hour shall not be hurried on by want, caused by culpable neglect on his part'.[6]

The avenue of sport would offer Aboriginal people some hope of acceptance, understanding and survival. In the contemporary twenty-first century Aboriginal people are regarded as having extraordinary gifts as sportsmen and sportswomen across a wide range of sporting endeavours particularly football, boxing and athletics. It certainly took Aboriginal Australians some time to gain not only acceptance on the sporting arena but even the right to take part.

Aboriginal Australia had developed a sporting culture long before European arrival on the Australian continent. Arguments have raged that in fact Aboriginal people were the original inventors of a form of Australian Football. Writer Jim Poulter has recognized, 'the Gunditjmara tribe played a game called *marn gook,* or "game ball". A ball was made of possum skin and filled with pounded charcoal and bound with kangaroo sinews. Between 50 and 100 men a side played for possession for hours on end.'[7]

Early settler accounts of the 1840s testify that this game was predominately a kicking game.[8] The Aboriginal players apparently kicked 'the ball with the instep of the bare foot, and they made strong leaps – sometimes reaching 5 feet above the ground'.[9] An early pioneer scientist who explored the Murray River region near Mildura in Victoria's northwest corner also noted an Aboriginal ball game in 1857. William Blandowski described 'watching the Yerre Yerre people now known as the Nyeri Nyeri, playing a kicking ball game at Mondellimin, near present day Merbein'.[10] Blandowski's notes were later etched by artist Gustav Murtzel:

> 'A group of children is playing with a ball', the notes say. 'The ball is made out of Typha roots (roots of the bulrush that would have been growing alongside the Murray); it is not thrown or hit with a bat, but it is kicked up in the air with the foot. Aim of the game never let the ball touch the ground.'[11]

Predominantly though, traditional Aboriginal games were all about teaching skills, particularly agility and athleticism, which were integral in the hunting and gathering lifestyle. All games were taught and encouraged from a very young age to teach skills that were so important for survival. Social behaviourist Desmond Morris reflected 'our early hunting ancestors became gradually more athletic' and using 'these advantages and working together as a team – a hunting pack – they were able to plan strategies, devise tactics, take risks, set traps and, finally, aim to kill. Already, you will admit, they are beginning to sound like the perfect prototype for a soccer team.'[12]

## A sporting introduction

Prior to the 1850s Aboriginal people had little connection with organized sport. However Christian humanitarians and those with a benevolent directive encouraged Aboriginal sporting participation as a paternalistic means of civilizing Aboriginal people.[13] In these early years horse racing and cricket were the most prominent arenas of sporting outlet. There were a number of prominent Aboriginal jockeys, including the brilliant Peter St Albans, who as a 13-year-old rode Briseis to win Australia's greatest race, the Melbourne Cup, in 1876.[14] By the mid-nineteenth century it was noted that good numbers of Aboriginal people played cricket on missions, reserves and country stock stations: 'Rev. Mathew Hale, who established a missionary institution at Poonindie, near Port Lincoln in South Australia in 1850, believed that games and cricket in particular, could make Aborigines more industrious and moral.'[15]

One of the most significant sporting moments of this period was the highly successful Aboriginal cricket team that toured England in 1868. Without question the stars of this very good team were Johnny Mullagh and Johnny Cuzens. Mullagh was afforded the tag of the 'black W.G. [Grace]' and his statistics were impressive; in 'England he played 43 matches, scoring 1679 runs at an average of 22.5'.[16] Sadly by the turn of the century Aboriginal opportunities to play cricket and many other sports had declined.

While it is difficult to give precise reasons for declining Aboriginal involvement in cricket, it was undoubtedly related to a benign paternalism by a more pessimistic institutionalized racism by the turn of the century. With greater segregation and less contact between Aborigines and Europeans at work, there were fewer opportunities and incentives for Aborigines to continue playing cricket.[17]

Placed under the strict control of government Protection Boards, Aboriginal people were largely segregated away from the wider community.

> The need to protect Aborigines from the depredations of white society was overwhelming, and the ensuing legislation produced both legislative fences and the administrative decisions to physically locate Aborigines as far away as possible from whites. The exclusion of Aborigines from Australian society had begun in earnest.[18]

This was compounded 'with the general acceptance of Social Darwinism, which popularised racist views that Aborigines were an inferior race doomed to wither and disappear'.[19] As a result of this process many Aboriginal sportsmen and women, despite outstanding talent, were denied the greater recognition and representative opportunities they richly deserved.

### Barriers to the 'world game'

Australia, like many of the other colonial outposts, tried to create its own distinct national identity, declaring its independence of the mother country in many subtle forms. One area for promoting a strong independent national identity has been sport:

> The precariousness of the dominions' English speaking populations made membership of the Empire a source of security and strength, and physically and culturally connected these far flung societies to the metropolis and the old world. On the other hand their very distance and increasing difference from Britain left them searching for an alternative and distinct identity. Sport – imperial sport – offered just the right combination of communality and difference, amity and enmity.[20]

Despite the fact that soccer had humble beginnings and was embedded in a working-class background, it did not take off in Britain's colonies to the same extent it did in other countries. In South Africa, until recent decades, cricket and rugby union held sway. But of course they were sports tied to the apartheid regimes of the past and soccer became the game of the majority black population: 'the more popular soccer became with the non-whites the more the whites looked down on it'.[21] Canada and the United States for their own reasons chose to make their own way with games like gridiron, basketball, baseball and ice hockey. New Zealand chose rugby union, or fell under its spell, from the late nineteenth century. In 1905 a touring all-conquering New Zealand All-Blacks side won 32 out of 33 matches in Britain.[22] Beating the mother country at anything was a moment of special significance and this played a part in establishing rugby union as New Zealand's game. By this time British soccer players were full-time professionals and there was a marked difference between them and the purely amateur teams that colonial countries could put on the field. Australia followed the pattern, with rugby league, rugby union and Australian football dominating the local scene. In 1901 with the Federation of Australian states into the Commonwealth of Australia, the country had at last cut the umbilical cord. Australian football chose the timing of this period to plant the nationalistic tone and direction of their code: 'In 1906 the Australasian Football Council chose to promote the code with the slogan "one flag, one destiny, one football game", and it was a game to be played with balls of only Australian manufacture and beneath an Australian flag at every stadium.'[23]

From the late nineteenth century soccer in Australia did have strongholds in areas like Newcastle and the coalfields in NSW. Many famous teams in this region have records as long as some of England's greatest clubs. But sporting opportunities for Aboriginal people during this period were extremely limited because of the restrictive segregated government policy of the day.

## Bondi Neal

Despite the severe handicap of many Aboriginal people being incarcerated on strict reserves and denied access to soccer, one outstanding individual overcame those obstacles, and his name was 'Bondi' Neal. He gained employment in the mines of the Hunter Valley coalfields, west of Newcastle in NSW. How he came to the area or escaped the restrictive government policy is unknown, but he would achieve local fame as an incredibly talented sportsman. Sid Grant recorded that: 'A part Aboriginal Bondi Neal was a keen, versatile sportsman. He played senior cricket with Kurri, senior soccer with Kurri, Weston and Pelaw Main, and Rugby Union and Rugby League with Kurri … He once threw a cricket ball 66 yards with both hands.'[24]

Despite his sporting versatility it was on the soccer pitch as an outstanding goalkeeper that Neal is best remembered. He was a member of the newly formed Pelaw Main team that was beaten by Broadmeadow in the 1904 Newcastle competition final 1–0.[25] During that 1904 season a large crowd of 400 people watched a fiercely fought local derby match between Pelaw Main and Heddon Greta. The match, which ended in a 2-2 draw, witnessed some exciting incidents, on and off the field:

> Pelaw Main's goalie Bondi Neil [*sic*] stopped two penalties. Thrice the referee, Harry Speers of Dudley, held up play as spectators crowded the visitor's goalmouth while stones were aimed at the 'keeper'. Play became heated in the final 20 minutes and fights broke out among partisan fans. Player Chris Picken, also a first grade Rugby Star, remarked, 'I was glad to hear the final whistle'. Strange but true, referee Speers was cheered by both teams and many of the crowd. Years later, when living at Kurri Kurri, Harry remarked – 'Yes, the strangest game I ever refereed. I gave a penalty to each side but when Neil fisted Picken's drive over the bar pandemonium broke forth'.[26]

Three years later Pelaw Main and their richly talented goalkeeper overcome the disappointment of losing in 1904 when they won the 1907 final, beating the Wallsend Royals. The two leading teams fought out a thrilling final played at Broadmeadow showground: 'It was an excellent game with the scores 2 all at 90 minutes. However in the extra time period, Pelaw Main excelled to win by 4 to 2 to take the first major soccer trophy to the coalfields.'[27]

Bondi Neal joined the Kurri Kurri club in 1908 and during the 1909 season his form was of such a high standard that he was selected as the representative goalkeeper for a combined Coalfields team that played against the visiting West Australian team at Maitland. He was undoubtedly the first Aboriginal player to gain representative honours as a soccer player. There was much anticipation in the local press of the visit of the West Australian team:

> The Albion Ground has been engaged for the match. The local team comprises a fairly strong combination and a good game of soccer is sure to result. 'Soccer' is the predominant

game of Great Britain and is very fascinating. Those who have the opportunity should not fail to see this match.[28]

Over a thousand spectators packed into the ground for the game. Match reports in both the *Newcastle Morning Herald* and the *Maitland Mercury* clearly reveal that the West Australian team had by far the better of the match, winning two goals to nil. But the win would have been by a much greater margin but for the brilliance of Bondi Neal in goal. In the opening minutes he was 'called upon on two occasions to save, which he did brilliantly'. The local goalkeeper was certainly in the centre of the action: 'Neal relieved splendidly', 'Neal saved well' and 'West Australian halfback Roskam put in a warm shot but Neal saved splendidly'.[29]

Bondi Neal left Kurri and moved to Weston for the 1910 season and played two seasons with the Weston club. About 1912, Bondi left the coalfields and returned to his native South Coast region. Neal is certainly the most famous early Aboriginal soccer player and was unquestionably an incredible athlete. To this point there has been no further evidence of Bondi Neal that has come to light after his return to the South Coast. So whatever became of this legendary player has disappeared from both archival and memory sources. There are a number of contributing factors to explain Bondi Neal's rise as a great goalkeeper. He had somehow escaped the tight government restrictive reserve policy that ruled over the lives of the majority of Aboriginal people, and he gained employment in the mines in and around the Newcastle region of NSW, with its heavily populated British mining population, a renowned soccer stronghold. It would be over 40 years before another Aboriginal soccer player of prominence would burst upon the Australian soccer scene.

## The global impact of the world game

Charles Perkins, arguably the most charismatic and recognized Aboriginal political leader of the twentieth century, was an outstanding soccer player. Perkins was in fact one of three great Aboriginal soccer players of the period that included John Moriarty and Gordon Briscoe. These men followed near identical and connected paths to the top. Perkins was adamant that: 'Aboriginal Affairs and soccer have been my passions and where I could work out my problems through both of those two things ... Soccer was where I got my satisfaction, my fulfillment'.[30]

Charles Perkins was born at the Aboriginal reserve near Alice Springs in the Northern Territory. His parents were Arrente and Kalkadoon people. He was taken from his mother at the age of 10 and placed in St Francis Anglican Home at Semaphore, SA, founded two years earlier by Father Percy Smith for Aboriginal boys. The practice of removing Aboriginal children from their families and communities had horrific implications for literally thousands of Aboriginal people for many decades. However, for Perkins it was here, amongst many other Aboriginal boys that had been taken from their families including his cousin Gordon Briscoe, Johnny Moriarty, Vince Copley and Wally McCarthur, that he attended school and learned to play soccer.

Later after leaving the home and working in a variety of jobs Perkins enrolled as a student with the University of Sydney and was only the second Aboriginal person to graduate from an Australian university. In 1965, he led a group of students, emulating the US civil rights movement 'Freedom Rides'. The Australian 'Freedom Rides' will remain forever one of the pivotal moments in Aboriginal history, and it provided the perfect political and public launching pad for Charles Perkins. The students, in visiting outback towns in New South Wales, used the media to draw attention to the deeply segregated inequality of Aboriginal existence. Aboriginal people were denied access to hotels, swimming pools and, in some cases, even the streets of these towns.

From that point and for the remainder of his life, Perkins was at the forefront of Aboriginal political activism. He played a role through the Foundation of Aboriginal Affairs in the campaign that led to the overwhelming 'yes' vote in the 1967 referendum, resulting in the federal government taking power over Aboriginal affairs from the states. Throughout his dynamic and often turbulent political career, Perkins was compared to such individuals as Martin Luther King Jr and Nelson Mandela. He died in 2000, leaving a void in Aboriginal political affairs that has been impossible to fill.

But it is the intersection and pivotal point of connection with other boys like Moriarty and Briscoe at the St Francis Home and their introduction to soccer that will be examined here. It was their acceptance not just onto the soccer field but into the wider cosmopolitan soccer community and international travel that played some part in moulding all three into inspiring Aboriginal political leaders in the decades ahead.

All of the boys were to feel the full brunt of racism and prejudice that was an everyday part of the Australian landscape during their young lives. Denied access to so much, Perkins' reflections clearly identify the pain he felt as a young man:

> It really hurts you; it slices right to your heart. You can't handle it. I thought to myself, what have I done? How can I rectify this? Can I scrub myself white? Can I do something to myself? Nothing. They really make you feel ashamed of yourself and you feel less of a person as a consequence. It undermines your confidence above all else, and your dignity and your self-respect. Then it develops a reaction within yourself of hatred. It pierced me right to the core of my heart. I've never forgotten those things and I never will. You carry them to your grave. They're scars on your mind.[31]

Acceptance 'as an equal was a powerful panacea for Dr Perkins. To achieve that sense of equality, on an individual level as well as on behalf of his people, was the summation of his life's mission'.[32] It was something that made a great and lasting impact on Charles Perkins. Soccer was responsible for opening doors and delivering a glimpse of a level playing field. Perkins was adamant that: 'It brought me into the migrant community where I found great satisfaction, no prejudice, no history of bad relations, no embarrassing comments or derogatory remarks, they welcomed me into the fold and I've been there ever since.'[33]

The large influx of European migrants into Australia after the end of the Second World War had a marked impact on, and explosion of interest in, soccer. Clubs formed with a diverse variety of ethnic backgrounds including Polish, Italian, Greek, Hungarian, Croatian and Jewish to name but a few. Gordon Briscoe reflected on the impact of these arrivals:

> when these 'New Australians' came onto the scene, they didn't question our background, because they were people who'd had difficulties, they'd suffered from war damage, they'd suffered from [not] having the freedom to move wherever they wanted to, they were probably being employed for the first time, struggling, but yet still wanting to prac- tice their culture, which was soccer ... So when they saw us, they didn't question our background and our racial heritage ... and they respected us, because we could do the things that entertained them.[34]

Of course the migrant interest in the game had an Achilles heel. In the racist xeno- phobic Australia of post-Second World War the game was targeted and undermined.

As Johnny Warren aptly described it, soccer was branded as only a game fit for 'wogs, sheilas and poofters'.[35] The mass media had a major role in this process as they had a vested interest in the other codes. As a consequence soccer was given little press coverage unless it could be portrayed in a negative light and as unAustralian.[36]

> The games challenge to the hegemony of the dominant football codes alienated many who had long held these codes to be symbols of what it was to be Australian. Soccer's strong immigrant element drew adverse reactions and ensured that the game received similar treatment from the Australian establishment as was meted out to immigrants in general.[37]

The vibrant migrant communities nevertheless worshipped the game and embraced their new homeland:

> Football connected them to their homelands rather than to Britain. They created a football revival which, in the context of the narrow and provincial racism of mid-century Australia, only served to reinforce the minority status of football or, as it was derisively known, 'wogball'. The entry of football into the Australian mainstream would only be possible when these new migrant communities had been allowed admission into 'white Australia' in the last quarter of the twentieth century.[38]

As such Aboriginal players and the migrant community were partners and victims of the entrenched Anglophone 'White Australia' policy. The football career of Charles Perkins:

> commenced before the 1967 referendum moved to include Aborigines as part of the 'official' population of Australia. The axiom of 'the enemy of my enemy is my friend' rang true and as such, both Charlie Perkins and non-English speaking migrants shared a common bond through the common enemy of racism.[39]

The launch of Perkins, Moriarty and Briscoe's soccer careers could all be tied to a now-legendary minor soccer game played whilst they were at the St Francis Home. A state under-18 representative team was practicing on a football pitch close to the Home. All of the Aboriginal boys were sitting on a fence watching the team practice when an official came over and asked if the boys would like to form a team and play a practice match against the State team. The Aboriginal boys jumped at the chance. The officials had no idea that these boys were mad on sport and were excellent at any football code. John Moriarty recalled that at the Home:

> We'd play during the holidays from eight o'clock in the morning, from after breakfast, right through till dark. Sometimes we'd even play in the moonlight; we were so full of energy. All we had to play soccer with was a tennis ball, but we'd play six, seven, eight, ten a side often in quite confined spaces in the courtyard at the home. That was good fun, learning to control the ball and so on.[40]

On the field the Aboriginal boys annihilated this representative team twelve to nil. There were a number of officials present from the Adelaide Port Thistle Soccer Club, and they immediately signed up a number of these budding stars. Perkins was a first grade soccer player at the age of 15, by the age of 21 he had moved to the most powerful club in South Australia at the time, Budapest. During this time period Budapest won a host of trophies and Perkins was awarded the South Australian Player of the Year award. John Moriarty, Gordon Briscoe and Vince Copley also initially joined

Port Thistle. Moriarty also made the first team before the age of 18. A number of the Aboriginal kids including Briscoe and Copley made the State intermediate team. Moriarty played for a number of clubs including International United, Birkalla and then back to Port Adelaide. Both Perkins and Moriarty made such an impact that they became regulars in the South Australian senior representative team.

On one interstate trip in 1960 Moriarty became aware that as an Aboriginal the soccer authorities had to gain permission from the Protector of Aborigines for him to travel with the team:

> This is an insult, having to seek permission from someone I've never met. Who is this person who has control over my life? Being an independent minded person, and having just turned twenty-two, I thought I was representing the State in soccer in my own right, which was as an Australian. I thought, 'this is an indignity that no-one should suffer'.[41]

Charles Perkins meanwhile received an invitation from the English first division club Everton to go to England for a trial in 1959. Perkins was encouraged by friends to take the chance as it could only broaden his knowledge of 'world situations' and benefit him on his return to Australia.[42] Perkins was faced with enormous disadvantages when travelling. He set sail on an Italian liner in the cheapest class, with little money or clothes. The trip to Europe was a nightmare, he suffered severe seasickness and ate little. He disembarked in Genoa and took a train to Paris where his bag was stolen. He arrived in London unshaven, with only the clothes on his back and must have resembled a tramp to the Everton officials there to meet him. He was given only two weeks to get himself into shape for his trial and received no encouragement from either the players or officials. Understandably the trial did not go well. Disheartened and lonely for home, he often walked the Liverpool streets at night. He gained employment at the Mersey shipyards as a fitter, but racism there forced him to look elsewhere. He gained a job as a coalminer in Wigan and lived with a former friend from the St Francis home, Wally McArthur, who was now a world class rugby league player. The mining community had no problem accepting Perkins as one of their own. He was given a football opportunity with Bishop Auckland, then regarded as the best amateur team in Britain. He was an outstanding success and, now fully fit and acclimatized, his performances warranted the notice of some first division clubs, including one offer of a trial by the legendary Matt Busby and Manchester United. Perkins, now suffering acute homesickness, turned down the offer and accepted a paid return ticket to Australia by the Croatia club back in Adelaide. Despite the negativity of his initial disappointments in Britain he could at the conclusion of his stay reflect:

> I've had a good time here. I've seen a lot of things, met a lot of people and found a lot of happiness. The English people in Wigan and Bishop Auckland or England generally, I suppose, are wonderful. They are decent people and give you a fair go. They treated me better than I was ever treated in Australia ... I was on my way back to my country, my people and problems.[43]

He encouraged his cousin Gordon Briscoe to join him with the Adelaide Croatia club. Initially Briscoe had played with Beograd and Polonia after leaving Port Adelaide but had moved to the country through work and had continued to play soccer in Port Lincoln where he had represented that district in both soccer and Australian Football. Perkins and Briscoe had a great season with Croatia winning the Ampol Cup, and Perkins was back in the South Australian representative side.

Meanwhile John Moriarty achieved a wonderful milestone at the conclusion of the 1960 state championships in Melbourne, where his performances were of such a level that he gained selection in the Australian side to tour South East Asia. He was the first Aboriginal selected to play soccer for his country. Sadly, he would be denied the opportunity. Australia was expelled by the world governing body FIFA for poaching players from European clubs without paying for them. The ban lasted nearly two years and sadly Moriarty would not be given the opportunity again:

> None of this changed the fact that I'd been picked to represent my country. I was on top of the world. I really felt I'd earned my place and I was walking on air. Of course, not getting to play was upsetting, but I was also still seething about needing permission to play soccer interstate. In fact, that was one of the things that brought me to the Aboriginal rights issues. And it did so at the beginning of a time of great activity.[44]

In 1961 Moriarty joined the Italian-supported Adelaide Juventus team; the perks were obvious: eating at fine Italian restaurants and wearing tailor-made Italian suits. Moriarty proved a great favourite with the Juventus fans. He had previously been approached about possible opportunities with English clubs Tottenham Hotspur, Arsenal and Everton, but a lack of financial resources had curtailed his ambitions. It was during this time period that Moriarty, along with Perkins, came into contact with a number of influential non-indigenous Aboriginal rights campaigners like Dr Charles Duguid and Don Dunstan who encouraged their involvement in Aboriginal affairs. Moriarty outlined, 'I started taking petitions around. Dunstan spurred us on, and we gained a lot of support, in the form of signatures and petitions, that were presented in the State Parliament.'[45]

Gordon Briscoe decided to follow the example of Charlie Perkins and travelled to England to further his football career. He started playing for an amateur team, Henal Rovers, just outside of London, but was spotted and signed by first division club Preston North End. Preston was a club with a proud past and also an Australian connection. Joe Marston spent five seasons with the club in the early 1950s, playing in a losing FA cup final in 1954. Briscoe during his stay more than held his own playing with the B and C teams, the reserves and made a couple of first team appearances. Famous England international Tom Finney was assistant coach at the time. Briscoe supported the comments of Perkins that in England he found great acceptance:

> Well, they didn't know what an Aboriginal person was, and because of our background, we'd say, 'I'm an Aboriginal' … and they'd say, 'Well what's that?', and then we'd have to explain our background. But, they treated you in the same European way, they were very self interested. And that's how we were able to get past some of the problems. If you could play soccer, amongst people who knew something about soccer, you were put on a pedestal … if the coach said, 'You do this and you do that', and you did that, and then you did that well, you were given an opportunity to go further up the slippery pole.[46]

After returning to Australia his soccer career scaled down, and in 1971 he accepted a position as a field officer with the recently established Aboriginal Legal Service in Sydney. In the same year Briscoe and Shirley Smith established the Aboriginal Medical Service in Redfern and persuaded Fred Hollows to become its first medical Director. Hollows as Director and Briscoe as Assistant Director later cooperated in running the national trachoma and eye health programme. The programme had screened 110,000 people by 1981, when they resigned from it in protest against

Commonwealth government proposals to pass Aboriginal health funding to the states. In 1972 Briscoe attempted to enter federal parliament. As an Australia Party candidate, he unsuccessfully contested the NT seat in the House of Representatives against the sitting Country Party member, Sam Calder. Briscoe moved to Canberra in 1974, where he worked for the Commonwealth department of Health, Aboriginal Hostels Ltd, Central Australian Aboriginal Congress and AIATSIS. Briscoe went to university, gaining a Bachelor of Arts, Master of Arts and PhD from the Australian National University. In 2004 in recognition of decades of work on behalf of his people he was awarded an Order of Australia.

In 1963 John Moriarty finally decided to join the European caravan and set sail for Europe with a group of friends. He made an error in timing. It had been his intention to break into European soccer, but he arrived in October: 'it was mid season and it was impossible to break into it'. He went on a European sojourn with his friends, visiting over 30 countries, but still carries disappointment over not pushing harder with his soccer opportunities:

> One of my big regrets of that time is that I didn't settle with a soccer club. I just trained in Sweden. The truth is, I was really enjoying myself. I was twenty six and what really stuck out for me was meeting and mixing with people. I had always been told I was very narrow in outlook; that trip overseas broadened my outlook considerably ... Even so I regretted not playing soccer in England, or not giving it a go there. I lived with that for the rest of my life. I'll never know if I'd have made it.[47]

Moriarty was also forthright on the difference of attitude between the people in England and Australia at that time: 'They enjoyed life; they enjoyed people for what they were. If you were a likeable person, they didn't discriminate on colour – at least the people I met didn't. In Australia discrimination was enshrined in law.'[48]

After nine months of wonderful memories and travel Moriarty was called back to Australia to play for Adelaide Juventus in the Australian soccer championships, the club paying for his flight back to Australia. He arrived back in Adelaide on 11 June 1964 'and went straight from the airport to a Juventus home game, at Hanson Reserve. When I walked onto the ground the crowd forgot the game for a moment and turned to greet me. I'll never forget that welcome. People still mention that moment to me.'[49] In 1965 his soccer career was prematurely brought to an end in a savage collision with a goalkeeper. The force of the impact ripped one cartilage completely off; the one on the other side was half off. Surgery attempted to put his knee back together. After months of rehabilitation he made a comeback, lasting only two games before his knee once more gave out, ending what had been a great career.

One stellar career ended and another began. Moriarty was a foundation member of the local Aborigines Progressive Association and the South Australian branch of the Federal Council for the Advancement of Aborigines and Torres Strait Islanders (FCAATSI). In 1967 he completed a Bachelor of Arts Degree in history and geography at Flinders University and in 1971 was awarded a Churchill Fellowship. He moved to Canberra in 1973 to take a position with the Department of Aboriginal Affairs (DAA) and rose rapidly. In 1974 he served with several advisory groups and subsequently moved to Melbourne and Adelaide as a regional head. The following year he was appointed national chairperson of National Aborigines and Islander Day Observance Committee (NAIDOC). Moriarty left the DAA in 1988 to work as a private consultant in Aboriginal affairs to public and business agencies. He and his wife Ros also run design firms, Jumbana (Moriarty's Aboriginal name) and Balarinji, producing high-quality fashion goods inspired by Aboriginal arts and crafts, most famously with the designs worn by Qantas staff and carried by a number of their elaborately decorated planes.

In 1963 Charles Perkins decided that Sydney was the place for him, and a university degree was high on his priority list: 'When I came to Sydney my deep interest in sport was transferred more to Aboriginal affairs. I realized that Sydney was the centre of the mass media and this was where I could get an opinion across to people in Australia.'[50] Perkins had hoped that soccer could pay his way through university and he trained with the Bankstown soccer club for a week, but was told he would not make the team. A fortunate meeting with an old soccer chum put him in touch with the wealthy Greek-backed club Pan Hellenic. He had a training session with the club and the following Sunday in a match against arch rivals Prague he was given a run in the second half. Perkins was never one to let an opportunity go begging. He had an outstanding debut scoring a second half hat-trick that sent the Greek fans mad with delight. He was an instant celebrity with the Greek community. Within three months he was captain of the club and in six months was captain coach. Perkins' goals and objectives were now fixed in sight: 'With my new status and the financial rewards it brought. I was now in a position to pursue my immediate objective of a university career, and beyond that, I hoped a revolution in race relations in Australia.'[51]

Perkins graduated from university. After so many years, soccer now took a back seat as Charles Perkins embarked with a group of students on the Freedom ride, and to Aboriginal political immortality. Johnny Warren had no hesitation in stating, 'Perkins was a champion – a real Ben Hur, smashing his way through Australia's race politics, and football was his first chariot.'[52] Charles Perkins, John Moriarty and Gordon Briscoe, against all odds made an indelible imprint on Australian soccer. Circumstances and place played a major part in their journey to the soccer pitch. Being taken from their families at a young age and placed in a boys' home in Adelaide in close proximity to a soccer playing area had a major part to play in their rise to prominence.

## Harry Williams

Interestingly, the inspirational exploits of Perkins, Moriarty and Briscoe did not play a part in the career choice of the man regarded by many as the greatest ever Aboriginal soccer player, Harry Williams. He was a lightning fast and extremely skilful fullback renowned for his electric overlapping runs down the line. Williams played in the all-conquering St George Budapest side of the early 1970s. This team bristled with international players such as Mike Denton, Adrian Alston, Johnny Warren, Manfred Schaffer, Mike Fraser and Allan Ainslie. St George was without doubt the glamour side of Australian soccer at the time and was coached by the tempestuous and brilliant Frank Arok. Harry Williams made 44 appearances for the Socceroos and will be forever remembered as a member of the Australian side that qualified for the 1974 World Cup Finals in Germany. William's rise was meteoric to say the least as he was selected to the national team after making only six first team appearances for St George. Immensely proud of his Aboriginal background he is adamant that his indigenous heritage was never an issue on the field: 'No one went about congratulating me because I was an Aboriginal soccer player.'[53] He was equally forthcoming in his thoughts on his own fortunate introduction to the game and the wider limited exposure of Aboriginal involvement:

The opportunity for indigenous Australians to play soccer was probably more limited. Most Aboriginal communities were introduced to league, union, AFL, boxing and to some degree basketball. I was exposed to soccer by a friend across the street at six years of age. For me, it was just a question of circumstances. It just happened. Maybe, it was fate, or maybe it was chance. In hindsight, maybe it could be called luck.[54]

Like the earlier Aboriginal soccer groundbreakers Perkins, Moriarty and Briscoe, Williams was also candid on the impact and connection with the migrant communities that he experienced:

I actually always felt at home with the migrant communities. We found common ground through the round ball, and the shared interest built up a great understanding. We were all soccer players, and it didn't matter where we were from. Soccer is a great leveller for that all over the world.[55]

After winning every honour available at club level with St George, Williams moved to Canberra City in 1977. He spent several seasons with the Canberra club playing in the National Soccer League. He had his last game at the age of 39 playing for Monaro in the ACT State league in 1990. He immediately began taking a more active role in Aboriginal affairs. He gained working opportunities within ATSIC (the Aboriginal and Torres Strait Islander Commission) working on social, economic and social justice issues and later as the Director of the Indigenous Services Unit, for ACT, Corrective Services. Through his work Williams had the good fortune to come into contact with the late Charles Perkins and acknowledged the long-lasting impression Perkins made upon him: 'Charlie loved to talk and was always on the go. He was a very good soccer player as well as politician, and did some great things for indigenous Australians. I am not exactly sure how I started doing the work I do, but while it is demanding, it can also be very rewarding and I enjoy it.'[56]

Williams has also taken on with a passion the development of young Indigenous soccer talent: 'I do have a tinge of disappointment that there haven't been more Aboriginal players that have made it through to national level ... I have seen so many Aboriginal kids with such tremendous talent, more talent than I ever had.'[57]

As a consequence he became the Ambassador for an initiative instigated by Soccer NSW to unearth and encourage indigenous soccer talent. The programme included conducting the inaugural Harry Williams Cup, which was held at Soccer NSW's Valentine Park, Parklea headquarters in early 2006. Williams was glowing from the success of this initial tournament: 'Some 19 teams participated including 5 Indigenous sides and some 80 plus young Indigenous players. We had 15 girls for the week, but due to the lack of numbers weren't able to organize a girl's comp, but rest assured that will happen next year.'[58] Williams is committed to the cause and is hoping to attract corporate funding to support indigenous junior soccer development.

**The awakening of the 'sleeping giant'**

In the last five years soccer has made incredible progress into the mainstream of Australian sporting culture. With the formation of Football Federation Australia and the backing, support and direction of business tycoon Frank Lowey, the leap forward has been beyond imagination. The appointment of CEO John O'Neil was a masterstroke and he initially presided over the formation of the now highly successful national competition, the Hyundai A-League, and the acceptance of Australia into the thriving Asian Confederation. But the qualification of the Socceroos into the 2006 World Cup Finals in Germany catapulted the Australian team onto the world stage and into the Australian public's imagination. Under the guidance of Dutch coaching wizard Guus Hiddinck Australia's performances at the World Cup against Japan, Brazil, Croatia and Italy were outstanding and gripped the public's heart like never before.

The once formidable barriers to the game have begun to crumble at the foundations and even the staunchest of supporters and commentators of other codes now recognize that trying to hold back the march of soccer will be like trying to hold back a tsunami. After Australia defeated Uruguay to qualify for the 2006 World Cup finals noted historian Geoffrey Blainey, himself a great follower of AFL and author of *A Game of Our Own,* recognized the changing landscape:

> Like thousands of others who admire Australian rules football, I watched the remarkable end of the soccer game in Sydney with split feelings … People brought up in Victoria – or in the three other strongholds of Aussie rules – have long sensed the fierce competition that soccer would some day give our game.

> If Australia's national soccer team performs well in the World Cup and goes on to win a fairly regular place in subsequent contests, the publicity for soccer here will be voluminous. Australian soccer then will probably attract more money than Aussie rules, and will increasingly recruit those talented youngsters who are mad about sport and have the natural football skills that both codes require.

> All this – if it comes to pass – will be to soccer's credit. But the spectacular game of our own, with its rich traditions could well be the loser.[59]

Marching hand in hand with this progressive and exciting development of the game at all levels has been a heightened indigenous presence. In the past several years a burgeoning group of indigenous players have broken through to play in the national league and gain national representative honours. Players like Jade North, Travis Dodd, Freddy Agius, Kasey Wehmann, Tajh Minniecon, David Williams and Morgan Cawley have made this important inroad. In late 2006 both North and Dodd were members of a Socceroo team that defeated Kuwait two nil in Sydney in an Asian Cup qualifier. John Moriarty was certainly uplifted by the moment and saw the potential for the future, hailing it as the 'great breakthrough':

> They're both fantastic footballers and they're great role models. I mean what more can you ask for? Playing for the Socceroos and putting on performances like they have. We can get many more Jade Norths and Travis Dodds into the national team. It's an old dream. If you can get an Australian team peppered with Aboriginal players, think of how well we could do … it's the ideal sport for Aboriginal people. Their bone structure. Their coordination, hands, feet, eye. They've got speed and dexterity. They're naturals, but we haven't tapped into it all.[60]

Of equal importance was the recognition by the indigenous players at this level of the crucial role they have to play:

> The way the game is progressing, with the spotlight we have now, hopefully we can be role models for Aboriginal kids.

> There just hasn't been that next step for kids to go before. AFL is in their face, so is rugby league. But now we're making some way on this. With the Socceroos, you do get

noticed more – kids can see that. It's such a big stage. To do what we're doing in front of so many people, it gives kids something to aspire to. People stand up and listen to what you've got to say. I can have an influence now.[61]

This rise in indigenous participation has been noted at all levels and informed commentators have remarked on this remarkable trend and the unease of the once dominant other codes:

Australia's 'traditional' football codes – Australian football and the two rugby codes – have long had their pick of the country's most promising indigenous athletes.

But this looks set to change with soccer finally waking up to the potential offered by the most athletic Aboriginal players – both boys and girls.

The growth in talent has been tremendous and there has been a real spike on the participation graph. At national championship level in soccer this year, 24 Indigenous youngsters were involved. In Australian football, there were 61, so that's still in front, but soccer has already outstripped rugby league, where there were 15.[62]

Outreach programmes to indigenous communities have begun in earnest. John Moriarty was quick to secure the support of Macarthur River Mines in the Gulf of Carpentaria to support a number of soccer clinics near his home town of Boorooloola. Travis Dodd, supported by former Socceroos John Kosmina, Alex Tobin and Craig Foster, all lent their time and support to the programme.[63] Former Socceroo star and national coach Frank Farina joined this exodus to a remote location with the backing of Football Federation Australia:

Farina went round the remote territories in the outback of Queensland earlier this year visiting some of them … The FFA is donating old kits to the remote communities to help them. The game is free flowing and oozes the exuberance and improvisation that young Indigenous kids love and are attracted to.[64]

That investment can only enhance the long-term future of the game in Australia. John Moriarty reflected that this commitment needs to be well planned and orchestrated from the highest levels of the game: 'It needs to be linked with the FFA so it's not done in isolation. We can't go on like we did with the old system. The FFA needs to be involved in a detailed structured way, to reach out to Aboriginal kids and bring them into football. It's long overdue, and I'd be happy to be involved.'[65]

The neglect of the soccer bodies of the past as highlighted by Johnny Warren can be finally laid to rest. Long term strategies and programmes are underway or in development.

The national body, which finally has the resources to introduce meaningful Indigenous programs, hears the call loud and clear. 'We've lagged behind the other sports in this area, and we know we have a lot of catching up to do', said (former) FFA Chief Executive John O'Neil. 'But we are committed to doing a lot more. We've now got some federal Government funding for Indigenous programs and we intend to do something about it.'[66]

## Conclusion

Aboriginal involvement with soccer has historically been one of denied access. The barriers to the game were undoubtedly a combination of government policy which severely restricted the movement of Aboriginal people and therefore their opportunities to connect with a game that was not located near the isolated reserves upon which they were incarcerated. Additionally there were barriers and hurdles placed before any Aboriginal participation in sport from the later stages of the nineteenth century which largely remained in place until the 1960s. The noted successful Aboriginal soccer players, like Bondi Neal, Charles Perkins, John Moriarty, Gordon Briscoe and Harry Williams, were fortunate in that circumstances placed them within localities that were soccer strongholds. The acceptance that these Aboriginal players found within the migrant communities had a profound impact upon their life directives and outlook. The multicultural environment of post-Second World War Australian soccer did provide these players with a haven from the prejudice and racism of wider Australian society. Like the Bob Dylan classic, for soccer and Aboriginal involvement, the 'times are a' changin'. Aboriginal initiatives like those instigated by Harry Williams and John Moriarty are now being supported by NSW Soccer and Football Federation Australia. The current crop of Australian Socceroos and Olyroos like Travis Dodd, Jade North, Kasey Wehrmann and David Williams are the advance party of what will undoubtedly prove to be an avalanche of outstanding Indigenous players of the future.

## Notes

1. Grant, *Jack Pollard's Soccer Records*, 11.
2. Cashman, *Paradise of Sport*, 142.
3. T. Lane, 'Aboriginal Players Could Take the Game Further'. *The Age,* November 19, 2005.
4. Personal correspondence with Johnny Warren, July 14, 2004.
5. Chase and Von Sturmer, '"Mental Man"', 7.
6. *Newcastle Chronicle*, November 13, 1869.
7. Booth and Tatz, *One Eyed*, 10; J. Poulter, *The Age*, June 8, 1993.
8. Goldblatt, *The Ball is Round*, 8.
9. G. Blainey, 'Why I Fear for Our Own Beautiful Game'. *The Age*, November 19, 2003, 95–6.
10. S. Rintoul, 'Aussie Rules Originally Aboriginal, Etching Shows'. *The Australian,* September 22–23, 2007, 3.
11. Ibid.
12. Morris, *The Soccer Tribe,* 10.
13. Cashman, *Paradise of Sport*, 132.
14. Maynard, *Aboriginal Stars of the Turf*, 28.
15. Cashman, *Paradise of Sport*, 132.
16. Whimpress, 'Johnny Mullagh', 98.
17. Cashman, *Paradise of Sport*, 135.
18. Booth and Tatz, *One Eyed*, 44.
19. Ibid.
20. Goldblatt, *The Ball is Round*, 88.
21. Murray, *The World Game*, 18.
22. Goldblatt, *The Ball is Round*, 90.
23. Ibid., 92.
24. Grant, *The History of Coalfields Soccer*, 137.
25. Hetherington, *History of Soccer.*
26. Ibid.
27. Ibid.
28. 'British Association Football', *Maitland Mercury*, May 5, 1909.
29. 'Soccer Football', *Maitland Mercury*, May 12, 1909.
30. Charles Perkins, video interview, 5 May 1998. Personal possession Eileen Perkins, Australian Biography VII (cameraroll2).
31. Read, *Charles Perkins*, 48.
32. Warren, *Sheilas, Wogs and Poofters*, xix–xx.
33. Charles Perkins, video interview, 5 May 1998.

34. Author interview with Gordon Briscoe, Canberra, October 7, 2004.
35. Warren, *Sheilas, Wogs and Poofters*.
36. Mosley *et al.*, *Sporting Immigrants*, 168–9; Warren, *Sheilas, Wogs and Poofters*, xxiv–xxv.
37. Mosley *et al.*, *Sporting Immigrants*, 168.
38. Goldblatt, *The Ball is Round*, 95.
39. Warren, *Sheilas, Wogs and Poofters*, xix.
40. Moriarty, *Saltwater Fella*, 105.
41. Ibid.
42. Perkins, *A Bastard Like Me*, 51.
43. Ibid., 41.
44. Moriarty, *Saltwater Fella*, 118.
45. Ibid.
46. Author interview with Gordon Briscoe.
47. Moriarty, *Saltwater Fella*, 136, 137, 138.
48. Ibid., 137.
49. Ibid., 138.
50. Perkins, *A Bastard Like Me*, 68.
51. Ibid., 66.
52. Warren, *Sheilas, Wogs and Poofters*, xx.
53. Wallace, *Our Socceroos*, 70.
54. Ibid.
55. Ibid.
56. Ibid., 72.
57. *Indigenous Times*, November 2, 2005.
58. Personal correspondence, Harry Williams, July 19, 2006.
59. Blainey, 'Why I Fear for Our Own Beautiful Game'.
60. M. Cockerill, 'Next Generation Can Turn Moriarty's Dreamtime into Reality'. *Sydney Morning Herald*, November 4–5, 2005, 80.
61. Ibid.
62. M. Lynch, 'Game Woos Aborigines'. *The Sunday Age*, December 19, 2004, Sport section, 14.
63. *The Sydney Morning Herald,* November 4–5, 2006.
64. Lynch, 'Game Woos Aborigines', 14.
65. Cockerill, 'Next Generation', 80.
66. Ibid.

## References

Blainey, G. *A Game of Our Own: The Origins of Australian Football.* Melbourne: Information Australia, 1990.
Booth, D., and C. Tatz. *One Eyed – A View of Australian Sport.* Sydney: Allen & Unwin, 2000.
Cashman, R. Paradise of Sport - *The Rise of Organised Sport in Australia,* Melbourne, Oxford, 2002.
Chase, A. and J. Von Sturmer. '"Mental Man" and Social Evolutionary Theory'. In *The Psychology of Aboriginal Australians,* ed. G.D. Kearney, P.R. De Lacey, and G.R. Davidson. Sydney: John Wiley and Sons Australasia Pty Ltd, 1973.
Goldblatt, D. *The Ball is Round – A Global History of Football.* London: Viking Press, 2006.
Grant, S. *Jack Pollard's Soccer Records.* Sydney: Jack Pollard Pty Ltd, 1974.
Grant, S. *The History of Coalfields Soccer.* Cessnock: Weastmead Printing, 1997.
Hetherington, H. *History of Soccer in Northern NSW & Sydney & South Coast.* Maitland: Self Published, 1979.
Maynard, J. *Aboriginal Stars of the Turf – Jockeys of Australian Racing History.* Canberra: Aboriginal Studies Press, 2003.
Moriarty, J. *Saltwater Fella.* Melbourne: Viking Books, 2000.
Morris, D. *The Soccer Tribe.* London: Jonathon Cape Ltd, 1981.
Mosley, P., R. Cashman, J. O'Hara, and H. Weatherburn. *Sporting Immigrants.* Sydney: Walla Walla Press, 1979.
Murray, B. *The World Game.* Urbana and Chicago, IL: University of Illinois Press, 1998.

Perkins, C. *A Bastard Like Me.* Sydney: Ure Smith, 1975.

Read, P. *Charles Perkins.* Sydney: Allen & Unwin, 2001.

Wallace, N. *Our Socceroos.* Sydney: Random House, 2004.

Warren, J. *Sheilas, Wogs and Poofters.* Sydney: Random House, 2002.

Whimpress, B. 'Johnny Mullagh: Western District Hero or the Black Grace?' *Aboriginal History* 18 (1994): 95–104.

# 'Holding their own': Australian football, British culture and globalization

Stephen Wagg[a] and Tim Crabbe[b]

[a]Carnegie Faculty of Sport and Education, Leeds Metropolitan University, Leeds, UK;
[b]Sheffield Hallam University, Sheffield, UK

'I want Australia to embrace this fabulous game. It's not "wog-ball". This is the game of the world.'

Johnny Warren, ex-captain of the Australian football team, on receiving FIFA's Centennial Order of Merit, 2004

This study looks historically at the Australian presence in English football culture. This, naturally, will involve describing a transition from Aussie-footballer-as-rarity to the contemporary situation in which Australians line up as simply one unremarkable nationality among the many represented in British football's contingent of migrant workers. To illustrate this transition we will discuss the case study of Craig Johnston, who, by definition, was an extraordinary presence in the English First Division between 1978 and 1988. We then reflect upon the representation of Australian football in the British sports press and of the British- (and Europe- ) based 'Socceroos' in the Australian media. These representations are considered alongside the first hand case study account of Aaron Downes, who, at the time of writing, captains Chesterfield in the English Coca Cola Football League Two representing one of hundreds of non-elite migrant Australian football workers contracted to clubs across Europe. We begin, though, with a brief consideration of Australians, and ideas of Australia, in British popular culture.

## Rolf, Richie, Barry and no poofters

There was an (admittedly minimal) Australian presence in British popular media culture throughout the 30 years that followed the Second World War. In a sense, and in different ways, we grew up with Rolf Harris who first appeared on British television in 1950 when one of us was 2 years old and the other yet to be born. He created (by drawing) a character called 'Willoughby' for the BBC children's programme *Whirligig* and has been seen many times since painting broad-brush pictures for young audiences. His soft, earnest voice and elephantine body movements were, and have remained, married to a clean-limbed lack of irony which together have made him a reassuring presence in the lives of Britons of a certain age and disposition. Embodying the Commonwealth loyalty of the Menzies era, Rolf reverenced, and was rewarded by, the British Establishment: he was made an MBE in 1968, an OBE in 1977, a CBE in 2006 and invited to paint the Queen's portrait to mark her 80th birthday in 2005. A popular Australian voice on British radio belonged to Bill Kerr who featured in *Hancock's Half Hour* between 1954 and 1959. Nostalgia websites attest that Kerr's character started out as a wise guy but was soon rewritten as the slow-witted butt of Tony Hancock's jokes.[1] A dozen years on and a broad streak of profanity had been added to this stereotype of the guileless Australian abroad in London. Barry Humphries' comic strip creation 'Barry Mackenzie' was carried by the satiric magazine *Private Eye* and translated to the cinema in *The Adventures of Barry Mackenzie* (1972) and *Barry Mackenzie Holds His Own* two years later. YouTube currently offers an extract from the first Mackenzie film. In it the comedy actor John Le Mesurier undertakes a spoof immigration interview, during which an otherwise genial game show host alights on the fact that he is not married and demands immediate confirmation that he not 'a poofter'.[2] This notion of the Australian as militantly heterosexual had already been mined by the Monty Python team for their famous 'Bruces' sketch, first broadcast on BBC1 on the 24 November 1970, in which four Mackenzie-esque Australian men, all called Bruce and wearing identical bush hats, purport to be the philosophy department at the University of Woolloomooloo. A new member of staff is told a number of times that the department admits 'no pooftahs'. This sketch is also available on YouTube and when visited on 14 December 2007 it had had over 97, 000 visitors. The most recent comment, by someone signing themselves only as 'D', read: 'this has got to be the best python sketch I've seen … its a pisser and so like us aussies'.[3]

At the heart of these representations of the Australian, irrespective of the degree of affection that they may have expressed or the possibilities of detecting postmodern, multi-layered irony in them, was a slightly embarrassing country cousin, deferential and devoid of sophistication. This, of course, was long since constituted by various writers as 'cultural cringe'.[4]

The area of popular activity where Britons and Australians met as apparent cultural equals was sport. For example, English rugby's leading historian Tony Collins writes of the 'kangaroo connection' to English Rugby League. Here, since the early 1900s a series of brutal encounters between the national sides had, if anything, strengthened 'the cultural affinities between the predominantly working class constituency of the sport in the two countries'. Rugby League footballers of the two nations communed as tough, egalitarian-minded men, united in their distaste for the class snobbery of the British elite.[5] Similarly Australians excelled at cricket and, in time, provided some of its most authoritative voices – for example, Richie Benaud, who began broadcasting to British cricket audiences in 1960 and was described recently by his fellow Australian cricket writer Gideon Haigh as 'perhaps the most influential cricketer and cricket personality since the Second World War'.[6] Cricket also provided an early glimpse of an Australian sporting celebrity in Britain: the test crick-eter Keith Miller, whose good looks and war record as a fighter pilot gave him access to the younger members of British high society, was called 'sport's Errol Flynn' in the late 1940s. Just before he boarded the boat home in 1948, Miller named the three most attractive sights in England as 'The hills of Derbyshire, the leg sweep of Denis Compton and Princess Margaret'.[7]

But, in the realm of association football, Britain's premier winter sport and long held to be one of England's greatest gifts to the world,[8] Australia carried no credibility in the 1950s and 1960s. To suggest at that time that England should play a full 'soccer' international against Australia would have been the cultural political equivalent of Barry Mackenzie promoting gay marriage or of Rolf Harris calling for the abolition of the monarchy. Even in 1978, four years after what many considered a respectable showing by the Australian team in the World Cup Finals in West Germany, when one of the most accomplished Australians to play in the English leagues, Craig Johnson, was approached about playing for Australia, he said no, adding that it would be 'akin to surfing for England'.[9]

### Coals to Newcastle – from Newcastle: Australian footballers come to England

Nevertheless, when he published his memoirs eleven years later, Johnston and his co-writer showed an acute appreciation of the game's history in Australia, identifying it with British migrants who had settled in the coalfields around Newcastle, New South Wales. He even takes the best part of a page to detail a lockout in the mines that lasted 15 months (1929–30) and perceives in the cultural origins of early twentieth-century Australian 'soccer' the same values cited by Collins for Rugby League:

> In this harsh environment, the intrinsic Aussie traits of mateship and suspicion of authority flourished and became the values by which people were judged. It was this history and these values that set Newcastle and the coalfields apart ... Today a soccer pitch exists on the spot where the men once went below ground with their lanterns and picks. Where I come from the histories of soccer and mining are inseparably linked.[10]

Very few of the men who played football at this time and place came to play in England. It's safe to assume that this was partly because the standard didn't match that of the English Football League, but also because of the widespread belief that other countries, particularly those with a negligible football tradition, had little to offer the nation that had given the game to the world. There was also the factor of accessibility – what the historian Bill Murray has called 'the tyranny of distance'.[11] Regular flights were not available between Australia and the UK until 1938 and a sea voyage, the only viable way of travelling from one country to the other, took between five and six weeks.

Very likely the first Australian footballer to come to Britain simply as a migrant worker, with no thought of settling there, was Joe Marston who arrived by plane in 1950. 'In what is a parable of Australian soccer, Marston is a legend', read a profile of him in the *Sydney Morning Herald* in 2004, 'but not in his own country'.[12] Joe has recently been rescued from historical obscurity and since 1990 the Joe Marston Medal has been awarded to the player deemed to have performed best in Australian football's

A-League Grand Final. Marston's re-discovery seems only partly to do with the increased interest in 'soccer' in Australia over the last 20 or so years. When Joe Marston first played for Australia against South Africa at the Sydney Cricket Ground in 1947 the crowd, as Joe told a surprised radio interviewer in 2006, had numbered 47, 000.[13] The match was one of a series of five, all played on the East coast: three in Sydney, one in Newcastle and one in Brisbane, implying that 'soccer' lacked not so much popularity as cultural legitimacy. It was largely confined at that time to its semi-official heartland and had no place in Australia's (equally semi-official) national sporting identity.

As is now well known, Joe Marston, then a part-timer at the Sydney club Leichhardt Annandale, was invited to a trial at Preston North End in 1949. He established a place in the Preston first team in 1951, played 196 consecutive games for the club and appeared for them in the FA Cup Final of 1954. In 1955 he was made captain and represented the Football League against the Scottish League and, as he introduced him to listeners prior to his interview in March 2006, host Mick O'Regan noted that Joe had been voted one of Preston's five greatest players by the club's supporters. Marston returned home to Australia in 1956.

The football culture that had spawned Joe Marston was, as we have noted, dominated by British-descended Australians. And as the sport historian Wray Vamplew made clear, British people dominated the inflow of migrants to Australia into the 1980s. By that time, however, contingents were also coming in significant numbers from Southern and Eastern European countries, notably Italy, Yugoslavia and Greece.[14] These were countries, of course, with strong association football traditions. These traditions, meeting 'a policy of assimilation at official level',[15] and racism at pitch level, deepened the estrangement of 'soccer' from mainstream Australian sport culture and had by now gained it the unpleasant soubriquet of 'wogball'.[16]

The peculiarly Australian use of this term and the racial epithet it contains – which in other contexts has more typically been related to people of Afro-Caribbean descent – reveals something of the degree of this estrangement. For whilst in the English game, such overt forms of racism helped to maintain a racialized hegemony based on a normative code of footballing 'whiteness',[17] here the game of football was itself ostracized as the racial 'other'. As Aaron Downes, the Australian captain of Chesterfield FC who we interviewed in the course of the research for this study, revealed:

> I used to play in the Sydney State League. We were the only country team – the rest were city teams and they were nearly all Italians, Greeks, Croatians … and they were often called 'Wogs'. [Winces slightly.] I mean I've got a mate who looks Italian and I might call him 'Wog', but that'd just be banter. I'd never use the word openly.

It was in this context that the sons and grandsons of the latter south European migration, many of them honing their skills at British and continental European clubs, were to become the architects of Australian football's final flourishing. But the player to establish the vital bridgehead here had been born in South Africa to globetrotting parents from New South Wales, whose family ancestry was in Britain.

## Craig Johnston: walking alone

Craig Johnston was born in 1960. He has a special place in the contemporary mythology of Australian football, but the reasons for this are more complex than they might at first appear. Certainly he was not the first Australian to prove himself at the highest level of English League football. Nor, in formal terms, was he necessarily the most accomplished Australian 'soccer' player of his generation. Johnston made his debut in the English First Division for Middlesbrough at the age of 17 in 1978 but, beyond this, his career entailed a number of important signifiers which, as he himself acknowledges in a thoughtful autobiography, were likely to endear him to an Aussie public. First, by the time Johnston had begun to establish himself in the Football League, ABC Television had begun showing BBC's *Match of the Day*. Johnston would later say that his childhood football references, like those of his friends, had all been English: 'Privately we dreamed our adolescent dreams about playing at places like Elland Road, Highbury, Stamford Bridge and Old Trafford'.[18] Moreover, in 1981, Johnston had moved to Liverpool, a club with an international following and five years later played for them in the FA Cup Final, which had by then become a global TV event. Johnston scored in a Liverpool victory and was immediately thereby confirmed as Australia's first representative in a world of global football celebrity, headquartered in the Old Country.

Recognizing that his performance in the final 'had gone down a storm in sports-mad Australia',[19] he straightaway began to perform the duties of such a celebrity. He brought the FA Cup back to Australia for public display and agreed to take part in Bob Geldof's *Sport Aid*, giving Australia representation in the pantheon of international pop stardom and fulfilling the now virtually mandatory obligation of the celebrity to 'give something back' via acts of visible altruism. Second, unlike subsequent Aussie 'soccer' luminaries like Mark Viduka and Harry Kewell, Johnston's success was widely accepted to have been down in large part to hard work, rather than natural endowment. As a child he had survived osteomyelitis and as a player his style was harrying and relentless, rather than suave or sophisticated: the Liverpool sports press dubbed him 'Skippy', invoking the bouncy marsupial character from the popular 1960s Australian television series *Skippy the Bush Kangaroo*. At Middlesbrough he had been famously told by manager Jack Charlton, pragmatic son of English football's first family, that 'you'll never be a footballer while your arse points to the ground'.[20] Nevertheless, a few years later he had been signed for Liverpool by Bob Paisley, widely seen as the shrewdest and most accomplished of post-war English football managers. Aussies, like most publics, are said to love a battler and this may have helped to mitigate Johnston's refusal to play for Australia when approached to do so in 1984. Third, when he retired in 1988, still only 27, he returned to Australia and it emerged that part of his reason for doing so was to help in the care of his sister Faye, who was critically ill.

In his memoir of the following year Craig Johnston argued once again that his reluctance to play for Australia had been down to the underdeveloped nature of Australian football culture. He also hinted at a harsh sink-or-swim social world in the English leagues, in which outsiders were scorned with stereotyping and summary judgments *à la* Jack Charlton not uncommon:

> In 1975 I was motivated by the desire to play full-time football. Back then, there was no such thing as the Australian Institute of Sport where talented players can now live and learn in a total football environment. Perhaps if the AIS [Australian Institute for Sport] had been founded when I was fifteen, I wouldn't have set foot outside Australia. While I was in England I met at least a hundred hopeful Australian teenagers who were trying their luck with pro clubs. Almost all went home sooner rather than later. Some were better for the experience; many were bruised by it.[21]

### 'We are what people call a pub team': the Australian football team on the English sports pages 1974–2003

The AIS had been established in 1981 and its principal motivation was thought to be national concern over Australia's mediocre performance in the Montreal Olympics of 1976. However, association football – seldom regarded as a sport of central Olympic importance - was one of the eight sports initially designated for the institute and its inclusion seems to have been an acknowledgement of the importance of the FIFA World Cup in maintaining national morale and international profile. Australia had taken part in the World Cup finals of 1974 and by the turn of the century the national side had progressed steadily toward global credibility. The coverage of this progress in the English press, which we now consider, occasionally acknowledged Australian achievement but, on the several occasions when the Australian and English teams met, the tabloid newspapers reported the matches within their dominant (and continuing) paradigm of English decline. In this representation Australia were seldom good; more probably, England, this once-great football nation now brought low by a bungling manager, were bad.[22]

Australia played two games in the World Cup of 1974, both in Hamburg. Their opponents were East and West Germany respectively. The English tabloids seem not to have reported on these matches, but *The Times* did. These (unattributed) reports certainly did not dismiss the Australians. In the East Germany game:

> Australia, against all expectations, dominated the play for long periods and in Alston they had the best ball player on the field. Schaefer and Wilson were pillars of strength in defence and the whole team fought for every ball. For weeks Germans had been told to expect uncompromising tackles from the Australians, but tonight it was the East Germans who were forced to resort to unfair tackling ... Australia had the better of the first half play, but a change in tactics by the East Germans and their youth proceeded to wear down the Australians in the second half.[23]

Perhaps predictably, Australia's Yugoslav Rale Rasic invoked national football immaturity to account for East Germany's 2-0 win:

> The Australian team showed that it still lacks experience. Both goals could have been prevented. The first goal was a case of sheer naiveté by our defence. This goal caused the team to disregard instructions and they opened up completely, giving the East Germans a chance for a prompt second goal.[24]

Four days later, the paper reported that, despite being beaten 3-0 by West Germany, 'Australia could feel well satisfied with the margin of their defeat', adding that 'Beckenbauer, a master at slowing down the game, dawdled with the ball in the closing stages as the Australians tired, and was whistled and booed. He made a spitting gesture towards the restless crowd and was booed louder than ever.'[25]

In May of 1980 Australia met England in Sydney in a match to mark the centenary of the Australian FA. Eyebrows were raised in the English press that the match had been accorded full international status since England had withheld a number of their first-choice players for the forthcoming European Championship Finals.[26] But in the game itself the Australians were once again rendered as plucky part-timers, giving it a go. England won 2-1. 'In the second half', reported *The Times*:

> the England defence were fortunate to hold out against persistent pressure from the part-time Australian team until two minutes from time when Gary Cole, a schoolteacher,

scored from the penalty spot. If the Australian forwards had made better use of their earlier chances, England could have met with an embarrassing defeat.[27]

The following November an England B team played Australia in Birmingham, before a small crowd of little more than 3,000 people. In *The Times* Norman Fox wrote that Australia 'are by no means a poor team, and have a fine goalkeeper, but could use more confidence … Certainly, by keeping England goalless until half time, they gained respect'.[28] None of the Australian team that night played his club football in the UK.

We see in these reports the sort of good natured condescension that seems to define the archetypal Australian in global popular culture: the Australian football team seems here to be consigned to the same clumsy, innocent, big-hearted and unsophisticated category that has at different times embraced Barry Mackenzie, Monty Python's Bruces, Crocodile Dundee, the sundry males of myriad lager advertisements and, perhaps, Rolf Harris. It is, of course, firmly within the paradigm of 'cultural cringe'. But, three years on, this condescension was beginning to evaporate, a consequence, it seems, of Australia's improvement, although the two aspects most apparent on the English sports pages were Australian brutality and English decline.

England visited Australia for a three match series in mid-summer 1983. The English football press gave the series extended coverage, *The Sun*'s beginning with a preview of the first game, scheduled for Sydney the following day. Here Frank Clough quotes England manager Bobby Robson at some length. Robson had dared to contemplate the possibility of defeat – albeit a remote one:

'The million-to-one shot can still come off if you're not careful … There'll be no complacency … We want to win. We know that the reaction back home, should we lose, will be, shall we say, of an unkind nature. And I find that perfectly understandable.' [Clough counters:] 'England should win by a handsome margin. If they don't, they need their backsides kicking.'[29]

Two days later, in the wake of a 0-0 draw, Clough wrote:

Bobby Robson's inept and awful England couldn't even claim the dubious distinction of a beer can in the back of the neck at Sydney Cricket Ground yesterday. Down the years brave Poms like Denis Compton and Fred Trueman have been pelted by fans on the famous Hill for incurring their displeasure. A sort of reluctant but admiring salute. This time they wisely held on to their amber nectar, drinking it to relieve the excruciating boredom …if England can't beat a bunch of sales reps, window cleaners, teachers, dole queuers and the like, what chance are they going to have when the European Championship Finals take place next summer, assuming we get there?[30]

Harry Miller, slightly more temperate in his reporting for the *Daily Mirror*, reminded readers of the commercial context of this football series – which was to boost the domestic marketability of Australian 'soccer':

England's footballers fly out of Sydney this morning as the super salesmen who couldn't produce the goods. The advance publicity that suggested they were coming here to put soccer up alongside rugby and cricket as a top spectator sport suddenly requires a major repair job. No Test Match drawn on Sydney's famous cricket ground can have been as dull as the one Australia and England put together yesterday. From The Hill to the members' stand the reaction at the final whistle was the same – sustained booing.[31]

Nor was there any pat on the head for an emergent football nation in *The Times*, whose correspondent argued that

> England's chances of enjoying a goal feast were thwarted by the Australian tactics. Their coach, Frank Arok, used five defenders but he said: 'We were the underdogs. Nobody expected us to do anything. Entertainment was the duty of England, not us' ... The Australian goalkeeper, Greedy, spent much of the game collecting back passes from his own team.[32]

The *Daily Telegraph*, like all the other papers, noted the derision that had followed the players 'into a Sydney pavilion, where generations of spectators have been accustomed to rise for the likes of Trumper, Bradman and the Chappells', adding that 'Mr Robson left the field meditating on these matters in what is now the traditional posture of England managers – shoulders hunched and hands thrust deep into pockets'.[33]

The following day, Clough of *The Sun*, with no football to report for a further 48 hours, suggested that 'England are no longer the glamorous darlings of European football who condescended to come Down Under to show the colonials how the game should really be played' and must now 'stop the Aussie sniggers'.[34] A further 24 hours and a number of papers were reporting Robson's displeasure that Australia's coach had been watching an England training session prior to the forthcoming second encounter in Brisbane. 'If Robson hadn't been so serious', scorned Clough, 'the incident would have been laughable. It's a sorry state of affairs when England, with all their star names, are afraid that a tiny soccer nation like Australia are attempting to find out their secrets.'[35] The *Daily Telegraph* reported that Arok had 'offered an immediate apology but accompanied it with ridicule: "Suddenly it's a war. Isn't it fantastic that little Australia can be so deadly dangerous to a big team like England". Mr Arok claimed that his intention was only to further his football education, saying: "We're so far away from big soccer, so every bit of information is valuable".'[36]

After the final game in Melbourne, which England won 1-0, the *Telegraph* branded Australia as 'part-timers of mostly Fourth Division class' and the *Sun* accused some of the Australian side of punitive treatment of England forward Trevor Francis. Having styled them as 'Aussie brutes' after the second game,[37] Clough claimed in his final dispatch that 'for three matches Down Under, [Francis] has been kicked like a mongrel stray by Aussie defenders, who haven't given a damn for his reputation or health'.[38] The consensus among English football reporters, though, was that the tour would have left those Australians not already interested in 'soccer' querulous as to the attractions of the 'round ball game'.

The chief subtext of this press discourse about the 1983 encounters is globalization. Across the English tabloids and broadsheets alike there was, to a greater or lesser extent, an acknowledgement of emergent global markets – for football and for sport generally. Each country is taxed with its own imagined history. England are indicted for failing to be the England of an almost wholly mythical past and, perhaps, for being an in-the-flesh disappointment for viewers of *Match of the Day* on Australia's ABC channel. For the most militantly populist sections of the English football press the preferred language, chosen with its readership in mind, was of national betrayal – usually by the team manager – although, in his final report from Australia, Miller did acknowledge in the *Daily Mirror* 'evidence which suggests that the gulf between the traditional giants and the upstarts of world soccer is narrowing all the time'.[39] Australia, on the other hand, were indicted for *not* transcending their status as part-timers on leave from their day jobs, often resorting to brawn to cover their lack of artistry. Metaphorically, in the summer of 1983, the faded ex-imperial power confronted her hefty unreconstructed dominion with the former's failure to dispose convincingly of the latter being the measure of how far it had fallen. As for Australia, now dubbed the Socceroos, it was made clear that they should not expect to dislodge cricket or rugby as the nation's premier ball game any time soon and, in football terms, their dominion status seemed to be confirmed by the fact that a number of their current players during this period were English-born with modest records in the English league. Indeed the *Daily Telegraph* identified the defender whose stud marks were allegedly imprinted on the body of Trevor Francis as David Ratcliffe, 'a free-transfer immigrant from Bradford City'.[40] Bradford were then in the English Third Division and had recently gone into administration, thus doubly signifying failure.

England returned to play the Socceroos in Sydney in 1991 and beat them 1-0. In the press box a framework of representation similar to that employed in 1983 was adopted by English reporters. Once again, the current England side were portrayed as pedestrian when measured, tacitly, against its mythical golden past: '[Manager Graham] Taylor's line-up was full of journeymen', wrote Stuart Jones in *The Times*, 'none of whom was capable of splashing colour across the evening for an expectant audience'.[41] Once again, a spokesperson for the Australian team stressed the underdog, still-learning status of the side and their corresponding disappointment with the performance of the mother country. Captain Paul Wade told Alex Montgomery of *The Sun* that he and his teammates were no more than 'backyard players', adding: 'In international terms we are what people call a pub team and, with a reputation like that, I felt England might try and play a bit against us – but they didn't.'[42] Once again, the England players were found guilty of that most signal of late twentieth-century cultural crimes – failing to live up to their TV image. 'I like David Platt and Nigel Clough', Wade continued. 'We see these guys on the telly working their magic week in, week out. But they didn't seem to do that against us.'[43] And once again the part-time, migrant nature of England's opposition was emphasized. Wade, readers were reminded, was 'a part-time footballer and full-time draughtsman', born in Altrincham, Cheshire and brought to Australia as a child.[44]

But there was an important new note struck in the English reports on this match. Wade shared the after-match commentary with 19-year-old Sydney central defender Nedijeljko ('Ned') Zelić, who, in his reflections both on his team's and his own capabilities, carried no trace of colonial inferiority. In the *Daily Mirror* Harry Harris wrote: 'Zelić revealed that he was always sure that Australia would give England a tough match. He said: "I enjoyed the game and I was always confident about how it would go. My nature is not to be nervous anyway".'[45] Moreover, not only had Zelic been approached to join Leeds United in England, but he was considering his options. 'Clearly Leeds do not represent his ideal' wrote an apparently affronted Stuart Jones in *The Times*.[46] Unfazed, Zelic expanded on his dilemma in the *Mirror*:

> They are still very keen on me to sign for them. But I haven't decided what I will do. I want to be financially secure, but I am not putting that as my priority. I want to go somewhere where my football will prosper, and this is the reason I won't rush into it … My parents are Croatian. I was born in Canberra and I have a good life. I don't know when I'll make up my mind. I suppose that will be when the right offer and the right club comes along. I don't want to make a decision I might later regret.[47]

This is the unequivocal voice of a new Australian 'soccer', confident, unburdened by colonial cultural baggage and patiently scanning the global football market for the best option. By the end of the decade, characterized by a steady progress in international competition, it was possible to regard the journalist Matthew Hall's assertion that Australia was 'a third-world nation on Planet Football' as an overstatement.[48] This was certainly apparent in Australia's first defeat of England in a full international at West Ham's Boleyn Ground in East London on 12 February 2003, although it was not wholly reflected on the sports pages of the English press, still largely wedded (as they remain) to their paradigm of England's National Decline and Disgrace. Australia won 3-1. All of the 18 players named in their squad played outside of Australia at the time – ten for British clubs and the remainder in Western Europe: three in Italy, and one each in Holland, Belgium, Switzerland, Spain and France. In *The Times* the almost experimental line up preferred by England's first foreign national coach, Sven Goran Eriksson was not allowed to diminish Australia's achievement, nor was there any suggestion that England had been roughed out of it:

> all [the England players'] combined efforts still amounted to less than the output from Harry Kewell, who tormented England even though he had been up until 2 am on the eve of the game suffering from a cold … If James had not tipped over a looping header from Mark Viduka, it could have been even worse for England's senior players. It was with bitter sarcasm, rather than light humour, that the crowd cheered the announcement of 11 substitutes.[49]

But, in the various tabloids, Kewell and the emergent football nation he represents are almost nowhere to be seen; instead Australia remains what she is presumed always to have been – a sport-mad country excelling at other sports, but not this one. The fact that Australia had outplayed England was rendered as a further massive dent to English national pride, not as a sign of the Socceroos' coming of age. 'KANGA POO', bawled the *Sun*'s headline, 'Stinking England dumped on by Aussies'.[50] On inside pages the paper mobilized two reporters to hammer home the full scale of England's latest humiliation. Shaun Curtis writes,

> We used to banish our convicts to Australia. Last night there were another 11 criminals who should have been frogmarched to the boat for a one-way trip Down Under. England's senior team, who played the first half, produced one of the most lamentable displays in our football history. Forty five minutes of cobblers against the cobbers … The Socceroos are football pygmies but they were a class above England.[51]

His colleague, Steve Howard, pointed out that 'Australia are ranked 50th in the world – below New Zealand, Trinidad and Tobago, Honduras and Saudi Arabia. And England, 42 places higher, had **NEVER** lost to the Socceroos – a country who last qualified for the World Cup Finals almost 30 years ago.'[52] Similarly, in the *Daily Mail* Jeff Powell fulminated: 'As if being patronised by their cricketers, thrashed by their tennis players and more often than not trampled by their rugby he-men were not humiliating enough, now they are embarrassing us at football.'[53] This is a sentiment shared by Martin Lipton of the *Daily Mirror*: 'Beyond belief, beyond a joke, beyond the pale … Losing to the Aussies at cricket and Davis Cup tennis was anticipated, if painful. Being humiliated by the green-and-golds at football is the final straw'.[54]

Ultimately two things were most noticeable about the Australian team that night. One is that its prior connection to England was minimal. Only one, Kevin Muscat (b.Crawley, 1973) was English-born. Harry Kewell, Australian-born and by common consent the most gifted member of the team, travelled on a British passport, for which he was eligible through his English father. The bulk of the remainder – came from families originating in countries outside of mainland Britain, including Northern Ireland, Croatia, Greece, Italy, Germany, Slovenia and Macedonia. This was a team substantially of New Australians, less likely to be touched by colonial heritage or football's version of cultural cringe. Secondly, most of them were playing at the top level in well-established leagues, including several in the Premiership (here by invitation, not 'trying their luck'). Taken collectively, these tabloid appraisals, written in their respective house styles and doubtless intended to stimulate a million pub arguments, were an oblique way of telling the Socceroos that they had arrived on the international stage.

### The away game: migrant labourers in the land of football celebrity

Australian football culture, as with all developed football cultures, now divides between an elite and a rank-and-file. Harry Kewell, Mark Viduka, Lucas Neill and others present in the Socceroo side that beat England in 2003 have led the Australian football public and Australian entrepreneurs to the rim of the honey pot that is the international football-media-celebrity nexus. Other Aussie players, meanwhile, gain a steady living in leagues in England and across the world.

In 2006 Melbourne's Visual Entertainment Group released a DVD called *The Away Game*. Based on Matthew Hall's book of the same name,[55] it was clearly precipitated by Australia's qualification for the World Cup finals of the same year. Whilst Marston and Johnston were the pioneers who left the door for Aussie soccer players ajar, the DVD declared a new Year Zero. 'On the night of November 16th 2005', ran the gravely enunciated commentary, 'Australia changed. Maybe forever. If ever a sporting event can be said to have altered the way a country sees itself, after 32 years of failure Australia's qualification for the World Cup did just that.'[56] But, adds the voiceover, the scorer of the decisive goal that night, John Aloisi, though born in Adelaide, 'had to leave his country to realise his dreams' (he played in England, as well as Belgium, Italy and Spain). There then follows a series of jaunty interviews with successful, young expatriate Australian footballers enjoying the good life across Europe. Joking in their kitchens and spacious living rooms, doting on their dogs or young families or relaxing in restaurants, they recall how they always wanted to play football and how, yes, the money's pretty good. The Socceroos assistant coach Graham Arnold refers to the 'lack of respect that we had overseas as Australian footballers' during his playing days of the 1980s and 1990s. Now, though, they have a healthy representation in the world's most conspicuous league. Josip Skoko, of Wigan Athletic, reflects:

> Er, the Premier League? Well, it's probably labelled the best league in the world. It's the most televised and probably got the most stars in the world and the salaries are probably the highest. So take your pick of any of those and you can probably see why someone wants to at least have a go ... mix it with the best. Here in England it's very professional.[57]

'Every week I play in front of 40 to 45,000 people', enthuses Everton's Samoan Australian Tim Cahill. 'They watch it in Australia.' Blackburn's Lucas Neill asserts that Premiership employers like the Australian players' 'Never-Say-Die kind of 100% commitment and the fact that this is our Once-in-a-Lifetime opportunity. We don't have these opportunities [at] our own back door, so we don't take them for granted.' His manager Mark Hughes confirms for the camera that Neill and Brett Emerton, his Australian teammate at Blackburn, 'are basically winners'.[58]

With their places in the first team secured, these men are now promoted as celebrities rather than Australians, offering all the appropriate ideological accoutrements. While occupying an ethereal world of wealth, fame and comfort they are at the same time accessible and Just-Like-You-and-Me. They are blokey and jokey, relaxed and domesticated, while quick to extol the virtues of hard work and football's disproportionate reward system. Neill, for example, is seen as lord of all he surveys outside his remote house in the countryside near Blackburn. While he concedes that the latter is a 'small town full of working people' he stresses to viewers that, as a teenager, he gave up parties to go to football training. Now some of his contemporaries are 'brickie's mates'.[59]

*The Away Game* commentary concludes that Australian footballers are now celebrities in the national sporting pantheon dominated hitherto by other sports. The next step, commercially, will be to try to transcend sport itself and become famous for their fame – the bottom rungs of the ladder to Beckham-style global known-ness. This is beginning to happen, the film says. The players are available for interviews, photo shoots and sponsors. Indeed the DVD is sponsored by Qantas, the Australian airline and the team was subsequently renamed the *Qantas Socceroos*.

There is a dual paradox, though, to the emergence of the (predominantly New) Australian footballers. First, as acknowledged in *The Away Game*, their success is largely predicated on the employment of virtually all its players in foreign leagues, all of which, especially the English Premiership, are financially and professionally more credible than the Australian Soccer League and, unlike the ASL, offer a global media profile. Given the responsibilities borne by global football celebrities, being a dutiful Socceroo can impose an especially punitive schedule. For instance, in late September 2007 Tim Cahill told Dave Lewis of the *Sydney Morning Herald* that although he would 'chew the arm off any coach who offered me the captaincy … for my own health and wellbeing, I can't see myself being there for every single match from now on'.[60] English clubs are reluctant to release their Socceroos for the long journeys entailed in representing Australia – Harry Kewell, for example, said while at Leeds that the club wanted him to quit the Socceroos[61] – and two Socceroo fixtures in 2007 were staged in London: against Denmark at Queens Park Rangers' Loftus Road ground on 6 February and against Nigeria at Craven Cottage in Fulham on 17 November. This, of course, can scarcely assist the promotion of indigenous Australian 'soccer'. Secondly, and moreover, the development of global football competition has brought dual, and often multiple, nationality into play. In 2007 around 90 Australian professional footballers qualified to play for at least one country other than Australia and over a dozen had opted to do so. 'Australian officials', wrote journalist Michael Lynch of *The Age* in 2004,

> have grown increasingly frustrated at the possibility of players, in whom the taxpayer has invested significant amounts, slipping through the net. 'When players come into our program now, they have to sign an agreement that commits them to making themselves fully available to represent Australia in international competition for at least two years after the agreement has concluded', an AIS spokesman said. 'If they refuse to give that undertaking, they don't get their scholarships. If they subsequently breach that clause, they may be required to pay back to the AIS the value of their scholarship.'[62]

In this development we see the realization of the transition of Australian footballers from pioneering sporting outcasts from the colonies to their presence as one more unremarkable nationality among the many represented in British football's contingent of migrant workers. Their employability is increasingly tied to their domestic productivity rather than national allegiance, even beyond the elite levels of the game, as revealed by Aaron Downes account to us in October 2007. Aaron is 22 and a first generation Australian who graduated through the Australian Institute of Sport and now captains Chesterfield in the English Coca Cola League Two having been spotted by scouts on a tour of England. As he revealed, his journey into the game was more about the harsh realities of a competitive labour market than pre-conceived romantic notions or national stereotypes:

> Well, there was some interest [during the tour]. Particularly because I've got an English passport and don't count as a foreign player. I was offered a trial at Bolton and I went there for a three month trial and was given digs. They told me basically that I was as good as players they already had, but no better. I also went down to Rushden and Diamonds. Several clubs said to come back pre-season, so I stayed the summer with an aunt in Yorkshire. An uncle got me work on a building site. I also got a game with Frickley ... they wanted me to train with them. And I played for them and got a small amount. Forty quid a game – something like that. Then I got a trial at Chesterfield and was offered a contract.

Even this development seems some way from the prevailing Australian view of football when Aaron was growing up in the 1990s, when football still lagged behind other sports in terms of cultural credibility:

> You know, there was rugby union, rugby league and cricket. They were the established sports. Then there was soccer. They still call it 'soccer' over there. And it was like [in mock condescension] 'Oh, *soccer*'. It was treated as ... like a girls' sport. We had no role models.

Interestingly, this situation appeared to change not with the organic development of the domestic game or even the arrival of a superstar player but with the country's improved performance at the 2002 FIFA World Cup Finals which seemed to generate new interest:

> The World Cup in 2002 had a big impact. Australia ... well, they got knocked out in the end, by Uruguay. But they nearly qualified and that created a lot of public interest. And gave the Australian team some credibility. Before that it was like 'Australia? We might as well play Fiji, or someone like that.' This coincided with the new A League, which began in Australia in 2002 ... It's on pay TV in Australia. And there are quite a few Australians playing in it now. They do promotion work on local TV and national radio. Viduka. Mark Schwarzer. Lucas Neill.

Whilst Aaron acknowledges that there are still more opportunities for aspiring footballers in England, partly as a consequence of the country's more accessible geography, the growing cultural appeal of football 'back home' means that English football can now increasingly be regarded as a temporary posting:

> If there's a coaching job I could stay. But I think when I'm 34-ish I'll go back to Australia. Things are happening there now. We were in the last World Cup and ... We never had that before ... Well, there was that guy who invented a special type of boot. Liverpool player. What was his name? ... Yeah, Craig Johnston. But he was never publicised in Australia. It wasn't like it is now.

What is significant here is that Australians plying their trade in the English leagues now carry a sense of cultural confidence both in their identification with the game but also a distinctive national 'style' with the AIS emphasizing a more technical approach to the game, where in Aaron's terms: 'We had to keep the ball on the floor. It's a different game here [in England]. It's crowd game. It's faster. More entertaining. In Australia they'll slow the game down for ten minutes.' Yet it remains his clear ambition to play for the full Australian side rather than England despite carrying a British passport as a result of his genetic and cultural antecedents, proudly declaring: 'I'm an Australian. I've got the Southern Cross tattoo [pulls up his sleeve to explain]. They're stars. They can only be seen in Australia.'

It is in this sense that Australian players might now be seen to have 'arrived' on their own terms, with Aaron finding it hard to discern anything distinctive in the way that his compatriots are now regarded in England, suggesting merely that: 'There might be a bit of banter, drawing on the history side. You know: "You're just a bunch of convicts". That kind of stuff. But no. We get the same respect. There's no difference.'

Yet, despite this normalization of the Australian presence in English football this discussion does seem once again to point up the continuing contradictions of Australian football. The Australian game and its exponents have undoubtedly gained a degree of acceptance and normalization 'over here' (in the UK) but this still lags behind their acceptance and degree of normalization 'over there' (Australia). Indeed this latter acceptance seems more conditional - on Australia's access to the global television shows that are the English Premiership and the World Cup Finals – both conferring global celebrity – than on the credibility of domestic competition.

## Acknowledgements
We'd like to thank Tony Collins, Aaron Downes, Stephen Hopkins, Bill Murray and Roy Williams for their help in preparing this study.

## Notes

1. See for example http://www.tonyhancock.org.uk/bill.html.
2. http://www.youtube.com/watch?v=8PfDro1UGUo.
3. http://www.youtube.com/watch?v=eqgnExSiS0s.
4. See, for example, Head and Walter, *Intellectual Movements*; McCallum, 'Cringe and Strut'.
5. Collins, *Rugby League*, 118–19.
6. http://content-aus.cricinfo.com/australia/content/player/4123.html.
7. Perry, *Keith Miller*, 231 and 257.
8. Wagg, 'Playing the Past'.
9. Johnston and Jameson, *Walk Alone*, 102.
10. Ibid., 35–6.
11. Murray, 'Cultural Revolution?', 154.
12. www.smh.com.au/studys/2004/04/23/1082719627573.html?from=storyrhs.
13. Interview with Mick O'Regan. Radio National, *The Sports Factor*, 3 March 2006. http://www.abc.net.au/rn/sportsfactor/stories/2006/1581120.htm.
14. Vamplew, '"Wogball"', 208.
15. Murray, 'Cultural Revolution?', 156.
16. Vamplew, '"Wogball"', 207–23.
17. Back, Crabbe and Solomos, *The Changing Face of Football*.
18. Johnston and Jameson, *Walk Alone*, 47.
19. Ibid., 19.
20. Ibid.,69.
21. Ibid., 243.

22. See, particularly, Wagg, 'Playing the Past'.
23. *The Times*, June 15, 1974, 17.
24. Ibid.
25. *The Times*, June 19, 1974, 10.
26. *The Times*, May 31, 1980, 15; *Daily Mirror*, May 31, 1980, 31.
27. *The Times*, June 2, 1980, 8.
28. *The Times*, November 18, 1980, 10.
29. *The Sun*, June 11, 1983, 30.
30. *The Sun*, June 13, 1983, 28.
31. *Daily Mirror*, June 12, 1983, 29.
32. *The Times*, June 13, 1983, 20.
33. *Daily Telegraph*, June13, 1983, 19.
34. *The Sun*, June 14, 1983, 25.
35. *The Sun*, June 15, 1983, 27.
36. *Daily Telegraph*, June 15, 1983, 27.
37. *The Sun*, June 17, 1983, 29.
38. *The Sun*, June 20, 1983, 24.
39. *Daily Mirror*, June 20, 1983, 24.
40. *Daily Telegraph*, June 20, 1983, 26.
41. *The Times*, June 3, 1991, 30.
42. Montgomery, 'You Couldn't Tan Our Pub Team, Taylor!' *The Sun*, June 3, 1991, 30–1.
43. Ibid.
44. Ibid.
45. *Daily Mirror*, June 3, 1991, 26–7.
46. *The Times*, June 3, 1991, 30.
47. *Daily Mirror*, June 3, 1991, 26–7.
48. Hall, *The Away Game*, 260.
49. M. Dickinson, 'Red-faced England See their Plans Torn to Shreds'. *The Times*, February 13, 2003, 50.
50. *The Sun*, February 13, 2003, 72.
51. Ibid., 71.
52. Ibid., 68–9.
53. *Daily Mail*, February 13, 2003, 85.
54. *Daily Mirror*, February 13, 2003, 71.
55. Hall, *The Away Game*.
56. *The Away Game*, 2006.
57. Ibid.
58. Ibid.
59. Ibid.
60. http://www.smh.com.au/news/football/ticking-tim- bomb/2007/09/22/1189881829406.
61. Hall, *The Away Game*, 259.
62. M. Lynch, 'Players Torn by National Loyalty and Hopes of Glory'. June19, 2004. http://www.theage.com.au/studys/2004/06/18/1087245104962.html?from=storyrhs.

## References

Back, L., T. Crabbe, and J. Solomos. *The Changing Face of Football: Racism, Identity and Multiculture in the English Game.* Oxford: Berg, 2001.
Collins, T. *Rugby League in Twentieth Century Britain: A Social and Cultural History.* London: Routledge, 2006.
Hall, M. *The Away Game: The Inside Story of Australian Footballers in Europe.* Sydney: HarperCollins Publishers, 2000.
Head, B., and J. Walter. *Intellectual Movements and Australian Society.* Melbourne: Oxford University Press, 1988.
Johnston, C., and N. Jameson. *Walk Alone: The Craig Johnston Story.* Sydney: Collins Publishers Australia, 1989.
McCallum, J. 'Cringe and Strut: Comedy and National Identity in Post-War Australia'. In *Because I Tell a Joke or Two: Comedy, Politics and Social Difference,* ed. S. Wagg, 202–20. London: Routledge, 1998.

Murray, B. 'Cultural Revolution? Football in the Societies of Asia and the Pacific'. In *Giving the Game Away: Football, Politics and Culture on Five Continents,* ed. S. Wagg, 138–62. London: Leicester University Press, 1995.

Perry, R. *Keith Miller: The Life of a Great All-Rounder.* London: Aurum Press, 2007.

*The Away Game* (Director: Scott Fergusson) DVD published by Visual Entertainment Group, Port Melbourne, Victoria, Australia, 2006.

Vamplew, W. '"Wogball": Ethnicity and Violence in Australian Soccer'. In *Game Without Frontiers: Football, Identity and Modernity,* ed. R. Giulianotti and J. Williams, 207–23. Aldershot: Arena, 1994.

Wagg, S. 'Playing the Past: The Media and the England Football Team'. In *British Football and Social Change,* J. Williams and S. Wagg, 220–38. Leicester: Leicester University Press, 1991.

# Sheilas, wogs and metrosexuals: masculinity, ethnicity and Australian soccer

Jessica Carniel

*The Australian Centre, University of Melbourne, Melbourne, Australia*

## Introduction

When David Beckham announced he would be moving to the United States to play for Los Angeles Galaxy and raise the profile of soccer in America, it was not just Mr Beckham the United States Soccer Federation were bargaining for, but also Mrs Beckham; they sought the entire Beckham brand. For that is what the Beckhams have notoriously become: a globally recognized and marketable brand. Since Beckham's rise to fame in the mid-1990s, he not only became a household name but Manchester United, his club for many years, also experienced an escalation in their international recognition and following. Photogenic and media-friendly, Beckham also became the poster-boy for the metrosexual look, a new trend in postmodern consumerist masculinity that allows (heterosexual) men to engage in practices stereo-typically associated with femininity and homosexuality, such as care for their appearance and the latest fashion trends, without threatening their straight masculinity. As Beckham became fashionable, so too did his club (drawing a distinction here, of course, between the popular support of a loyal fan base and fashionable cachet). This is not to argue, however, that the Beckhams or Victoria Beckham's posse of fellow soccer wives-and-girlfriends (WAGs) are responsible for the growing success of soccer around the world. Rather they are symptomatic of the global phenomenon into which soccer has rapidly developed – a phenomenon that is a marketing dream and occasionally a nationalist nightmare.

In Australia, both the dream and the nightmare have had their collisions. Soccer's popularity has grown immensely in the past few years, accelerated by the national team's qualification for the 2006 FIFA World Cup. For many years soccer in Australia had experienced something of a PR problem. It was derided as a migrants' sport and subsequently associated negatively with ethnic conflict and violence. In addition to this, soccer was deemed, at best, the effeminate cousin in the hyper-masculine family of football codes in Australia. As former Socceroo Johnny Warren observed in his autobiography, '"Sheilas", "wogs" and "poofters" were considered the second-class citizens [during his youth] and if you played soccer you were considered one of them.'[1]

Soccer's rise in popularity in Australia and across the world coincides with various significant trends, such as postmodern consumerism, globalization and transnational identification, which have further complicated the already complex relationships between sport, gender, ethnicity, nationality and identity. This paper utilizes metrosexuality and soccer as two important and interconnected texts to illuminate how new forms of consumption have altered understandings of ethnicity and masculinity. It argues that soccer's recent rise in popularity in Australia and the rise of the metrosexual throughout the 1990s and 2000s are both related to new forms of postmodern consumerism that are significantly influenced by the shift from multiculturalism to cosmopolitanism. This argument is applied to the Australian context in order to explore the complex processes of the de-ethnicization of soccer in the 1990s and its lingering effects as Australia moves to become recognized as a major player on the world scene, both on and off the pitch.

## Metrosexuality: the consumption of postmodern masculinity

In the influential book, *Masculinities*, R.W. Connell argues that masculinities are historical, that they 'come into existence at particular times and places, and are always subject to change'.[2] As his plural indicates, there is no single masculinity but multiple and often intersecting masculinities that emerge from their historical and cultural context which are often understood in relation to the hegemonic masculinity at the time. Connell identifies individualism, imperialism, capitalism and war as four major influences upon Western masculinities that can be traced throughout this historical period. Although Connell's book predates the rise of metrosexuality as a significant trend in Western masculinity and its exact manifestation is beyond the scope of his projections and observations, he does argue that contemporary masculinities are influenced by the climate of increased consumerism and globalization.[3]

The term 'metrosexual' first emerged in the *fin de siècle* Western world and in many ways can be seen as the materialistic counterpart to the SNAGs (Sensitive New Age Guys) of the late 1980s and early 1990s. The play upon 'metropolitan' and 'heterosexual' succinctly locates the term as an expression of urban and straight masculinity. SNAGs were also urban and heterosexual but where they were men ostensibly sensitive to women's needs and sympathetic to feminism, metrosexuality is based largely upon the consumer practices and superficial appearance of men rather than their politics or emotions. A metrosexual is a straight male who takes an interest in fashion and personal care, such as hairstyle, facial cleansing regimes and the aesthetic benefits of regular gym attendance, but whose masculinity, in the hegemonic heterosexual sense of the term, is not called into question.

Although I refer throughout this paper to the 'metrosexual aesthetic' and the 'metrosexual look', it is important to remember that the 'look' of the metrosexual, in true postmodern form, is not in itself static; it is based upon the principle of grooming, fashion and consumption. In previous gender orders such practices were largely feminized, particularly throughout the twentieth century, and men who engaged in them were labelled effeminate or gay. The trend of metrosexuality indicates the successful opening of a new market sector; it describes the straight, male consumer of particular goods and services previously only successfully marketed to women and, to rely upon stereotype, homosexual men.

Mark Simpson, the journalist whose writing on metrosexuality is believed to have popularized the term, describes a metrosexual as 'the single young man with a high disposable income, living or working in the city (because that's where all the best shops are), [who is] perhaps the most promising consumer market of the decade'.[4] Simpson further argues that rather than being a new idea or image, metrosexuals moved from the confines of the fashion pages to the streets and mainstream culture. 'Metrosexual man is a commodity fetishist: a collector of fantasies about the male sold to him by advertising ... Traditionally heterosexual men were the world's worst consumers ... In a consumerist world, heterosexual men had no future.'[5] The emergence of the metrosexual therefore signals the survival of the heterosexual male within this consumerist world, an adaptation to its market expectations within the context of broader shifts in postmodernity, cosmopolitanism and globalization.

While metrosexuality may not be the hegemonic form of masculinity, it is perhaps the most pervasive in terms of marketing and advertising and has rapidly become normalized. More accurately, metrosexuals are growing in number because of the symbiotic relationship they have with postmodern consumerism: they sustain and are sustained by consumer capitalism and the contemporary marketplace. Susan Alexander argues that certain texts, such as *Men's Health* magazine which is the focus of her analysis, seek to 'shape the reader's views of masculinity so as to transform modern men into postmodern consumers. In other words, male gender role resocialisation *is* the product.'[6] Alexander refers to this as 'branded masculinity', which shares all the hallmarks of metrosexuality.[7] At their most, metrosexuality and branded masculinity have the potential for gender revolution; at their least, they are merely repackaging. As mentioned above, it is not overtly attached to any particular politics or emotions but it does imply that aesthetics do not have to detract from perceived 'manliness'. Alexander finds that *Men's Health* uses covers and features to both covertly and overtly advertise certain consumer products and behaviours that 'promise to create real men'.[8] The only real resocialisation, therefore, is in getting men to practice certain consumerist behaviours to support this image without feeling that they are in any way being feminized, but rather that they are asserting and reinforcing 'real' masculinity.

The image of the metrosexual is one that is packaged and sold perhaps even more self-consciously than other images before it; to achieve this look requires regular clothes shopping, a hairstylist, a range of skin care products. Metrosexuality has emerged within a particular historical moment wherein consumerism has reached a new height, egged on by increased advertising and marketing, new media, globalization and the cult of celebrity. The celebrities are desirable, groomed and selling the very products needed to achieve the metrosexual look.

## The Beckham brand: metrosexuality, masculinity and the postmodern 'world game'

An article in the *Economist* examining David Beckham as a brand observes that his 'most powerful role' is that of a 'lifestyle icon':[9] 'Beckham can cause a sensation simply by getting a new hair style. Once, after he shaved his head, thousands of young men, from Manchester to Tokyo, trooped to their hairdressers to be scalped.'[10] The *Economist* relates his power as a lifestyle icon directly to his recognition as a metrosexual but does not, however, make the critical leap between Beckham as a brand and the consumerist aesthetic of metrosexuality. While his appeal as an elite soccer player has gradually diminished due to relatively lacklustre performances and the rise of new young players who are arguably even more talented, Beckham still holds commercial appeal. A game with Beckham will sell tickets around the world arguably because of the spectacle of his celebrity rather than because of his often questionable talent as a sportsman. More importantly, Beckham's appeal extends beyond the pitch. While many other soccer players and sportsmen enter into fairly lucrative sponsorship deals, Beckham has been most successful in marketing himself (or being marketed) as a branded image that can be used to help market other brands in turn.

It is this complex relationship between his celebrity status and his marketing appeal that, Graham Scambler argues, makes Beckham a hero of postmodern culture in the same manner that Muhammad Ali was a hero of modern culture: 'Beckham, in short, is a paradigmatic – that is, an almost infinitely marketable – (post-Diana) postmodern text: he is everything to everybody, a perfect malleable resource for the everyday *business* of identity-formation.'[11] His fans include those who are traditionally excluded from much of sports culture, such as women and gay men, as well as traditional sports fans, heterosexual men. His ability to bridge these three groups mirrors the role metrosexuality plays in contemporary culture; just as the metrosexual aesthetic allows heterosexual men to participate in postmodern consumer culture, Beckham's metrosexual appeal opens up his image, and therefore his sport, to women and gay men.

A further consequence of this shift in consumption is therefore also a shift in the gender messages encoded in soccer-related marketing and advertising. Michael A. Messner, Michele Dunbar and Darnell Hunt argue that televised sports events and their accompanying advertisements present to boys, young men and adult males a 'narrow portrait of masculinity', which they call the 'Televised Sports Manhood Formula'.[12] This formula presents complex ideas about gender, race, violence and consumption which, they argue, provides a 'remarkably stable and concrete view of masculinity as grounded in bravery, risk taking, violence, bodily strength and heterosexuality' at a time when hegemonic masculinity has been destabilized by socioeconomic change and social and political movements.[13] The Televised Sports Manhood Formula is therefore as much a reaction to contemporary consumerism as metrosexuality. The crucial difference, I would argue, is that the Televised Sports Manhood Formula promotes modern masculinity, whereas metrosexuality promotes a postmodern masculinity.

This, of course, hinges upon an understanding of the relationship between postmodernism and sport, which is also linked in many ways to globalization and its influence upon trends in consumption. Geneviève Rail argues that postmodernism is useful in discussing sport as it 'considers subjectivity as mobile and culturally constructed at the intersection of various social categories'.[14] In particular, it is useful for examining the body, image and text in sport, therefore it is most useful in a consideration of metrosexuality, which can be seen as an intersection of these three categories. Sport in the postmodern era is aestheticized, appropriating artistic forms, in order to become an 'object of hyper-consumption for postmodern clients'.[15] Bob Stewart and Aaron Smith state, 'Postmodern sport is mainly about re-working its cultural and social traditions to produce a desirable consumer experience, and therefore add to its commercial value.'[16] Postmodernism pluralized possible lifestyle and identities influenced by sporting culture; the use of clubs brands, team images and player personalities, Stewart and Smith argue, undermined traditional identities based upon local loyalties to form a 'fluid but often superficial and shifting sense of self'.[17] Furthermore, they identify developments in global communications as a key factor in the postmodernization of sport, arguing that improved communications technologies allow viewers to experience multiple identities and loyalties within and beyond the nation.[18] Garry Crawford, examining the consumption habits of sports fans, argues that consumption is an active process; it 'can involve the production of meanings, further consumable texts and can also play a significant role in the users' construction of identity'.[19] A distinct feature of postmodern sport, Stewart and Smith claim, is the element of choice, also a key feature of postmodern consumption. While Alan Bairner dismisses the relationship of globalization to postmodernity as irrelevant, he too highlights the element of choice in the globalized sporting economy, relating it to the international brand recognition enjoyed by large sporting clubs, such as Manchester United and Inter Milan.[20]

Scambler argues that the 'hyper-commodification of football' is related to new forms of fame and fandom in the postmodern era.[21] As discussed above, Scambler views Beckham as a postmodern text that is also an efficient and lucrative 'resource' in the postmodern marketplace. What Beckham sells in addition to more overt product spruiking is an image that constantly shifts, and that requires many and varied products to maintain. In Scambler's comparison of modern sporting heroes Ali and Paul Gascoigne to postmodern heroes Beckham and Michael Jordan, a key difference is admiration for the man as opposed to desire for the product. As argued above, the metrosexual is not about a particular political subject position in the way that the SNAG was a response to feminism; it is about encouraging heterosexual men to practice consumerism in ways that they previously had not. While it does involve a significant shift in our understanding of men as consumers – that is, that they can enjoy to shop in the same way that women have been encouraged to enjoy consumerism for a long time – it does little to destabilize other characteristics of hegemonic masculinity. Where Messner *et al.*'s Televised Sports Manhood Formula was about both product and personality, this postmodern masculinity simply addresses surface.

This, of course, is a very cynical view based upon the inferred meaning of certain consumer practices. Ben Clayton and John Harris suggest that Beckham does challenge assumptions about traditional masculinity and patriarchy beyond his hairstyle and fashion sense due to his active domestic role and his relationship with his wife.[22] Until stories of his alleged infidelity surfaced, Beckham was often feminized by the media and presented as emasculated by his domineering wife. Clayton and Harris argue that Beckham's alleged infidelity acted as a 'reaffirmation of the frequently questioned masculinised Beckham character, declaring a previously unseen side to his image where he engaged in a subculturally fashionable (and masculinised) display of sexual promiscuity'.[23] Although Beckham's agency in style choices has also been called into question throughout his relationship with his wife,[24] it is important to be critical of drawing any strong relationship between his metrosexual image, his emasculation by the media and any political repercussions of metrosexuality. What the narrative of his alleged infidelity does is establish that the aesthetic of metrosexuality has done little to destabilize a view of masculinity based upon *his* sexual prowess and *her* fragile victimhood. Rather, it demonstrates that the same sexual relations and understanding of masculinity were simply repackaged.

**Football but not as you know it: the global game down under**

Soccer in Australia has over the years experienced a repackaging similar to that undergone by masculinity and, I argue, is related to it through discourses of postmodernism, globalization and cosmopolitanism. The sport's troubled history in Australia is a rich site for investigation, the exploration of which illuminates the nation's colonial and migrant past. Soccer has notoriously never achieved the same large following as Australia's indigenous code of Australian Rules football or other colonial imports, such as rugby league, rugby union and cricket. Indeed soccer has been more readily associated with post-war waves of immigration from continental Europe than it has with earlier Anglo Celtic immigration and settlement. Interestingly, as Alan Bairner notes, soccer has spread more rapidly and successfully in countries beyond the British Empire despite its origins.[25] Richard Cashman argues that the sport's association with ethnic communities and working-class migrants in Australia contributed to its lack of success in the nineteenth and twentieth centuries;[26] this accessibility to marginalized groups is arguably what led to its success elsewhere, such as in Central and South America, but is widely accepted as the reason for soccer's downfall in Australia. Largely supported by migrant social and sports clubs, teams became associated with particular ethnic groups. James Bradley, in a 1990 report prepared for the Australian Soccer Federation, identified this ethnic association as one of the greatest 'image' problems faced by soccer.[27] As a result of this influential report and growing concerns about ethnic violence amongst spectators, Australian soccer underwent a 'de-ethnicisation' wherein all ethnic names, emblems, flags and logos were banned from clubs and matches.[28]

In an analysis of the marketing problems faced by Australian soccer in the 1990s Damon Kobe observes that match attendance levels at important soccer events, such as the grand final or World Cup qualifiers, were equal to those of other sports. From this he argued that soccer's success in Australia would depend upon its qualification in a World Cup final or, failing that, a successful bid to host the tournament.[29] Kobe was correct to bank upon Australia's vibrant sporting nationalism, which has certainly grown since the Socceroos' World Cup debut in 1974. Their qualification in the 2006 FIFA World Cup finals garnered national attention and lucrative sponsorship deals for the team from such companies as Nike and Powerade. In addition to this, television shows and books about the World Cup and soccer more generally proliferated; the opportunity to market soccer through Australia's World Cup qualification was well and truly seized, and was largely successful.

The atmosphere for this success was, however, generated prior to the Socceroos' qualification. In 2005 the Australian Football Federation (formerly the Australian Soccer Federation and Soccer Australia) relaunched its A-League tournament together with a slick marketing campaign that drew upon soccer's reputation as the 'world game' as well as the physical appeal of its players to both female and male audiences, while its tagline – 'It's football but not as you know it' – played upon soccer's ambiguous status as a football code in football-mad Australia. The television commercial for the campaign featured attractive young players from the league playing a fast and furious match as they move through a city and using balls to graffiti walls with the names of various soccer skills. The players are well-dressed in stylish urban street wear rather than soccer uniforms or other overtly sports-related clothing and display artfully dishevelled hairstyles. Their deliberate styling together with their placement in an urban landscape visually references the aesthetic of metrosexuality:

the young, urban, heterosexual male who displays an interest in fashion and appearance yet still engages in manly activities, such as sport.

While Beckham's association and popularization of this particular aesthetic is both convenient and useful for understanding how the ASF were attempting to package and sell soccer in Australia, it is even more interesting and revealing to explore the intersection of ethnicity and masculinity in this. In the Australian context the metrosexual aesthetic also draws heavily upon a pre-existing aesthetic of ethnic masculinity – that is, the 'wog look'.[30] Like the metrosexual aesthetic, the wog look features a groomed appearance and stylish (usually European) clothes, certainly more groomed than the mythic Australian masculine ideals of the bushman and the digger that are fading from popular interest as an increasingly urban and cosmopolitan Australia searches for a new national iconography. Beyond the Australian context, a similar aesthetic can be found in the image of the exotic continental male frequently placed at the centre of heterosexual women's romantic and sexual fantasies in popular culture. There is also a significant connection between the wog look and football hooligans. Hughson observes that ethnic supporter groups, such as the Bad Boys Blue, the Hellas Hooligans and the Stallions 'share with the predominant *casual* hooligan style in Europe an interest in fashionable menswear and, particularly, expensive accessories such as sunglasses and jewellery'.[31] Crawford also recognizes English 'lads' as a particular type of sports fan whose consumption of casual designer wear distinguishes them from newer fans of the sport, who are more likely to wear official merchandise.[32] The lads' consumption of designer clothes is therefore in a sense sports-related and certainly expresses a particular form of working-class masculinity.

On the one hand, the association of the wog look and that of the soccer hooligan is problematic in that it encourages a conflation of hooliganism and ethnicity. On the other hand, it demonstrates an intersection between soccer and this particular aestheticised masculinity that is unconfined by national borders, demonstrating the cosmopolitanism of both the game and its supporters. For the marginalized wog or hooligan look to undergo an evolution into more widely practiced metrosexuality does, however, involve complex shifts in understandings of ethnicity, race and masculinity that help illuminate soccer's transformation from the marginalized ethnic sport to the cosmopolitan world game in the eyes of Australian spectators. In a sense, it could be argued, this look itself had to be de-ethnicised but to begin to understand the complexities of these transformations, it is important to consider the broader social and theoretical shift from multiculturalism to cosmopolitanism.

Multiculturalism was introduced to Australia in the early 1970s as a new settlement policy. It initially addressed the provision of services and support to immigrants, including translation services and support for the establishment of ethnic organizations, but was later taken up as a potential national cultural identity and, as its political cachet was diminished under Howard's Liberal government, simply as a descriptor for Australian society.[33] From its outset, multiculturalism was beset with criticisms that it was not a unifying policy for Australian culture and society; Geoffrey Blainey, for example, famously stated that the policy would turn Australia into a 'nation of tribes'.[34] More recently Peter Costello, then Federal Treasurer, derided multiculturalism as 'mushy [and] misguided'[35] in a speech addressing immigration and citizenship in February 2006. Even multicultural theorists Ien Ang and Jon Stratton observe that 'the discourse of multiculturalism has failed to provide "old" Australians with ways of re-imagining themselves as an integral part of the "new" Australia'.[36] Given multiculturalism's purported failure to capture the imagination on a national level, it can be difficult to see how it could assist the nation of Australia on the global scale. Australia's diverse cultural make-up together with increased global communications and internationalization has, however, contributed to large and complex transnational networks that promote the maintenance of diasporic cultures and identities. Sneja Gunew suggests that when talking about globalization and diasporic issues it is perhaps more useful to use the term cosmopolitanism, as opposed to internationalism or the arguably more parochial multiculturalism.[37] Popular understandings of cosmopolitanism relate it to an urbane worldliness that better equips individuals to deal with globalizing trends. Due to their transnational networks and diasporic cultural and political identities, those from migrant and ethnic backgrounds are believed to have an easier or even naturalized access to this worldliness. Ien Ang, however, observes that multiculturalism and cosmopolitanism are further interconnected through trends in postmodern consumption:

> An oft-expressed view is that multiculturalism – with its emphasis on the celebration of cultural diversity – advances and privileges the way of life of so-called cosmopolitan elites (who relish the consumption of diversity) at the expense of those who are both economically disadvantaged and culturally marginalised in an increasingly fluid, globalised and postmodern world, where no 'identity' is secure any longer.[38]

The consumption of diversity and the expression of transnational identity (often through consumption) are thereby legitimized in postmodern forms of globalization.

Cosmopolitanism lends itself well to discussions of sport, particularly within the context of internationalism and globalization. Grant Jarvie argues that cosmopolitanism 'allows for the blending or merging of customary differences that may emerge from multiple local sporting customs [and it] projects a theory of world sporting governance and corresponding citizenship'.[39] In this light, the de-ethnicisation of Australian soccer and the formation of the new A-League can be seen as an act of cosmopolitanism (albeit a highly fraught and problematic one due to its dependency on the eradication of non-Australian nationalism) as it sought to unify to local scene in order to facilitate Australia's serious participation in the global soccer scene. By promoting a strong professional league – and one that participates in international commerce of player transfers at that – Australia was arguably able to develop a strong national team and following that would sustain their participation in major world and regional tournaments, such as the World Cup and the Asia Cup.

The de-ethnicisation of soccer in Australia sought to destablize its reputation as an 'ethnic' sport and establish it as an 'Australian' sport,[40] although the precise meaning of this is certainly contestable. As Hughson has demonstrated through his examination of the Bad Boys Blue in Sydney the 'success' of this de-ethnicisation must be called into question as fans have developed encoded ways of demonstrating and displaying ethnic nationalism without disrupting the ban.[41] It may, however, have played an important role in minimizing ethnic conflict at games and disrupting popular affiliation of the sport and migrant groups. Nonetheless, it is its marketed transformation from the negatively associated ethnic/multicultural game to the positively associated world/cosmopolitan game that should really be credited with its more recent success. The savvy marketing of the most recent incarnation of the A-League and the Socceroos's involvement in the World Cup cashed in upon soccer's cosmopolitan global appeal. The ad campaign developed by Nike, the Socceroos' major sportswear sponsor, deliberately mocked Australia's small presence on soccer's global scene in a way that would have nagged at its strong sporting nationalism. In a series of television commercials, the Socceroos were taunted by the personification of History, an old man in a brown robe with an undefinable (and not incidentally) European accent. As Martin Polley observes, 'A national team can, in media and popular discourse, take on the guise of the nation itself'.[42] To be a global player, the campaign therefore seemed to say, Australia had to prove itself in the world game.

Just as Australia was urged to shrug off its provincial, colonial reputation, the revamped image of Australian soccer encourages its supporters to make the shift from divided ethnic supporters to hybridized cosmopolitan elites. This is the crux of the transformation: the popularization of the consumption of diversity encouraged forays into areas of both fashion and sport once deemed 'ethnic', 'woggy' or 'effeminate', helping to merge the principles of both the wog look and the metrosexual aesthetic. It was not necessarily that the wog look was de-ethnicised in any real sense but that the cultural diversity from which it drew and that it represented gained a particular cultural and consumer cache. Similarly, soccer cannot be said to have been successfully and completely de-ethnicised. The 'ethnicity' of the game, so to speak, has simply been successfully encoded into the notion of the 'world game' in Australia by drawing upon broader social and cultural trends where the marginalized ethnic – through the socio-economic mobility of migrant groups and shifting trends in postmodern consumption – becomes the cosmopolitan elite.

## Conclusions

Both the trend in metrosexuality and the increased popularity of soccer in Australia are linked to cosmopolitanism and postmodern consumerism in an increasingly globalized world. Where metrosexuality has developed to encourage the participation of heterosexual men in consumer practices that have traditionally been the domain of women, the appeal of cosmopolitanism has been used in marketing soccer in Australia to likewise draw in spectators who had previously felt excluded from its target audience due to its reputation as an 'ethnic game'. As this essay has demonstrated, both metrosexuality and cosmopolitanism are hybridized developments of existing paradigms in masculinity and multiculturalism. While metrosexuality re-socializes men as consumers, it does not necessarily alter other fundamental characteristics of hegemonic masculinity. Similarly, cosmopolitanism is still rooted in the same principles of cultural diversity as multiculturalism. What alters both masculinity and multiculturalism is their intersection with postmodernism, globalization and transnationalism.

In the contemporary context of globalization and postmodern consumerism, soccer's reputation as the 'world game' makes it the perfect foil for marketing products internationally. Add to this the obsession with celebrity, such as the example of David Beckham, and the possibilities for new and perhaps even more insidious forms of marketing and consumerism are limitless. There are, however, more positive possibilities to be gained from this context, as the cosmopolitan reading of soccer in Australia performed in this essay has shown. Rather than viewing the Australian spectator as either a disenfranchised ethnic supporter or a colonizing anti-ethnic supporter, we can begin to examine them as a hybrid form replete with complex sporting, ethnic, national and gender identities.

## Notes

1. Warren, *Sheilas, Wogs and Poofters*, xiv.
2. Connell, *Masculinities*, 185.

3. Ibid., 199–202.
4. Mark Simpson, 'Here Come the Mirror Men'. *Independent*, November 15, 1994. This article is largely believed to be the first appearance of the term 'metrosexual' in print.
5. Ibid.
6. Alexander, 'Stylish Hard Bodies', 540.
7. Ibid., 550–1.
8. Ibid., 547.
9. 'Branded like Beckham'. *Economist*, May 7, 2003, 57.
10. Ibid., 56.
11. Scambler, *Sport and Society*, 132, 135, original emphasis.
12. Messner, Dunbar and Hunt, 'The Televised Sports Manhood Formula', 229.
13. Ibid., 243.
14. Rail, 'Postmodernism and Sports Studies', 190.
15. Scambler, *Sport and Society*, 160.
16. Stewart and Smith, 'Australian sport in a postmodern age', 291.
17. Ibid., 288.
18. Ibid., 296.
19. Crawford, *Consuming Sport*, 112.
20. Bairner, *Sport, Nationalism and Globalisation*, 166.
21. Scambler, *Sport and Society*, 116.
22. Clayton and Harris, 'Footballers' Wives', 330.
23. Ibid., 331.
24. Ibid.
25. Bairner, *Sport, Nationalism and Globalisation*, 13.
26. Cashman, *Paradise of Sport*, 116.
27. Hughson, 'Football, Folk Dancing and Fascism', 170.
28. Booth and Tatz, *One-Eyed*, 166.
29. Kobe, 'Soccer in Australia'.
30. Baldassar, 'Italo-Australian Youth in Perth'.
31. Hughson, 'Fandom in Australian Soccer's A-League', 21.
32. Crawford, *Consuming Sport*, 125.
33. For a useful history of multiculturalism, particularly its evolution as policy, see Lopez, *The Origins of Multiculturalism*.
34. Blainey, G. 'Australia must Break Down the Walls of the Ghettos', *Weekend Australian*, March 12–13, 2008, 18.
35. Quoted in Josh Gordon and Jewel Topsfield, 'Our Values or Go Home: Costello'. *The Age*, February 24, 2006.
36. Ang and Stratton, 'Multiculturalism in Crisis', 100.
37. Gunew, *Haunted Nations*, 55.
38. Ang, *On Not Speaking Chinese*, 15.
39. Jarvie, *Sport, Culture and Society*, 123.
40. Hughson, 'Football, Folk Dancing and Fascism', 170.
41. Hughson, 'The Boys in Blue and the Bad Boys Blue', 167–82.
42. Polley, *Moving the Goalposts*, 35.

## References

Alexander, S.M. 'Stylish Hard Bodies: Branded Masculinity in "Men's Health" Magazine'. *Sociological Perspectives* Media, Popular Culture, and the Arts, 46, no. 4 (Winter 2003): 535–54.

Ang, I. *On Not Speaking Chinese: Living between Asia and the West.* London: Routledge, 2001.

Ang, I., and J. Stratton. 'Multiculturalism in Crisis: The New Politics of Race and National Identity in Australia'. In *On Not Speaking Chinese: living between Asia and the West*, 95–111. London: Routledge, 2001.

Bairner, A. *Sport, Nationalism and Globalisation: European and American Perspectives.* Albany, NY: SUNY Press, 2001.

Baldassar, L. 'Italo-Australian Youth in Perth (Space Speaks and Clothes Communicate)'. In *War, Internment and Mass Migration : The Italo-Australian Experience, 1940–1990,* ed. Richard Bosworth and Romano Ugolini, 207–23. Rome: Gruppo editoriale internazionale, 1992.

Booth, D., and C. Tatz. *One-Eyed: A View of Australian Sport.* St Leonards: Allen & Unwin, 2000.

Cashman, R. *Paradise of Sport: The Rise of Organized Sport in Australia.* Melbourne: Oxford University Press, 1995.

Clayton, B., and J. Harris. 'Footballers' Wives: The Role of the Soccer Player's Partner in the Construction of Idealised Masculinity'. *Soccer and Society* 5, no. 3 (Autumn 2004): 317–35.

Connell, R. *Masculinities.* Oxford: Polity Press, 1995.

Crawford, G. *Consuming Sport: Fans, Sport and Culture.* London: Routledge, 2004.

Gunew, S. *Haunted Nations: The Colonial Dimensions of Multiculturalisms.* London: Routledge, 2004.

Hughson, J. 'Football, Folk Dancing and Fascism: Diversity and Difference in Multicultural Australia'. *ANZJS* 33, no. 2 (1997): 167–86.

Hughson, J. 'The Boys in Blue and the Bad Boys Blue: A Case Study of Interactive Relations Between the Police and Ethnic Youth in Western Sydney'. *Australian Journal of Social Issues* 34, no. 2 (1999): 167–82.

Hughson, J. 'A Tale of Two Tribes: Fandom in Australian Soccer's A-League'. *Culture, Sport, Society,* 2, no. 3 (1999): 10–30.

Jarvie, G. *Sport, Culture and Society: An Introduction.* London: Routledge, 2006.

Kobe, D. 'Soccer in Australia: What's Going Wrong?' *The Cyber-Journal of Sport Marketing* 3, no. 1 (1999). http://www.ausport.gov.au/fulltext/1999/cjsm/v3n1/kobe31/htm.

Lopez, M. *The Origins of Multiculturalism in Australian Politics 1945–1975.* Melbourne: Melbourne University Press, 2000.

Messner, M.A., M. Dunbar, and D. Hunt. 'The Televised Sports Manhood Formula'. In *Critical Readings: Sport, Culture and the Media,* ed. D. Rowe, 229–45. Maidenhead: Open University Press, 2004.

Polley, M. *Moving the Goalposts: A History of Sport and Society Since 1945.* London: Routledge, 1998.

Rail, G. 'Postmodernism and Sports Studies'. In *Theory, Sport and Society,* ed. J Maguire and K. Young, 179–207. Amsterdam: JAI, 2002.

Scambler, G. *Sport and Society: History, Power and Culture.* Maidenhead: Open University Press, 2005.

Stewart, B., and A. Smith. 'Australian Sport in a Postmodern Age'. In *Sport in Australasian Society: Past and Present,* ed. J.A. Mangan and J. Nauright, 278–304. London: Frank Cass, 2000.

Warren, J. *Sheilas, Wogs and Poofters: An Incomplete Biography of Johnny Warren and Soccer in Australia.* Milsons Point: Random House, 2002.

# Soccer in the west: the world game in Australia's western periphery

Philip Moore

*Faculty of Media, Society and Culture, Curtin University of Technology, Perth, Australia*

## Introduction

While it is now a recognized truism that '[d]uring the twentieth century, soccer emerged as the world's most popular sport',[1] it is not the case that Dunning's authoritative assertion is true for every sporting nation. In Australia, to note but one exception, there are three other codes of football that will lay claim to greater popularity than 'the world game'. In the burgeoning offshore literature about this most international of games Australia receives but scant attention.[2] Yet, if we take seriously the claim that the globalizing of sport entails a process of 'diminishing contrasts and increasing varieties',[3] so that even while we may well be playing the same game we are likely to be playing it in different ways, then there may well be much to be gained from a closer examination of the culture of the game as it has been organized and played in the antipodes.

Association Football, known locally as 'soccer' for most of its history in Australia, has changed a great deal over the past century; and, particularly recently, it has done so very quickly. After languishing as an 'ethnic' game for many decades, interest in the game now shows signs of having broken through, with a push to claim a more central place for the sport in Australian society. The recent national restructuring of the sport, that has included the cessation of the men's National Soccer League and the creation of the new elite A-League, the presence of the Australian men's team in the World Cup in 2006, an acceptance into the Asian Football Confederation by FIFA, and the shift in name from 'soccer' to 'football' are perhaps some of the more significant markers of the repositioning of the game in Australian society. To say this, of course, is not to assume that the hard work done repositioning the game will necessarily have the desired outcome. Australians may well be 'obsessed' by sports, as has often been noted – and now increasingly contested by some academics,[4] but even more than sport Australians love winners. A core task ahead for those committed to this code of football in Australia is to build on the recent success and to entrench the game in Australian society and the Australian sporting calendar. Given the history of the game on this continent, this will be no easy task.

Soccer in Australia, at least since the end of the Second World War, has been understood by most as a sport riven by ethnic differences.[5] The ethnic differences played out through and around soccer in Australia have developed a distinctly local sense to them.[6] These are not simply 'old' enmities, brought like luggage from other places, transferred to Australia and retaining all the same meanings, significances and understandings. Rather, the ethnic differences played out in soccer have an Australian significance precisely because of where they happen and who is involved: where diverse peoples meet and interact in ways that are different to their traditions elsewhere and in political and sporting contexts that are distinctly Australian. This is not to deny that the near mythical 'elsewheres' so often invoked have influenced what happens in Australian soccer; it is, rather, to assert that such ethnic differences are made differently here because the relationships must be contextualized here to take account of the particular social forces that the game has faced in Australia – and, perhaps in even more complex ways, in different parts of Australia. The Australian state(s), in different guises, the national and local soccer organizations and the particular communities where people live and play have reshaped the possibilities for the game in Australia.

In this study I seek to explore some aspects of the history of soccer in Perth, Western Australia (WA). In particular, through an approach that owes much to the figurational sociology of Norbert Elias, this study uses notions of established and outsider relations in order to tease out an overview of aspects of the historical complexity of the organizational development of the game after the Second World War, even as the sport has remained on the margins of WA society. The established sporting organizations could fairly easily resist the push from the newly arrived and unorganized outsiders. The limited focus on the particular figuration of soccer in Perth is, of course, only a small part of much broader social and historical processes. The account that emerges is of a complex and perduring struggle over control and organization of this game – the particularly Australian figuration, if you will. After briefly noting the debt to Elias, the study will locate soccer in the west in the context of WA sport and then work through some of the complex organizational difficulties associated with the game in Perth, locating the establishment of the Perth Glory in the National Soccer League and the development of the newly structured A-League and Football Federation of Australia before ending with some comments about the trajectory of the development of the game in the West of Australia more generally.

## Elias and sport

The process or figurational sociology of Norbert Elias provides a useful way of conceptualizing and understanding the social dynamics of the development of soccer in Western Australia. In particular, two aspects of Elias's work are particularly helpful in guiding this account of the history of the game in the western third of Australia. First, Elias's emphasis on an historical dimension to his sociology is fundamental to understanding the dynamics of the game. The emphasis on a figurational approach is central to the need to understand the shifting power relationships in the development and organization of the game. Also, the focus on the relations between those he identified as 'the established' and 'the outsiders',[7] as the location of important social resources provides a way of conceptualizing how relations within a figuration are given shape through time.

The historical emphasis found in Elias's work and his concern that sociology – I would want to insist for all social analysis – should not retreat into the present is foundational for his theoretical insight. It is the basis for his anti-essentialist approach. Elias's work focused on figurations, and particularly their changing or shifting arrangement, as the core problem in social analysis. The analyst must be sensitive to the shifting figurational relationships through time. In *The Civilizing Process* Elias seeks to understand the shifting political figuration that leads to the development of the modern state in Western Europe.[8] His point is that the rise of the modern state has been the result of planned and unplanned processes that have seen culture and social relations shaped by an historical trajectory that has civilized social life. My concern here is not so much with Elias's conclusions as it is with how he arrives at them, the underlying theoretical assumptions that render his analysis possible.

*The Civilizing Process* was central to the development of Elias's work but it was not his only contribution to the development of the figurational sociology attributed to him. Elias's involvement in a community study, of a small community just outside the city of Leicester, would also see him make another important contribution to social theory.[9] Rather than focusing on long-term changes in the figuration of social life, this community study saw Elias working in a more ethnographic vein, in a shorter time-span and with a wealth of evidence collected by a diverse array of contemporary social research methods. In this community study it was the relationship between an established set of residents and the newly arrived outsiders that moved into the community that became the central focus of the work. Understanding the relationships between the established and the outsiders provided a means for Elias and his postgraduate student, Scotson, to make sense of the shifting pattern of local social relations. While members of both groups shared about equally in material goods – they were working class – and most other resources, the established members of the community had well developed local social networks that could be used as a resource to exclude and disadvantage the relatively newly-arrived outsiders. The power of Elias's insight was to demonstrate both the clear and subtle ways that relationships between members of these two groups could be played out. However, as an ethnographer reading *The Established and the Outsiders* as an ethnographic community study, one would have to conclude that this was not a genre of work for which Elias had great capacity. The evidence is presented in ways that would hardly satisfy a more ethnographic researcher in terms of the sense of everyday life it allows. Indeed, the text pales when read beside the works of, say, Ronald Frankenberg or Tony Cohen.[10] However, it is Elias's sense of the importance of the complex tenor of the relationships between established groups and outsiders, and the subtle ways that such relationships can be played out among a variety of social groups at different analytical levels of a figuration, which is theoretically provocative and will rightly survive his otherwise rather mundane community study.

When Elias turned his attention to sport, in what has become a separate yet intellectually connected body of work, his sociological understanding remained grounded in his historical account of the civilizing process in Western Europe. A central first task was to identify where and why what we recognize as modern sport had developed. For Elias, it was in England that the particular form of sporting organizations and competitions would be created and then spread around the world. This process, that he referred to rather inelegantly as the 'sportization' of games, was a crucial step in shaping the development of international sports as we know them today. The sportization of games grew out of the habitus that developed with the growth of parliamentary democracy – hence his equally inelegant phrase 'parliamentarization' to describe this process; just as people had to take responsibility for managing politics, they also took to themselves the responsibility for organizing games in a rational, rule-guided manner. This has tended to generate something of a top-down focus in most studies. It is the concern with how sport has come to be organized that will be of considerable interest in the study of soccer in Western Australia and that will shape the particular use of figuration here.

## Sport in Western Australia

The task in this section is to identify some key aspects of the figuration of sport in Western Australia. Using Stoddart's insightful account of the history of WA sport prior to the Second World War I show that in the history of WA sport the relationships between established social groups and those made into outsiders was accomplished mainly on the basis of social class. This created a hierarchical arrangement that fits nicely with the sense of the historical social organization of WA. It is hardly surprising that social relations within sports would be organized in ways similar to the rest of social life at that time.

In Stoddart's account of the history of sport in Western Australia between 1890 and 1940, he sets out the social and cultural contexts that have shaped sporting activities in the state. He sets out to demonstrate that: 'between 1890 and 1940 organized sport in Perth did not just reflect general social developments, but helped shape and sustain the city's social structure, as well as relationships within it'.[11] Stoddart's account is not written from a figurational perspective. However, because it is so insightful, his analysis is amenable to reframing in this way. Most importantly because he identifies the fairly limited range of sports that were organized and played and, more importantly, as he is clear about the relationships between and among the social groups that were central to the organizing and control of the different sports.

Horse racing was the earliest sport organized in WA, with the Turf Club being established in 1852 by elite members of the community. English in origin or orientation, the social elite would control both horse racing and local politics. Trotting was to be established by local business people who, while they were financially successful, were without the social 'credentials' to move among the elite of local society; they had the desire and money to engage with horses and were able to organize themselves to do so. Passing over the Englishness of another sport, Stoddart again gives emphasis to matters associated with social class when he tells us that: 'Cricket was played mainly by the small number of government servants in the city, while football [Australian Rules] was concentrated in the fledgling industrial working class.'[12]With the growth in size of an increasingly diverse population in Western Australia a number of other sports were also established. Stoddart tells us that: 'By the turn of the century there were regular competitions in cycling, lacrosse, tennis, swimming, athletics, golf, boxing, wrestling, rugby union, soccer and other sports.'[13] Stoddart does not much dwell on these sports. The point of his passing reference to other sports seems to be that the socially significant sports in WA during the time about which he writes were horse racing, trotting, cricket and Australian Rules football.

While he does not assert it immediately, the thrust of his argument is that each sport was organized by a distinct group of devotees. Soccer, like the many other sports noted immediately above, receives a mention but there is no significant engagement with soccer in Stoddart's account. Yet it is quite clear that there was much going on within this game during the time that interests him in his account. While soccer had been played in WA for over a decade, it was in 1896 that the game was first formally organized. Soccer in WA was originally organized by public school administrators.[14] By 1909 there was sufficient interest in both Western Australia and the eastern states for a tour from WA, organized by the British Football Association of Western Australia, to travel from WA through New South Wales, Victoria and what is now South Australia.[15] Kreider's recent account of 'the Soccerites' provides wonderful evidence about the strength of the early development of soccer in the west. The history of WA soccer before the Second World War shows that the league was culturally dominated by a sense of connection with the United Kingdom. Indeed, except for the 'Maccabeans' the winners in Division One of the local league are overwhelmingly sport names that identify them either with their cultural heritage in the UK or else by local location, such as: Thistle and Caledonians or else Perth City United, Victoria Park, Claremont and so on.[16]

There are two things that are clear from Stoddart's account: firstly, that for much of the twentieth century the state was, in a formal sense, little interested in any direct control over the development of sport,[17] and secondly, that sporting practices in Western Australia were historically constructed and socially distributed along lines of social class. Stoddart summarizes this insight noting that: 'the use of sports connections to promote or consolidate position within social groups; the boundaries between groups were rarely crossed. Sport reinforced the boundaries, if anything, so that individuals seeking mobility knew the heights to which they might aspire.'[18] Rather than a pathway to upward social mobility, the engagement with sports was a means of maintaining boundaries between the social groups. Effectively, what was happening in WA was that the established, beginning with the initial control of horse racing by the socially elite, had successfully set the agenda for the development of sporting organizations in the state. As others were not welcomed into the horse racing community there was a need for them to develop their own sporting activities in order to make community for themselves. This, Stoddart tells us clearly, was accomplished along class lines.

Near the end of this overview of the development of sport in Western Australia Stoddart suggests that by about 1940 this local social organization of sport might have reached a point where social change was a possibility.[19] It would indeed seem reasonable that the social disruption created by the Second World War would be felt in myriad ways within the local community. However, there are continuities in what happened locally with soccer after the end of the Second World War that make such a claim difficult to accept in its entirety. Indeed, while the figuration of sport in WA may have begun to change, the changing play of relationships between the established and the outsiders would be a central force in the development of soccer for the next 50 years as the new Australians were made and maintained as marginal outsiders.

## Soccer after the war

In the study of sporting organizations, grounded in organizational theory, there is a tendency for the analysis to be carried out in timeless analytical categories that, in the end, are not sufficiently sensitive to local conditions and history. In the work of Slack, for example, there are three variables that are understood as foundational for analysing any sporting organization: complexity, formalization and centrality.[20] Any sporting organization can be characterized with these notions. But they do not lead us very far if we seek to understand how such sporting organizations have come into being. In Elias's terms, the use of such analytical concepts leads us to a 'retreat into the present'. Understood through such timeless analytical concepts there tends to be a holistic, structural emphasis in accounts that renders the overall structure of the organization the focus of attention rather than focusing on the social processes that have produced the organization. From an Eliasian perspective, this is unsatisfactory because it removes the historical dimension of the development of the particular organizational figuration that must also include what those engaged in the activity understood they were doing. To shift to this perspective leads us to understand the politics of sporting organization in a clearer and analytically more satisfactory way.

At the end of the Second World War there followed a massive migration of Europeans to Australia, including Western Australia. The effect of this migration on Australian society and on sports in particular was enormous. The local impact of this migration on the development of soccer has been the focus of a large, and still growing, academic literature in/from Australia. The papers in O'Hara's study of *Ethnicity and Soccer in Australia*, those in the *Sporting Immigrants* volume produced by Mosely and his contributors, and the recent collection by Bill Murray and Roy Hay nicely demonstrate the nature of this literature.[21] In WA, this focus has also shaped the accounts produced although the authors have tended to approach the topic in different ways.[22] What is of particular interest in this section of the study are the ways that the organization of the sport has altered in the years after the war. The so-called 'new Australians' brought the game with them as an integral part of their own traditions, and on settling in Australia they sought ways to express themselves through their sport. Significantly, this meant not just playing the game within the existing organizational structures but also working to create and maintain their organizations for managing and controlling the sport. It was this shifting organizational context – the contests over control of the way the game was organized – that would be central in shaping the figuration of soccer in WA and in other part of Australia.

As I have already noted, soccer had been organized in WA since 1896. With the arrival of the new Australians from Europe at the end of the Second World War the game started to change as they found their way into the sport in Australia. Kreider identifies this as a 'continental shift' in the game.[23] As new soccer teams were established by the migrants, typically growing out of the social clubs that were the centre of much of their social life, their names identified ongoing connections to the past – such as Perth Azzurri, East Fremantle Tricolore, Fremantle Benfica and so on. Azzurri, the first new team to become a major power in the local game, was established in 1948. The new teams, and their styles of play, would lead to a range of issues that the game would have to confront in the coming years.

The relationships between the new teams (the outsiders) and the existing teams (the established) in the league were not always cordial. Kreider notes that:

> Azzurri's initial rival in the top division was North Perth, and it was not uncommon to see crowds of 4,000 when these two sides met. But while Azzurri's somewhat animated or passionate attacking style, unique in the local game, might have been pleasing to watch for some, it also started to gain a few enemies.[24]

Kreider's felicitous phrasing of their style as 'animated or passionate' is, of course, code for a style of play that was seen as different from the local style and that marked the players as outsiders. The public, as Kreider notes, was divided on what should be done.[25] There were some that wanted to see the new Australians playing in their own league even while there were others who argued that the European style of play had brought out or improved the skills of the 'local players'. Along with a number of ethnic confrontations off the field, the relations within the local sporting organization over the administration of the game were at times very difficult. Indeed, this testiness between the older, established clubs, and the clubs of the new Australians would remain a bone of contention for many years to come with recurrent criticisms of the style of play of the 'new' teams and the sometimes rowdy behaviour of their fans. The new teams and their fans, for their part, were not shy about claiming that a bias against non-British clubs permeated the organization of the sport. Style of play, on and off the field, became a way of marking the differences between the established and the outsiders, and for keeping the outsiders on the margins of the organization of this already marginal sport.

These relationships would run through the game for decades to come. Looking back on the game in WA, Kreider notes that:

> While the 1960s and early 1970s were mostly dominated by the Italian-backed clubs, the mid-1970s saw the emergence of clubs from a diversity of nationalities including those linked with the sensitive regions of Yugoslavia. This has been a national trend, and one that cast the mould for soccer in the 1990s. Athena (Greece), Olympic (Greece/Macedonia), Dalmatinac (Dalmation area of the Adriatic Sea), Croatia (Croatia) and Macedonia (Macedonia) made up the new force and have continued to show the way, despite the incessant presence of a minority of politically minded spectators who show no consideration for the sport.[26]

While the focus on the ethnic origins of particular clubs does reveal something of the changing relationships in the sport, there is more to it than just this.

There were organizational matters that also shaped the relationships between the established and the outsiders in WA soccer. In 1956, in the middle of the season, the Western Australian Soccer Football Association (WASFA) changed its constitution, getting rid of its Board of Control and replacing it with a League Management Committee and a Council. This was a clear sign that there was something wrong in the administration of the sport. By mid-1960 there was a breakaway from the Association by a number of teams who set up a semi-professional league on their own. Indeed, the ability of some clubs in the WASFA to pay their players 'under the table' had become a growing concern. Some teams believed that they were losing their best players to those clubs who could better reward the players. The Australian Soccer Football Association (ASFA) even sent senior national representatives to WA to try to reconcile the differences, and to bring the game back under a single administration, but to no avail. Kreider notes that the ASFA was having similar problems with other state bodies where the arguments were the same: that 'old school' administrators 'lacked leadership qualities suited to the new wave migrants'.[27]

The national association (ASFA) was embroiled in a number of difficulties. The state organizations were pushing in ways similar to that in WA, with the newer clubs wanting a greater say in the organization of the sport. But also, the national body was struggling in its relations with the FIFA. The international body had suspended the Australian association (1960–63) because some clubs in the eastern states had contracted and fielded players before the appropriate transfer arrangements had been worked out. The ASFA became the Australian Soccer Federation at the end of 1960 and the WASFA mirrored this by becoming the Soccer Federation of Western Australia (SFWA).

In Western Australia a number of other events have been significant in shaping the organization of soccer. Some of the highlights of the shifting organizational features of the sport include a range of new associations and the creation of new relationships among existing associations. According to Kreider,[28] this included a group of people who got together in 1966 to found the Westralian Amateur Soccer League, a league whose competitions would take place on Sundays, instead of the usual Saturday offerings, and so would offer the opportunity to compete to those who wanted to play but whose employment had precluded their involvement. This organization would later become the Amateur Soccer Association of Western Australia. In 1969 this organization would join the national Australian Amateur Soccer Association, and would be dissolved in 1971 only to be reformed some six years later.[29] Also in 1971 the WASL affiliated with the SFWA. The relationships continued to be strained and took a variety of shapes. The appearance of the Perth Friendly Soccer League (PFSL) in 1975 is a clear sign that everyone was not happy with the existing management and direction of the game. Playing matches on Sundays instead of the traditional Saturdays saw the PFSL quickly grow into a sizeable organization.

By 1983 the Amateur Soccer Association of WA sought association with the SFWA and was accepted. In the late 1980s the Western Australian government became involved in an attempt to bring order to the chaos of soccer administration in the state. With offers of a significant contribution to resourcing the sport, along with other help, the state led the charge for the game to be managed in a more rational manner. However, because such a set of changes would necessarily involve a reshaping of all of soccer administration in the state, and a loss of positions and resources by many, it was rejected,[30] even though many would see it as one more lost opportunity for the sport. In 1991 eleven clubs once again broke away from the SFWA to form a new semi-professional league, with its own administration under the Soccer Association of Western Australia, the lead body for the state. When this happened, the SFWA disaffiliated from the lead organization. The Professional Soccer League would return to the fold after two seasons, in serious financial strife but having established that they had particular interests that needed to be taken into account.

In the midst of it all there was a concerted move by many in Perth to get a team into the National Soccer League, the premier competition in the country. Western Australia had been excluded since the founding of this competition due, primarily, to the costs associated with travel to and from Perth. In the 1990s the most concerted effort to get a team into the league came through the building of Perth Italia into a powerhouse team. It was a dominant, and likely expensive, team that struggled for about nine years before financial problems began to bite. In the midst of this the National Soccer League moved to rid itself of ethnic labels in team names. Perth would finally get a berth in the national competition, but it would be a new club and would be financed from outside the existing league and sport organizations. Perth Glory would make its debut in the competition in 1996. Perth Glory was a team created from outside any 'ethnic' concerns in Perth soccer. It was founded on solid business principles rather than from a social club representing other interests and it would set the tone for the future development of the game across the country.[31] The team colours of the Glory and its traditions all had to be created to encourage supporters to barrack for the team and not for some ethnic organization.

Clearly there were problems associated with the organization of the game, with different interests forming associations, dissolving them and reforming through time. The picture is of a fluid bundle of relationships as individuals, teams and other groups shifted and changed to look after their own interests – whether we see these as ethnic or not. With so many different organizations coming into being during this period there was an increase in administrative positions, so that more people became involved in the management of the game, and, simultaneously, there was a clearer sense of being able to look after one's own interests within the game. The established teams and their managements could control the organization of the leagues. The outsiders, the new Australians, were without a central organizing body that could pursue their interests. They came at the game through their separate clubs rather than as an organizational force. Even the creation of new leagues and competitions speaks to the inability of the 'ethnic' clubs to manage the game in ways they thought appropriate.

The figuration of this sport that emerges from this lengthy period in the history of the game as it was organized and played in WA is one of near chaos, with matters being contested and organized at the level of teams and individuals rather than from any perspective that makes the overall health and organization of the sport its primary focus. The interests of individuals and teams reigns supreme and are protected and fought over with considerable vehemence, making established and outsider groups into those whose relationship shift as crucial resources shift. And yet, running through such an account is a sense of great love and enormous service to the sport by a great many people, and Richard Kreider and Peter Reynolds have both captured this sense very nicely.[32]

Organizational theory is little help in understanding the historical development of soccer in Western Australia precisely because the game was organized and controlled more from the bottom than from the top. Yet all this would change decisively in the twenty-first century. The most thoroughgoing change in the history of soccer in Australia, and therefore in Western Australia as well, has been the restructuring of the sport and the establishment of the new professional A-League. The Crawford report into soccer in Australia[33] provided an opportunity to restructure the organization of the entire sport, across the country, and to transform a failing 'national league' into one that had a greater chance of surviving, and perhaps even thriving. The report into the 'structure, governance and management of soccer in Australia' was carried out within a set of terms of reference that made ethnicity irrelevant and which stressed the concerns of a more timeless and structural organizational theory. The civilizing of the game has come about from above.

What is significant in this is that the federal government, through the Prime Minister, became involved in making this happen. The federal government found it could support the restructuring of the game if the sport was not associated primarily with ethnic minorities – the Prime Minister at the time was no fan of multiculturalism – and as long as there was reason to see that the government was not financially propping up an industry that should stand on its own two feet. The government could not just give support to the sport as a commercial activity; there had to be provisions for the development of the game and the Australian national team. This reorganization of the entire sport was no easy feat but after long negotiations, threats and a full share of brinksmanship all round, the recommended changes were put in place. Indeed, it would be one of Australia's most successful ethnic businessmen, Frank Lowy, who would act as go-between for the government. Solly has provided perhaps the best account of this to date.[34] The organization of the sport both in the states and at the national level was carried, even if it was seen as contentious by many, and the new eight team A-League competition began. The new national league saw all teams begin on solid financial footings and very much adopted the sort of business practices that were pioneered by the Perth Glory. This reorganization was achieved from the top down and has changed the game across the country and in all the states – even if the Glory have not done so well out of it. It was not this reorganization that got Australia to the World Cup in Germany – the push to qualification had been in the works for some time before – but the excitement created through that appearance has fed back into the game played in Australia.

### Elias, soccer and the Antipodes?

The relationship between sport and ethnicity has been used to sharpen the analytical focus on sport, beyond the Australian case, on several other occasions.[35] However, it is from an Eliasian perspective that I think a better account of what has taken place in the development of soccer in Western Australia can be articulated. Still, the present account provides more than just an overview – there is insufficient space to present all the evidence here – and works to show how figuration of soccer in WA, focusing on the relationships between the established and outsiders, changed through time as control over the game was shaped through particular contestations. It was not an equal contest, however, as the established clubs controlled the organization of the league and the administration of the sport. The new clubs – those of the outsiders – more often competed with each other, on and off the field, rather than cooperating to take a greater role in the management and administration of the game. The historical organization of the game in WA presents itself as complex and in flux for most of the time since the Second World War. The sport was organized as it was precisely because of the historical relationships that were being worked out in it and through it.

While those writing from the social and cultural centres associated with the world game do not make much of the Australian evidence, it should not be assumed that Australia therefore developed in isolation. Prior to the Second World War the game in Australia was indeed played and enjoyed by many. Indeed, the game arrived in Australia not long after it was codified in the UK. And it arrived in the context of the arrival of competing codes – rugby was also on the scene early on. However, the game had to contend both with a growing nationalism in Australia and the appearance of a particularly Australian form of the game, Australian Rules football. Soccer in Australia would for some time remain a sport played by many, but that was not professionally supported by many.

Following the Second World War and the arrival of many immigrants from Europe and elsewhere, the game slowly became entrenched in the control of the new Australians. They were 'outsiders' to the established settlers in Australia and struggled to build institutions in which they could control some aspects of their lives. Soccer did indeed experience a distinct ethnic influx during this period. This relationship lasted for several decades. By the 1970s early attempts were being made to remove the overt ethnic markers from the game. The identification of the game with the ethnic 'outsiders' was seen as a boundary to encouraging the established community from embracing the game. Over time, of course, the outsiders became the established controllers of the game and become more centrally engaged in Australian society and public life. Early in the twenty-first century the Australian federal government was ready to contribute funding to reshaping the sport, as long as it could claim that it was in the national interest rather than just the interest of minority (ethnic) interests or, worse, the owners of the professional teams. The clear and unambiguous connections between ethnic communities and their teams would be severed – and the world game would begin to be less marginal than it had during its history in Australia.

## Notes

1. Dunning, *Sport Matters*, 103.
2. Three recent examples include Giulianotti, *Football*, Goldblatt, *The Ball is Round* and the volume by Sugden and Tomlinson dealing with *FIFA and the Context for World Football*.
3. Maguire, *Globalsport* develops this insight from Elias's *The Civilizing Process*.
4. Phillips and Magdalinska nicely capture this in their chapter 'Sport in Australia', 313.
5. See, for example, O'Hara, *Ethnicity and Soccer in Australia*; Mosely and Murray 'Soccer'; Mosely, *Ethnic Involvement in Australian Soccer*; Mosely *et al.*, *Sporting Immigrants*; Hughson, 'Football, Folk Dancing and Fascism'; Moore, 'Scouting an Anthropology of Sport'; and Murray and Hay, *The World Game Downunder*.
6. Danforth, 'Is the "World Game" an "ethnic game" or an "Aussie game"?'
7. Elias and Scotson, *The Established and the Outsiders*.
8. Elias, *The Civilizing Process*.
9. Elias and Scotson, *The Established and the Outsiders*.
10. See Frankenberg, *A Village on the Border*; and Cohen, *Whalsay*.
11. Stoddart, 'Sport and Society 1890-1940', 653.
12. Ibid., 655.
13. Ibid.
14. Kreider, *A Soccer Century*, 8, 51; Reynolds, 'The New History of Soccer'.
15. Kreider, *The Soccerites*, 9.
16. Kreider, *A Soccer Century*, 49.
17. See Stewart *et al.*, *Australian Sport*.
18. Stoddart, 'Sport and Society 1890–1940', 670.
19. Ibid., 674.
20. Slack, *Understanding Sport Organizations*; Amis and Slack, 'Analysing Sports Organisations'.
21. O'Hara, *Ethnicity and Soccer in Australia*; Mosely *et al.*, *Sporting Immigrants*; Murray and Hay, *The World Game Downunder*.
22. Jones and Moore, '"He only has eyes for Poms"'; Evans, 'From Grisla to Wisla'; Moore, 'Scouting an Anthropology of Sport', and 'Soccer and the Politics of Culture'; and Jones, 'Home and Away'. The State Library of Western Australia holds a wonderful collection of documents and interviews with many people who were involved in the development of the game in this state.
23. Reynolds, 'The New History of Soccer'; Kreider, *A Soccer Century*, 47–59.
24. Kreider, *A Soccer Century*, 56. Kreider's involvement in soccer has been as a player, administrator, journalist and, most recently, historian of Western Australian soccer.
25. Ibid., 57.
26. Ibid., 73.
27. Ibid., 65.
28. Ibid., 118–50
29. Ibid., 119.
30. Moore, 'Soccer and the Politics of Culture'.
31. Solly, *Shoot Out*.
32. Kreider, *A Soccer Century*; Reynolds, 'The New History of Soccer'.
33. Crawford, *Report of the Independent Soccer Review Committee*.
34. Solly, *Shoot Out*.
35. Eisen and Wiggins, *Ethnicity and Sport*; MacClancy, *Sport, Identity and Ethnicity*; Cronin and Mayall, *Sporting Nationalisms*.

## References

Amis, J., and T. Slack. 'Analysing Sports Organisations: Theory and Practice'. In *Sport and Society,* ed. B. Houlihan, 201–17. London: Sage, 2003.
Cohen, A.P. *Whalsay: Symbol, Segment, and Boundary in a Shetland Island Community.* Manchester: Manchester University Press, 1987.

Crawford, D. *Report of the Independent Soccer Review Committee into the Structure, Governance and Management of Soccer in Australia.* Canberra: Australian Sports Commission, 2003.

Cronin, M., and David Mayall, eds. *Sporting Nationalisms: Identity, Ethnicity, Immigration and Assimilation.* London: Frank Cass, 1998.

Danforth, L.M. 'Is the "World Game" an "Ethnic Game" or an "Aussie Game"? Narrating the Nation in Australian Soccer'. *American Ethnologist* 28, no. 2 (2001): 363–81.

Dunning, E. *Sport Matters: Sociological Studies of Sport, Violence and Civilization.* London: Routledge, 1999.

Eisen, G., and D.K. Wiggins, eds. *Ethnicity and Sport in North American History and Culture.* Westport, CT: Greenwood Press, 1994.

Elias, N. *The Civilizing Process.* Rev. ed. Oxford: Blackwells, 2000.

Elias, N., and J.L. Scotson. *The Established and the Outsiders.* 2nd ed. London: Sage, 1994.

Evans, K. 'From Grisla to Wisla – Soccer in Collie 1950–1971'. In *Perspectives on Sport and Society. Studies in Western Australian History* No. 18, ed. E. Jaggard and J. Ryan, 51–63. Nedlands: Centre for Western Australian History, 1997.

Frankenberg, R. *A Village on the Border.* London: Cohen & West, 1957.

Giulianotti, R. *Football: A Sociology of the World Game.* London: Routledge, 2002.

Goldblatt, D. *The Ball is Round. A Global History of Football.* London: Viking Books, 2006.

Hughson, J. 'Football, Folk Dancing and Fascism: Diversity and Difference in Multicultural Australia'. *Australian and New Zealand Journal of Sociology* 33, no. 2 (1997): 167–86.

Jones, R. 'Home and Away: The Grounding of New Football Teams in Perth, Western Australia'. *The Australian Journal of Anthropology* 13, no. 3 (2002): 270–82.

Jones, R., and P. Moore. '"He only has eyes for Poms": Soccer, Ethnicity and Locality in Perth, WA'. In *Ethnicity and Soccer in Australia,* ed. J. O'Hara, 16–32. ASSH Studies in Sports History No.10. Sydney: Australian Society for Sports History, 1994.

Kreider, R. *A Soccer Century: A Chronicle of Western Australian Soccer from 1896 to1996.* Cloverdale, WA: SportsWest Media, 1996.

Kreider, R. *The Soccerites.* Cloverdale, WA: SportsWest Media, 2005.

MacClancy, J., ed. *Sport, Identity and Ethnicity.* Oxford: Berg, 1996.

Maguire, J. *Globalsport: Identities, Societies, Civilizations.* Cambridge: Polity Press, 1999.

Moore, P. 'Soccer and the Politics of Culture in Western Australia'. In *Games, Sports and Cultures,* ed. N. Dyck, 117–34. Oxford and New York: Berg, 2000.

Moore, P. 'Scouting an Anthropology of Sport'. *Anthropologica* 46, no. 1 (2004): 37–46.

Mosely, P. *Ethnic Involvement in Australian Soccer: A History 1950–1990.* Canberra: Australian Sports Commission, 1995.

Mosely, P., and B. Murray. 'Soccer'. In *Sport in Australia: a Social History,* ed. W. Wamplew and B. Stoddart, 213–30. Melbourne: Cambridge University Press, 1994.

Mosely, P.A., R. Cashman, J. O'Hara, and H. Weatherburn. *Sporting Immigrants.* Crows Nest, NSW: Walla Walla Press, 1997.

Murray, B., and R. Hay, eds. *The World Game Downunder.* ASSH Studies in Sports History No. 19. Melbourne: Australian Society for Sports History, 2006.

O'Hara, J., ed. *Ethnicity and Soccer in Australia.* ASSH Studies in Sports History No. 10. Sydney: Australian Society for Sports History, 1994.

Phillips, M., and T. Magdalinska. 'Sport in Australia'. In *Sport and Society,* ed. B. Houlihan, 312–29. London: Sage Publications, 2003.

Reynolds, P. 'The New History of Soccer in Western Australia. Volume One'. Unpublished report prepared for The Soccer Federation of WA, n.d.

Slack, T. *Understanding Sport Organizations: The Application of Organization Theory.* Champaign, IL: Human Kinetics, 1997.

Solly, R. *Shoot Out: The Passion and the Politics of Soccer's Fight for Survival in Australia.* Milton, QLD: John Wiley & Sons, Australia, 2004.

Stewart, B., M. Nicholson, A. Smith, and H. Westerbeek. *Australian Sport: Better by Design? The Evolution of Australian Sport Policy.* London and New York: Routledge, 2004.

Stoddart, R. 'Sport and Society 1890–1940: A Foray'. In *A New History of Western Australia.,* ed. C.T. Stannage, 652–74. Nedlands: The University of Western Australia Press, 1981.

Sugden, J., and A. Tomlinson. *FIFA and the Context for World Football.* Cambridge: Polity Press, 1998.

# You have the right to remain violent: power and resistance in the club

Bily Bosevski and Chris Hallinan

*School of Sport and Exercise Science and Centre for Ageing, Rehabilitation, Exercise and Sport, Victoria University, Melbourne, Victoria, Australia*

For the most part, research involving sociocultural examinations of non-Anglo soccer football in Australia has examined rivalries between ethnic groups such as Serbs and Croats, persistence of identities, connections to gendered behaviours, ethnic differentiation, and perspectives of second and third generation Australians.[1] Against the backdrop of the sanitized cosmopolitanism evinced by the A-League and Football Federation of Australia (FFA), the Preston Lions have continued to place a premium on Macedonian identity and affiliation. The club members also present evidence of all of the aforementioned elements. However, in recent times, a faction within the club has contested the cultural heritage model and sought to position itself as 'progressive' by advocating a corporatised model of structure and management. In response, other factions combined to actively confront and resist this model. In this study we seek to examine the aggressive commodification of the club's administration relative to its alignment with Macedonian identity. We contend that our study is of interest because we are able to focus on a relatively untouched area of internal club politics. We conduct our analysis with regard to Bhabha's notions of cultural identity and internal differentiation.[2] Like Bhabha and others we reject the essentialism idea of singularized ethnic communities. As with Bhabha,[3] we are mindful of locality, neighbourhood, generation, ethnic background, cultural tradition, political tradition, political outlook, class gradation, gender and sexuality. More simply, we incorporate the notion of cultural hybridity and our study concerns the particulars of various groups within the Preston Lions. However, our principal focus is the intimidatory 'hooligan' behaviour of the self-named Preston Boys and the ways in which their behaviour is directed at other groups *within* the club.

In its generic sociological construct, 'football hooliganism' is often presented as a variant of deviant behaviour and other anti-social activities, which are commonly the result of 'excessive drinking and incidents on the field of play (including violent conduct and over-exuberance on the part of the players or questionable decisions by referees and their assistants)'.[4] Roversi adds that these activities are a 'combination of acts of vandalism and systematic, often bloody aggression, carried out by specific groups of young fans against others like themselves both inside and outside the grounds'.[5] The general consensus amongst contemporary scholars suggests football hooligan subcultures exist in two primary models.

(1) The 'English model' – referred to as *'casuals'*, is typical among Dutch and Swedish *'firms'* albeit stamped with their own cultural signatures.
(2) The 'Italian model' – known as *'ultras'*, is prevalent across Argentina, Spain and many Eastern bloc countries in unique cultural deviations.

Both models have evolved since their inception in the 1970s. A brief synopsis of the two models suggests supporters adopting the English model obscure club colours to avoid detection of their activities in and around grounds. Supporters subscribing to the Italian model produce colourful displays via various forms of supporter paraphernalia, including replica kits, banners and a hefty arsenal of fireworks in promoting their activities.

## Preston Lions – a cultural history

Preston Lions Football Club was founded in 1959 and has since evolved into the largest Macedonian football club outside Macedonia. Its history reflects an immigrant identity which not only catered for sport participation, but also provided ethnic Macedonians with a setting within which they could socialize and observe their cultural heritage. Currently, the primary function of the club centres on football, but this does not accurately represent the role it plays for the greater community. The club also has social connections with Macedonian churches, community groups and language schools, which collaborate to organize and promote cultural festivals and community picnics. Its facilities, including a social club, are often used as a site for hosting various cultural activities, ranging from a concert venue for touring international folk singers and groups, a dance hall for youth groups and traditional folk dance rehearsals, as well as a place where seniors assemble midweek to play cards and board games. The Preston Lions service a Victorian-Macedonian community of approximately 18,500,[6] and a broader Australian-Macedonian community of 41,000.[7] Many Macedonians in Australia trace their home to the annexed regions of Aegean Macedonia (Greece) and Pirin Macedonia (Bulgaria), with others also referring to themselves as Yugoslavs. Figures published by the United Macedonian Diaspora in 2006 estimate approximately 80,000[8] Macedonians live in Australia. Preston Lions attendances typically vary from 1,500–4,000 spectators, and on derby occasions can draw in excess of 6,000 spectators. But, even with a steady fan base (the Victoria Premier League [VPL]'s highest) and relative on-field successes, financial solvency has always eluded the club. Victorian football traditionally is not a lucrative competition; a recent increase in prize money for the 2007 Minor Premiership offers $30,000, just enough to blanket four weeks of player wages. Therefore, the club relies on alterative means to raise revenue, namely through volunteer work, fundraising, donations and local sponsorship. Ultimately the generosity of supporters and the broader Victorian-Macedonian community keep it functioning. Using an analogy to express the clubs chronic financial status, it is 'a cloud without a silver lining'.

Preston Lions' on-field achievements prior to the 1980s comprise of one Victorian State League championship title, four lower divisional titles in various Victorian state and metropolitan competitions, and two Victorian State League Cups. In 1981 it was promoted to the now defunct National Soccer League (NSL), then Australia's premier football competition prior to the 2005 inception of the A-League, twice finishing runners up in 1987 and 1991. Arguably, its greatest success came in winning the 1992 Docherty Cup Final (Victorian football's FA Cup equivalent) against traditional rivals South Melbourne. In 1993 they were relegated from the NSL to the Victorian Premier League (VPL), following points table deductions for financial irregularities. In 1994 they were crowned VPL champions, but due to recommendations made by the Bradley Report (1994) to abolish the promotion-relegation system, coupled with new financial criteria needed to gain admission into a revamped NSL, they would never appear in Australia's national competition again. The following year (1995), the Preston Lions were relegated to Victorian State League Division One, and promoted again in 1996 after finishing runners-up. Following a lean spell of eight years without success they were crowned VPL champions in 2002. Following on from their 2002 triumph the Lions were crowned minor premiers in 2003, missing a Grand Final appearance in a dramatic penalty shoot-out, and once again in 2007. Over the course of their history, Preston Lions players have won the Victorian Player of the Year (VPL Gold Medal) on three occasions. The club has produced eleven players who have represented the Australian youth team in various age groups, and a further seven players with Australian representative honours at senior level. As a feeder club the Lions have been relatively successful in nurturing talent, having sold-on players to A-League and European clubs, the latest being Isyan Erdogan (Adelaide United – AU) and Ljupche Acevski (FK Said Most – CZE), both moving in 2007. The ability to attract foreign players, albeit generally ethnic Macedonians, saw Zarko Odzakov (still regarded by many as the greatest ever overseas player to represent Australia at international level) grace its former playing ranks.

Analysis of the club's cultural and sporting histories subsequently positions the moral and intrinsic value of the club over its extrinsic material value. Five decades as a social hub within the broader community put alongside the consolation prize of finishing twice runners-up in the NSL (the club's highest sporting achievement) allows for minimal latitude in weighting its cultural significance beneath its sporting pedigree.

### Gathering the data firsthand

Whilst both authors assume the role of ethnographers for this study, it should be noted that the first author is a constituent of the greater Australian-Macedonian community as well as an enduring supporter of Preston Lions FC. The first author's association with Preston Lions FC began in his early adolescence where he eagerly attended games with his father and older brother in father-son bonding affairs, with close relatives, or with friends. His absorption with football even possessed him to travel unaccompanied to games when a minor via the metropolitan public transport service without parental consent. The status-quo in venturing to games remained until the club was relegated from the National Soccer League to the Victorian State League in 1993. Post relegation the first author spent four years on hiatus as a substandard squad, and a large dip in crowds left his support exhausted. For the period 1997 through to 2001 the authors' attendances were sporadic (a dozen or so games) only choosing to attend the fashionable derby games. In 2002 the first author began casually attending games again, and easily familiarised himself with the 'Lions'. He has spent the last five years as a regular on the outer wing watching the club win two Premier League titles and intermittently battle relegation. In adulthood the club is viewed strictly through a social pane, with camaraderie between close friends, accompanied by excessive side-line chatter which becomes highly engaging. Admittedly, following the club from a personal viewpoint has waned as his current interests are neither supporter based, nor football (on field) related. Rather, he is now more charmed by the stereotypical kebapi (skinless mince sausages) and salted pumpkin seed culture that subsists within the club marketing strategies of Victorian football.

A descendant of proud Macedonian immigrant parents, the first author has been allowed freedom in pursuit of his own cultural offerings whether they are Australian, Macedonian or other. His parents are particularly proud of their Macedonian lineage, but have been lax in passing these cultural fibres onto their children, as ultimately they are content with the Australian guise as representative of the family's cultural portrait. The first author is not an active participant of the greater Australian-Macedonian community. Typically, a 'Macedonian' community member will attend Macedonian school into their late teens, frequent church and associated gatherings, be a member of a folk dance group, and attend the monthly Macedonian disco nights. The first author has forgone Macedonian school, only attends church on significant religious events (Christmas and Easter), and declined membership in a folk dance group. He attended disco nights into his mid teens but soon substituted them in favour of heavier music interests. Thus, Preston Lions FC's position in the community has served as insight into his own cultural template, and he would have little connection with his Macedonian roots if it wasn't for soccer.

## Preston Boys

The supporter collective now known as 'Preston Boys' or 'PB' lacks the physicality found in traditional hooligan definitions. However, it overtly preserves its intimida-tory mechanisms which are intentionally threatening and excessively amplified via supporter paraphernalia which commonly consist of banners embellished with fists, lions, devils and even rock n' roll clown motifs, illustrated in typically aggressive postures. Drums are used to choreograph routines, and to tempo chants which are at times rebellious and blatantly offensive. Fireworks are used on carnival occasions, such as local derby games and/or night matches. It is our view that these intimidatory mechanisms become a cultural symbol of football support and cannot always be interpreted as hooliganism, which implies violent and destructive behaviour.

The aim of the following section is to introduce the reader to the PB as a constit-uent of the greater Preston Lions supporter community. The Preston Boys collective espouse the conventional ultra model in its functions as a supporter body, albeit stamped with a unique broad-based cultural signature. The deliberate outward mani-festation of a transcendent Macedonian guise is accentuated via a disproportionate use of red and yellow supporter paraphernalia that serves to connect the PB syndicate to club and country via its analogous use of Macedonian national colours and symbols. Beyond the monotones of red and yellow, an Australian nuance is apparent via the use of contextually minimalist symbols; including the Australian national flag, sporadic appearances of an Aboriginal flag, seemingly appropriate as its composition embodies shades of red and yellow, and the St Georges Cross, with the characters PMFC (Preston Makedonia Football Club) printed in each quadrant. As a newcomer, immediate exposure to these symbols announces the club as being primarily of Macedonian origins, with its Australian influence accepted as secondary.

Chants are predominantly sung in English and Macedonian languages, but on occasions PB members have vocalized chants in German, Italian and Spanish, and adapted various other foreign chants into English and/or Macedonian, thus reflecting a diversely cosmopolitan pedigree amongst its supporting ranks. With a multiplicity of chant styles conveyed on match days, the members facilitate a range similar to the Eurovision song contest. The PB repertoire of soccer pop chants is usually light fun – smooth, entertaining, at times cheesy, but ultimately catchy. However, replace the 'love me', 'kiss me', 'hold me' lyrics and choreographed dance routines found in conventional Euro-pop, with overtly narcissistic lyrics compounded by excessively aggressive pomposity, and the ultras terrace songs soon have potential to become battle hymns.

Taking these cosmopolitan influences further, the PB have intentionally sculpted themselves from the matching clay used in producing the commercially stylised effigy of the ultra, thus mimicking the celebrated ultra groups from across the globe. This affinity with clay is dually represented by the material holding both practical and decorative applications. Practicality in a football framework allocates the PB collective greater agency in its own affairs as an independent body, and its decorative applications are further represented by the production of choreographed 'grandstand play' used to announce the group on match days. Further galvanizing the clay analogy, and positioning the material's fundamental property as malleability, the group is able to adapt and evolve with the shifting global football culture phenomenon. The latest evolution has been the accession of an internet forum which, used as a group asset, augments it's capacity as a supporter body. The persuasive force of the internet forum within the greater Preston Lions supporter community cannot be undervalued as it underpins the day-to-day goings-on of the PB alliance.

Informal conversations held with various PB members about their individual supporter styles and histories with a view to deciphering which continental ultra mode the PB collective should absorb in fashioning its overall supporter behaviours, gave a typically varied response. Several members of the group believe the PB ought to centre its chants and routines from established Macedonian Clubs in an identical manner to FK Vardar's Komiti, who promote a pronounced emphasis on sodality (a devotional or charitable association), which is commonly weighted above choreographed routines and banner displays. Equally other group members boast a desire to mimic the support modes of prominent ultra groups from the European continent, approximating with the likes of AC Milan's Fossa De Leoni, with vividly choreographed supporter displays using copious quantities of fireworks coupled with auxiliary supporter paraphernalia being a particular fan favourite. Less committed members simply wish to stamp their own unique cultural signature amongst the supporter lines opting not to adopt any of the traditions of established ultra groups. The group structure is not wholly based on one particular model. It is a continental cocktail of football culture which at times reflects the individual identities of PB members. Ultimately, regardless of its origins, the general consensus amongst the group on its supporting style is that it must reflect the community's Macedonian roots.

Considering the spurious nature of the existing Australian football supporter climate, the PB can be colloquially positioned as a 'bastardized' amalgam of the globally renowned ultra groups. It absorbs the best, and at times the worst, of what ultra culture from across the globe has to offer football as a spectacle and applies it to its uniquely Australian-Macedonian setting. Notwithstanding these variations, the PB maintain a fundamentally emblematic configuration, as at its core it is undeniably an ultra group. The PB ultras can and should be distinguished from orthodox ultra groups. The ultras are traditionally born of a coagulation of youths from local boroughs, with analogous geopolitical consciousness in turn creating fierce intra/inter-city rivalries with football as the sideshow. Two prime examples are used to highlight the origins of these relationships. The first example subsists in the Argentinean capital of Buenos Aries, between city rivals River Plate and Boca Juniors. This fierce rivalry is chiefly derived of socio-economic backgrounds and can be classified as a case of football's bourgeoisie (CA River Plate) versus football's proletariat (CA Boca Juniors), with each club representing communities at opposite ends of the social continuum. The typical ultra group origins are represented in the derby of Milan, Italy, where AC Milan's socialist legacy places it in conflict with the fervently right-wing ultra groups of FC Internazionale Milano. In this example, football serves as pretence to deep-seated animosity based upon political affiliations.

Using the aforementioned ultra models to illustrate the typical setup of conventional ultra groups, it is critical here to note that the PB structure digresses from the traditional ultras groups found in contemporary football circles. They do not subsist entirely through socio-economic, nor geopolitical, ties. Rather, PB group members have come together via social connections made in the broader Australian-Macedonian community. These social connections are forged at events such as church functions, Macedonian language schools, youth disco nights and community picnics, and further aided by modern technology (internet forums and Macedonian chat rooms). Taking into consideration these community institutions as propagation for developing strong/ useful social connections based principally on Macedonian ethnicity, the Preston Lions Football Club can no longer be viewed solely as a sporting club by its members and supporters. The proud ethnic undertone attached to the club represents a strong-weak duality. The strength is typified by the generosity of supporters and the broader community – trumpets and all. The trumpet is symbolic, as it is the instrument utilized by fans as the key to a cultural portal that opens on match days and is demonstrated by orchestration of an '*oro*' (group dance) and renditions of traditional Macedonian anthems played on festive occasions. The flipside of this strong-weak duality also subsists in the club's staunch ethnic base. On occasion, the club's own fans have 'blown their own trumpet'. In the last two decades (coinciding with the break up of the former Yugoslavia) the club has been weakened by fans who subscribe to political tensions abroad arising over the 'Macedonian' name issue, and subsequent contestations over sovereignty rights and Macedonian identity. These international contentions place it in direct conflict with rival Australian clubs of Greek origin, such as South Melbourne FC, Heidelberg Warriors FC and Oakleigh Cannons FC, all of whom are as staunch about their own ethnic being, resulting in intermittent clashes of an aggressive nature, making the club (Preston Lions) an unremitting target of national media outlets, the authorities and Victorian soccer's governing body the Football Federation of Victoria (FFV) which have resulted in sanctions, culminating in points deductions and heavy fines.

This 'us against them' mindset serves as an avid introduction to Preston Lions FC supporter community; and the PB, operating as the primary supporter group, has a reputation that precedes it. The fans are notorious. Without detailing its dealings, the fans are proud of the reputation they have earned. However, we must emphasize that this reputation is not fashioned of 'real violence'.[9] The emphasis here is on intimidation and reinforcing its status via its 'symbolic opposition and ritualised aggression'.[10] Whether the focal point of this intimidation is intra-club and centred on committee members, an opposition club, or one of the football bodies within Victorian football, the PB aren't short of antagonists. Supporters have a drawn out abhorrence for the FFV as it feels it's a victim of a larger FFV agenda to see the club fail and ultimately disband. Historically, fans have challenged the FFV on every front. In 2005 the FFV introduced fresh Codes of Conduct apropos of supporter paraphernalia. The determination declared the use of fireworks, ethnic symbols and/or slogans contained within league venues would be met with sanctions in the shape of financial penalties and/or points table deductions. The PB's response was typically defiant, but deliberately astute. Firework displays were temporarily discontinued; mockingly toned banners featuring humanitarian messages such as 'SAVE THE WHALES' soon replaced traditional banners. Others were also penned with topical issues, most notably a 'FREE SCHAPELLE' banner recognizing the plight of Schapelle Corby, an Australian woman convicted of attempting to smuggle marijuana into Bali in 2004.

The PB's disdain for the FFV continues. By the halfway point of the 2007 season, the club had accumulated fines totalling in excess of $10,000 associated with fractious supporter behaviours. The bulk of this fine was a consequence of an incident where a linesman was verbally abused by an indiscriminate Preston Lions fan from behind a 1.8 metre high cyclone fence. A FFV representative who witnessed the incident submitted an official report which resulted in the fine. Thus fans feel they are the victim of a subjective FFV strategy, as similar occurrences are profuse at other league venues but are rarely met with an equivalent sentence. The substantial size of the fine was felt harder off the field, particularly as in the pre-season the club commenced 'rattling the tins' in search of financial salvation. A banner made for the sole purpose of confronting the FFV read, '$7500 FOR ABUSING A REF?! ... IT ONLY COSTS $500 TO DROP A COP! FFV = CRIMINALS!' A concluding note to the FFV appeared on the final day of fixtures in the 2007 home and away season. The club began the season on minus six table points for failing to pay the annual contribution fees connected with VPL registration as a result of its chronic financial status. In response to the severity and potential impact of the point's table deduction, relegation being the most obvious hurdle to contend with in the early season, the PB fired a parting shot at the FFV in the form of a banner that read, 'FFV DOES IT HURT? -6 AND STILL MINOR PREMIERS!' and was dually accompanied by a chorus of 'Who Are Ya', a chant, which is typically used in football circles to denounce esteemed opposition. These actions may loosely be interpreted as an end to the PB's obsession with the FFV as a standpoint.

The level of organization of the PB collective on match days is remarkable, especially considering the relatively ad hoc configuration of the group. Notably, there is an absence of a hierarchical structure; there is no designated leader, just an armada/ fleet of followers. The only clue to any hierarchy is represented in their match day apparel. Producing its own merchandise, the PB has come up with a novel signifier of an individual's involvement within the group, as it endeavours to increase active participation amongst group members. Those who chant wear black hooded sweaters, whereas the 'mutes' wear the less fashionable light grey marl version. Despite these colour variations, all apparel is finished with a suavely designed motif bearing the characters PB inside a U-shaped wreath, which bears no resemblance to the Preston

Lions FC official crest (a prancing lion upon a shield). This can be viewed as a clear indicator of its mission to operate as an autonomous body, and further establish itself as a rival to those who culturally mismanage the club. Despite the obvious sodality among its members, there is a revolving door effect within its supporter ranks. Up to a dozen fresh faces enter the group each season, but this is balanced by equal numbers parting for the greener football pastures offered by the A-League franchise Melbourne Victory FC. Aggrandized analysis surrounding the deficient hierarchical arrangement within the group serves as precursor to central tensions. Without a formal leader, the group lacks stability at times, especially under the strain of below-par on-field performances by the squad. Within the group there are factions centred on their boroughs, and whether fans come from the North or West suburbs of Melbourne. On occasions these groups have refused to stand next to each other at home games. Any attempted chant by the North faction is given the razz by the West faction, and vice versa. It's a dysfunctional family at home that seems only to function at away games.

The reach of the group extends to on field participants also, as the PB has close relationships with the club's playing staff. When the players win, the supporter wins. This mindset is reflected each week pending the reward of the three points, when PB members are invited into the changing rooms post match to bond with the players in delivering the club's theme song. Individual players have shown their appreciation for the group by removing their playing shirts during goal celebrations to reveal a PB t-shirt, despite this action carrying an automatic booking. The kind gesture offered by the club captain, who made a promise to deliver his playing jersey from the Grand Final to a member of PB in anticipation of winning the 2007 VPL title, is a typical example of the close relationship between the players and supporters. Not only did he fulfil his promise, but the captain presented it to him in front of the fans directly after the final whistle had blown. The reputation of the group also extends beyond state lines. PB members travelled to Sydney to watch the encounter between sister club Bankstown City Lions FC and Bonnyrigg White Eagles SC in the 2005 NSWPL Grand Final. A PB member took it upon himself to scout a Bankstown City player as a self-appointed representative of the Preston Lions. The accomplished forward agreed to terms in principle in what seemed a win-win relationship for all parties as the playing position had traditionally been the club's Achilles heel. The player in question called Preston officials seeking a contract, but was denied a deal as club officials didn't take kindly to 'supporters' negotiating on behalf of the club.

In the total framework of Victorian football, notwithstanding the four Greek-backed clubs in VPL, the football community is forever welcoming of travelling Preston Lions fans due, for the most part, to increased earnings from gate receipts and canteen sales associated with Preston Lions famously large contingent of travelling fans – at times outnumbering home fans 10 to 1. Less significantly, this appreciation extends to the uniquely festive atmosphere created by Preston supporters. This posture is demonstrated by the PB having a healthy handshake pre-game, a spirited contest throughout the game, and a larger post-game relationship with equally parochial fans from opposition clubs such as Melbourne Knights FC as representative of the Croatian community and Sunshine George Cross SC and its Maltese roots.

**Supporter-committee power relationship**

A brief chronological analysis of the period from 2002 to 2006 is used to shed light on the transitions in intra-supporter dynamics, and their power relationship with the club's administrators (committee). This analysis is critical in the contextual analysis of power and social resistance.

### 2002 season

The Preston Lions committee-supporter relationship was harmonious, functioning through a strong volunteer community work ethic. There was an absence of an organized group structure amongst its supporter dynamics. Supporter connections were based on informal socio-cultural friendships. Battling relegation in the early season, the coach was replaced by club legend John Markovski. After a 13-game undefeated run, the Lions finished sixth and qualified for the final series in the ultimate round of the home and away season, after also relying on results from other games. The committee contributed resources (both financial and material) in soliciting supporters to create an 'atmosphere' for the 2002 VPL Grand Final. Preston won in each game en route to, and including, the Grand Final by the score line of 2-1 in sudden death extra time via the 'golden goal' rule. Many supporters affectionately tagged the 2002 final series as 'Ground Hog Day.'

### 2003 season

The committee-supporter relationship remained status quo. However, the first shift in supporter dynamics was evident, and a collection of youths and young adults united under the name 'Lions Pride' adopting the Italian 'ultra' model for its official fan base. Funds were collected for exclusive membership into the 'Lions Pride'. Fans produced official supporter merchandise. Lions Pride apparel featured a derivative of the Preston Lions club logo – the only resemblance being the prancing lion. As a reward for past volunteer services as fan representatives, Two Lions Pride members were elected onto the committee and later assumed general administrative and marketing roles in a volunteer capacity. The club led the competition all season and finished minor premiers but narrowly missed another VPL Grand appearance on a penalty shootout.

### 2004 season

A new faction called the 'Truck Drivers' took over administrative control of the club and promised a $250,000 investment to upgrade facilities, and sign 'big name' players. Championship winning coach John Markovski, a supporter and player favourite, was dismissed in the pre-season after requesting a $100 per week pay rise. The new committee appointed Zoran Trajcevski, a former Preston player with close connections to the Truck Drivers, as coach. A player revolt in protest of Markovski's sacking saw three long-serving Preston players, including the captain, leave the club in the pre-season. Two of those followed Markovski to his new club, the Whittlesea Stallions. The Lions Pride created a public internet forum for its existing and aspiring members. Topical discussions centred upon football and various community events. Thus, it simultaneously increased its presence within the power structures of the club and the greater Macedonian community. A further two fans were elected onto the Preston committee obtaining further specialized roles, such as player registrations, and inception and maintenance of the clubs official website. The Club qualified for the finals series, but was eliminated in the first round, finishing sixth overall.

## *2005 season*

The Truck Drivers failed to fulfil their promise of $250,000 investment, with little evidence of any upgrades to facilities or big name signings. Instead, they announce a new youth policy, and promote three youth players to the first team. A further three senior players left the club and joined former Preston coach John Markovski at Whittlesea Stallions. Rumours surfaced claiming the Truck Drivers were in arrears with senior players' match payments. The Lions began the season with seven games without a win. Round eight fixtures saw Preston play Whittlesea at home. Supporters organized a 'critical' banner display in protest of sub-par performances, the two most famous being 'TRUCK FOR SALE ... 13 13 FUCK OFF' and 'COACH OUT, UPRAVA PEDERI' (the committee is gay). Trailing 3-1 during the first half, a dozen Lions Pride members' gathered behind the technical area and released a barrage of insults aimed at the coach, questioning his tactical strategies coupled with personal slurs. Supporters of various ages soon joined them, with a critical mass of approximately 200 'animated' supporters assembled at The Truck Drivers corporate box, protesting verbally and gesturing physically at the clubs mismanagement. By the end of the game, the coach handed in his resignation, and members called an Extraordinary General Meeting (EGM) to nominate a new committee. To demonstrate the clout now available amongst Preston Lions supporters the first author witnessed various senior players thanking the protagonists for their role in getting rid of the coach. The committee–supporter relationship remained equable. The result of the EGM saw a new quasi-corporate consortium comprised of influential community and local business-men assume administrative control of the club. Having a purely business background, with limited technical football knowledge, they relied on assistance from past commit-tee members. Following the appointment of the coach, (the fans suggested Vlado Vanis) the club's on field performances improved dramatically. Supporters labelled the new committee 'The Silver Lining' before the team narrowly missed another finals campaign. A loss on the final day of the season saw it slip from fourth to seventh and out of finals contention. One of the supporters remarked how the club structure was now 'cloudy'.

## *2006 season (The cloud gets it's silver lining)*

After having a season to acclimatize to both administrative and football operations, the new consortium announced they had inherited a substantial, albeit longstanding, debt of $130,000. In pursuit of a 'professional' image, they dismissed two Lions Pride representatives and kept the other two in reduced capacities that focused on selling memberships and minor promotional duties. Against the advice of club members who wanted to instil the successful Club 1000 initiative from the early 1990s (1,000 memberships at $100), they introduced new membership packages with a corporate focus, with the basic silver membership priced 150% higher than the previous season, also charging higher prices at the gate, canteen and merchandise stand. Erecting a corporate marquee and excluding members from once freely accessible areas resulted in increased tensions between supporters and the new committee. New rules outlawing chants in Macedonian and clothing with Macedonian symbols were put in place. Many fans began to feel the club was losing its cultural identity. This view was further authen-ticated by the first author having overhead a conversation between two fans, one declar-ing 'money forgets culture'. Once again, rumours surfaced of players not being paid, and when a supporter of 20 years was removed from his seat in what was reclaimed as a corporate seating, the supporter collective mobilized themselves through peaceful means, hanging banners upside down in protest (mimicking European fans), using anti-committee chants, and refusing to celebrate when the team scored. The committee responded in a typically aggressive and swift fashion, using the print media to circulate exaggerated reports of deviant supporter behaviour in Macedonian newspapers, which labelled the protesters as 'drunks', 'hooligans', and 'undesirables'. Here the term hooligan must be revisited, as during the period under analysis, there was no actual violent physical conduct, and all forms of aggression were symbolic in opposition to these changes. However, the committee invoked stadium bans for continually resistant supporters, took long-range paparazzi style photos of 'trouble makers', and supplied their personal details to the FFV and the authorities.

## Power and social resistance within the Lions

Examination of these key points over this five-year period sees two key themes emerge: the primary being an evolution in inter-supporter dynamics, from an informal collective of fans, to an organized/cohesive group based on the Italian ultra model. Roversi's summation of this model illustrates the dynamics of these groups, and common methodologies used by ultras; defining them as, 'small groups of young fans who gather behind banners with intentionally threatening messages, and who stand out from the rest of the supporters because of their more colourful, lively way in which they expressed their passion for the game'.[11] The reference to the term 'game' in this context refers to their ability to influence the club's internal management objectives as a direct result of their 'passion'. Adopting the ultra model also proves successful in increasing supporters' cultural capital and its ability to control its own interests in relation to the clubs socio-cultural identity/responsibilities. The development of an internet-based community is an example of an increase in supporter capital within the club's social structure which becomes a powerful tool in expressing supporter views and gaining further allies. The production of merchandise as a source of revenue, and having Lions Pride members elected onto the committee as official representatives, further enhances it's agency as a supporter body.

The secondary theme to emerge is the deterioration of the hegemonic committee-supporter relationship. Over time supporters who were forced to adopt and internalize the committee's new corporate values and norms, at the expense of the clubs cultural identity, challenged this relationship. Interestingly, this counter-hegemonic form of social resistance links closely to broader issues of power and resistance in sport. In the context of this study, supporters (acting as human agents) and the committee (assuming a structural role) contest power. As noted by Tomlinson, power is 'the capacity to produce, or contribute to, outcomes – to make a difference to the world. In social life, we may say, power is the capacity to do this through social relationships: it is the capacity to produce, or contribute to, outcomes by significantly affecting another or others.'[12]

The application of Tomlinson's definition to the supporter-committee conflict within the Preston Lions Football Club makes clear that the Lions Pride operate as a 'point of resistance' within the club's power relations. Expressing their agency (ability to act independently, to make a difference and produce outcomes), the Lions Pride subsequently increased their power within the clubs social stratum. The committee response saw it become more stringent and less tolerant of the supporter body as it tried to limit or influence the power that the supporter body exhibited in maintenance of its new corporate structure. In what is a complex strategical situation likened to a game of chess, a key point arose – the contestation of power between the supporter and committee bodies indicated that as one group became increasingly organized and threatened the other's capability to make a difference and produce outcomes, the opposing group organized itself further in an effort to preserve its power. Ultimately, the issues of power and social resistance relate directly to the question of moral versus financial ownership, and establishing the importance of one over the other and/or achieving a balance in the power relationship where moral and financial ownership exist in equilibrium.

## Conclusion

This case study has examined how the Preston Lions Football Club operates as a social arm in the larger Australian-Macedonian community and its pivotal role in maintaining its ethno-cultural identity within a social football setting. The closeness of the community in resisting any change to both its cultural and football identities has seen a group of youths and young adults bond together and adopt the 'ultra' model in extending itself as a supporter body; subsequently providing a point of resistance to the gradual quasi-corporatisation of the club. As Bhabha notes,

> the 'locality' of national culture is neither unified nor unitary in relation to itself, nor must it be seen simply as 'other' in relation to what is outside or beyond it. The boundary is Janus-faced and the problem of outside/inside must always itself be a process of hybridity, incorporating new 'people' in relation to the body politic, generating other sites of meaning and, inevitably, in the political process, producing unmanned sites of political antagonism and unpredictable forces for political representation.[13]

The Preston Boys established itself within the Macedonian club not only as an official supporter body, but it further increased it's agency by independently operating within the clubs social sphere, evolving into a group with enough clout to make a difference on various fronts. These included the general supporter scene, the management and preservation of its cultural objectives/identity, and, at committee level, with an uncanny ability to influence the club's internal football operations. In the broader issue of power and resistance in sport, we have discussed how power is contested and how both supporter and committee bodies continue to organize themselves further to minimize any loss of power. In closing, this case study postulates that issues of power and social resistance in the Preston Lions relate directly to the question of supporters' moral ownership versus a corporate body's financial ownership; and their abilities to either preserve or alter cultural identity.

## Notes

1. For example, see Danforth, 'Is the "World Game" an "Ethnic Game" or an "Aussie Game"?', 363–87; Hallinan and Krotee, 'Conceptions of Nationalism', 125–33; Hughson,'Australian Soccer', 12–16; Hughson, 'Football, Folk Dancing and Fascism', 167–86; Hughson, 'The Bad Blue Boys', 239–59; Miller, 'The Unmarking of Soccer', 104–20; Mosely, Entry for 'Soccer', 316 and 321–3; Mosely, 'Balkans Politics in Australian Soccer', 33–43.
2. Bhabha, *Nation and Narration*.
3. Ibid.; Bhabha, *Location of Culture*.
4. Bairner, 'The Leicester School', 584–5.
5. Roversi, 'Football Violence in Italy', 312.
6. Australian Bureau of Statistics, 2006.

7. Australian Bureau of Statistics, 2006.
8. United Macedonian Diaspora, *UMD Quarterly*, 2006.
9. Marsh, *Aggro*, 80.
10. Ibid.
11. Roversi, 'Football Violence in Italy', 317–18.
12. Tomlinson, 'Domination, Negotiation, and Resistance', 237.
13. Bhabha, *Location of Culture*, 4.

## References

Australian Bureau of Statistics, '20680 – Country of Birth of Person (Full Classification List) by Sex – Australia' (Microsoft Excel Download). 2006 Census. Australian Bureau of Statistics, 2006. Retrieved on 2 June 2008. Total Count of Persons: 19, 855, 288.

Bairner, A. 'The Leicester School and the Study of Football Hooliganism'. *Sport in Society* 9, no. 4 (2006): 583–98.

Bhabha, H. *Nation and Narration.* London: Routledge, 1994.

Bhabha, H. *Location of Culture.* London: Routledge, 2004.

Danforth, L.M. 'Is the "World Game" an "Ethnic Game" or an "Aussie Game"? Narrating the Nation in Australian Soccer'. *American Ethnologist* 28, no. 2 (2001): 363–87.

Hallinan, C.J., and M.L. Krotee. 'Conceptions of Nationalism and Citizenship among non-Anglo-Celtic Soccer Clubs in an Australian City'. *Journal of Sport and Social Issues* 17, no. 2 (1993): 125–33.

Hughson, J. 'Australian Soccer: "Ethnic" or "Aussie"? The Search for an Image'. *Current Affairs Bulletin* 68, no. 10 (1992): 12–16.

Hughson, J. 'Football, Folk Dancing and Fascism: Diversity and Difference in Multicultural Australia'. *Journal of Sociology* 33, no. 2 (1997): 167–86.

Hughson, J. 'The Bad Blue Boys and the "Magical Recovery" of John Clarke'. In *Entering the Field: New Perspectives on World Football,* ed. G. Armstrong and R. Giulianotti, 239–59. Oxford: Berg, 1997.

Marsh, P. *Aggro: The Illusion of Violence.* London: Dent, 1978.

Miller, T. 'The Unmarking of Soccer: Making a Brand New Subject'. In *Celebrating the Nation: A Critical Study of Australia's Bicentenary,* ed. T. Bennett, P. Buckridge, D. Carter, and C. Mercer, 104–20. Sydney: Allen and Unwin, 1992.

Mosely, P. Entry for 'Soccer'. In *The Oxford Companion to Australian Sport,* ed. W. Vamplew, K. Moore, and J. O'Hara. 311–30. Melbourne: Oxford University Press.

Mosely, P. 'Balkans Politics in Australian Soccer'. In Ethnicity and Soccer in Australia, ASSH: 33–43.

Roversi, A. 'Football Violence in Italy'. *International Review for Sociology of Sport* 26, no. 4 (1991): 317–18.

Tomlinson, A. 'Power: Domination, Negotiation, and Resistance in Sports Cultures'. *Journal of Sport & Social Issues* 22, no. 3 (1998): 235–40.

United Macedonian Diaspora. 'Macedonians Take Active Role in Australian Census', *UMD Quarterly* 1 (2006): 13–15.

# Fan perspectives of change in the A-League

Daniel Lock

*School of Leisure, Sport and Tourism, University of Technology, Sydney, Australia*

## Introduction

Soccer, or new football as it is being marketed by the Football Federation Australia, has long been conceptualized and framed on the basis of ethnic involvement. Despite attempts to 'de-ethnicise' the National Soccer League (NSL) during its 17-year existence[1] the competition was marginalized and widely perceived as an ethnic affair.[2]. Conjecture has placed ethnicity as a root problem in the dwindling attendance figures experienced by the NSL. Graham Bradley alluded to the inherent issues associated with fan bases formed around ethnicity, instead arguing for a league model which included clubs based around 'areas and regions', to engage football's huge participant base.[3] As Cockerill described them, 'football's silent majority, the hundreds of thousands of youngsters playing the game who have never felt connected to it at professional level'.[4]

In 2003 the first step in restructuring football in Australia was taken. The Federal Government commissioned a report into the structure and function of Soccer Australia,[5] which was ailing following the Socceroos failures to qualify for the Confederations Cup in 2001 and the World Cup in 2002. *The Crawford Report* instigated a process of revolutionary change in Australia's football governance. Business tycoon Frank Lowy accepted the Chairmanship of the reformed body and set about assembling an administration to implement the structural recommendations provided. At the start of his tenure, Lowy commissioned an independent report into the structure of a new National Soccer League, to replace the existing model.[6] The report was commissioned in an attempt to outline a clear model for a successful league, based upon the recommendations of a highly qualified panel.

The recommendations of the report were clear and broad ranging. In terms of support for a new league and club structure it was clear that 'A-League' clubs would be spread more evenly across Australia (instead of concentrated in Sydney and Melbourne) and clubs would be established to cater for districts, not ethnic groups.[7]

The FFA took the recommendations of the *Report of the NSL Task-Force* further, implementing a one-team-per-city model containing only eight teams. In developing a league structure without intra-city competition (during the first five seasons at least), the FFA (from a fan perspective) initiated a clear departure from the NSL competition in two respects. Firstly, the A-League provided an opportunity for entire cities to amorphously support the same team, without inner-city divides. Secondly, as clubs didn't represent an expressive ethnicity, it provided the potential for clubs to attract a more culturally diverse following. In this study two central questions are addressed. Firstly, does the A-League represent a significant change from the NSL, and secondly, why do individuals identify with a specific A-League club? These questions are addressed through a qualitative method drawing on 21 in-depth interviews with members of Sydney FC.

## Football in Australia

The historical context of football in Australia has received much attention in the literature to date.[8] This body of research has clearly articulated the introduction of the game to Australia,[9] but has focussed more prominently on football's history post-Second World War and the role that football played in the lives and acculturation of non-English speaking migrants.[10] On an individual level football provided a pastime in which migrants could outshine their native oppressors,[11] whilst socially the local football club served as a focal point within ethnic communities.[12] The football club served 'as an instrument through which all elements of social life could be aided. They enabled people to interact, to establish patronage links, support networks and social contacts.'[13] At a time when assimilation was enforced, football clubs provided a clear point of sanctuary to migrant communities. The consequent traditions that developed around football clubs created an avenue for migrants to gain prominence through playing and administrative roles as well as through club patronage.[14]

The extent of involvement with ethnically based clubs differed based on ethnicity.[15] In his discussion of the Croatian community Hughson defined the role that the football club played within this ethnic group – specifically at Croatian club Sydney United. Hughson argued that Croatian ethnicity was a far more binding factor than Italian heritage at Marconi in relation to both football clubs. An attributing factor to this was the efforts of Marconi to broaden their support base within their community. Hughson's research is supported by Mosely,[16] who articulated the role that Croatian soccer clubs played in educating young Croats in the traditional loyalties of their homeland. The Croatian 'soccer club helped not only to build migrant communities but to perpetuate them as well'.[17] This is not to say Croatian supporter bases were necessarily the most fervent or nationalistically driven, but to articulate the extent of the role that ethnicity played in the formation and maintenance of national identity in some ethnic groups.

Football and its distinct role and social function in ethnic communities across Australia created an image of it being a marginalized and multicultural affair.[18] This perception coupled with a hooligan problem that perpetuated itself in Australian football developed an environment that was viewed as exclusive and intimidating by football fans outside of the existing support network. The role of the media in perpetuating this perception has been discussed;[19] see Kent for a recent example of bad press.[20] Hughson's provocative titling for his case study: 'The wogs are at it again' articulated the role the media played in developing public perspectives of the 'soccer riot' and its inextricable ethnic links.[21] Hughson linked inflammatory media reportage as a precursor to de-ethnicising the sport. Moreover 'the de-ethnicising case has always hinged on the perception that soccer will only move into the mainstream of Australian sport once it has freed itself from controversies associated with ethnic identity'.[22] Inflammatory media reportage, as Hughson contended, provided 'a stark image of "ethnicity" against which "Australianness" might be celebrated'.[23] The broader connotations of this media-developed perspective have provided a backdrop against which de-ethnicising the NSL was founded.

Broader discussions regarding de-ethnicisation are mainly superfluous to the topic of this study; however their role in defining the change process is relevant. Pertinent arguments regarding the positive and negative aspects of the de-ethnicisation agenda have already been written.[24] The conceptual dimensions of this problem centre upon the right of individuals to express their cultural heritage. However, as Mosely conceded, de-ethnicisation, to football's governance, has been less about removing ethnicity and more about good business and developing the games following outside of locally based, insular football clubs.[25] More specifically, de-ethnicisation was designed in the NSL (not its early attempts in Canberra[26]) to broaden the game's appeal and capitalize on football's significant grass-roots participation levels. As Vamplew argued, ethnic communities were no longer providing the support to the football clubs that had played such a fundamental role in the acculturation process of Western European migrants, post-1940.[27] Vamplew viewed a de-ethnicised competition as a means to grow the game, despite its problematic standing in relation to multicultural policy.

It is from this foundation that the focus of this study stems. Namely, that changes to Australian football have occurred based upon the premise that new clubs devoid of expressive ethnicity are the best way to grow football to a broad audience in Australia. The reformed governing body of the game in the antipodes, the Football Federation Australia (FFA), quickly developed media links and attempted to boldly outline the vision for the reformed national competition. As Chief Executive John O'Neill told reporters, the A-League was an attempt to 'unite the tribes' that had served to divide football in Australia.[28] O'Neill was referring to the rival ethnic groups that had been seen by many as the fundamental problem with the NSL. The A-League presented an opportunity for the FFA to develop 'a strong, credible, vibrant A-League, where long-time fans, recent converts and bandwagon jumpers can see their heroes play'.[29] In essence, the A-League marked a clear attempt to give all fans of football, or curious others, the opportunity to support domestic football in Australia.

In the following paragraphs the discussion focuses on literature published on the A-League in order to frame the new competition, prior to presenting initial findings outlining how the supporter environment has changed and how fans of Sydney FC identify with the club.

**The A-League: research to date**

There is general consensus that A-League presents a notable shift from the NSL, both in culture and focus. Studies to date include Hay's ethnographic work with fans of Melbourne Victory;[30] Lock, Taylor and Darcy's quantitative work with members of Sydney FC;[31] and Hallinan, Hughson and Burke's comparative study between fans of Melbourne Victory and the Springvale White Eagles in Victoria.[32] Hay alluded to the changes that had taken place in the support of Australia's national competition arguing that: 'The current [football] boom is different from all those which have gone before. Those were precipitated and sustained by high levels of inward migration of football-cognisant people; this one is virtually entirely driven by the interest of the existing domestic population.'[33]

The comments of Hay are important when addressing the A-League's following. Of particular importance is the notion that support for the A-League is drawn from Australia's 'existing population'. Hay's argument supports the perspective that A-League clubs draw from a broad cross-section of 'Australian' society, which was an explicit recommendation of the *Bradley Report* (1990)[34] and *The Report of the NSL Task-Force* (2003).[35] This shift has been indicated through research into Sydney FC's club membership.[36] Findings in this study indicate that the A-League has succeeded in attracting a young market, which identifies strongly with Sydney FC, despite the lack of club history. The quantitative nature of these findings provides an insight into the broader makeup of Sydney FC's membership base. However, further qualitative research is required to elicit the thoughts and feelings[37] of participants in order to develop understanding in this specific case.

Hallinan, Hughson and Burke provide a fascinating insight into fan perspectives on the A-League.[38] Fans interviewed purported that the A-League was far more professional than its predecessor. Furthermore, it was evident that fans believed the playing standard had improved due to an influx of quality foreign imports. However, Hallinan, Hughson and Burke invoke significant discussion regarding how the development of the A-League impacted upon a specific ethnically orientated football club. The comparative discussion, between the Melbourne Victory and the Springvale White Eagles addresses a vital aspect of the new milieu: namely, how the restructure of Australia's domestic football competition affected a specific ethnically based club. The findings of this study indicated that it was unlikely that ethnically based clubs would feature at the top-level of Australian football again. However, the role of ethnically orientated clubs in the suburbs and margins of Australia's cities has not abated. Football's role in the social fabric and networking of migrant communities demonstrably continued in the case of the Serbian football club Springvale White Eagles. There is a need for further research to explore this milieu in order to replicate, or contrast the findings of this study in a range of ethnic backgrounds and clubs.

## Framing the study

This study is structured in two primary sections as articulated in the introduction. The first area of this study concerns the extent to which fans of the A-League perceive it to represent a change either positive or negative from the NSL. Theoretically, this aspect of the study will be framed by the detailed histories, narratives and sociological studies that served to develop the social context of football in Australia.[39] It is from this clear basis of ethnic involvement that arguments regarding change post-2004 are founded within this study.

Secondly, the process of social identification, post-NSL, is explored to elicit what motivates fans to support the A-League. This aspect of the study is designed to address what factors members of Sydney FC deem salient in their decision to support an essentially 'new team'.[40] Moreover, following the changes to league structure and the removal of expressive ethnicity, why do individuals identify with a club? Literature on social identity posits that for an individual to attach to a group they must perceive or gain some 'emotional significance' from categorization.[41] Perspectives on the NSL purvey the view that the central process in social identification with football clubs was ethnicity and nationalistic celebration.[42] This theory is used to frame motivations of Sydney FC fans.

**Method**

This research employed a case study of A-League foundation club, Sydney FC: firstly, to explore how Australia's domestic football competition had changed; secondly, to examine what attracted Sydney FC members to join and support the club. The sample was drawn from club members of Sydney and is part of a broader doctoral study examining the development of social identity in Sydney FC's fan base.[43] This study employs a wholly qualitative methodology, designed to examine the thoughts and feelings of participants. The use of a qualitative method in this case exemplifies a desire to provide a deeper understanding of this social phenomena.[44] To investigate the research problems, 21 in-depth interviews were conducted with members of Sydney Football Club.

In-depth interviews were conducted following the conclusion of version one of the A-League. During version one of the A-League, the researcher attended every one of Sydney FC's home games to develop understanding of the home-ground environment and develop a level of cultural competency for the interview stage.[45] A pass provided by Sydney FC allowed access to all areas in the ground, which provided an opportunity for the researcher to move freely and explore all areas of the stadium on match day. This base understanding initiated a point of common ground from which each interview was initiated. Due to ethical constraints applied to the doctoral research process in this case, participant names are not provided. Instead, subjects were assigned a number from 1 to 21 to denote their views without divulging their personal identity. The findings of this research process are discussed in the following paragraphs.

**Findings and discussion**

The discussion is structured into two primary sections defined by the research questions posed in the introduction. Firstly, fan perspectives on changes since the restructure are presented; secondly, the process of social identification is discussed. The re-developed A-League demonstrated a clear attempt to align football with a more mainstream audience than was attracted by the NSL. This process of change relied on a clear departure being made from the perceived NSL culture of ethnic involvement. Research on the A-League to date suggests that it represents a marked shift from the NSL in Melbourne. Discussion addresses the application of these findings within Sydney FC's supporter base. Members of Sydney FC formed a dualist group in relation to the NSL. Firstly, the group that did not support the NSL, which provided a basis to explore the market the NSL didn't attract through an articulation of why non-NSL fans were put off supporting the previous national competition. Secondly, those that did support the NSL provided an outline of their experiences. These two groups provided an opportunity to explore some indicative differences between the NSL and the A-League.

**Non-NSL fans**

Research into Australian football has, as discussed previously, concentrated on ethnic communities and groups.[46] There has been little focus on groups that did not support the NSL and the underlying reasons for their abstention. As Bradley discussed, ethnically based clubs did not apply to broader areas and regions.[47] In this respect, many NSL clubs were exclusive to individuals outside of the cultural heritage of their team.[48] This notion was highlighted by subject 5, who espoused the following reasons for not supporting the NSL: 'I'm of Anglo-Saxon background, I guess that's something to do with it, I'm not Croatian or an ethnic group that I could feel affiliated with any [NSL] clubs and it was kind of, you were ostracized if you weren't part of those groups, so there was no team to support.' Fans that didn't follow the NSL often alluded to the negative aspects of the competition's ethnic ties during the interview process. These perspectives included two central issues with the presence of expressive ethnicity. First, as the comments of subject 5 allude to, ethnicity in some football clubs created distinct and powerful communities,[49] and as influential as these groups were in the development of cultural identity in migrant groups,[50] they made involvement for individuals outside of the cultural fabric of football clubs difficult.

Second, respondents alluded to issues of perceived safety in-ground. Subject 4 commented that, 'you'd go to games at Edensor Park [home of Sydney United] and you'd be frisked for knives ... you felt like an outsider, you felt excluded from it'. This comment underlined the reason that subject 4 reneged on supporting an NSL club and the issue of perceived safety at games was clear. Subject 3 commented on the safety and general atmosphere at NSL games, stating: 'I didn't think it was a great environment to have the kids in'. This perspective envelops the view that to some supporters the NSL appeared inaccessible and violent (after attendance). It is important to state, that at no time during the interview process did subjects allude to being physically threatened during attendance at games.

Both subjects 3 and 4 commented on the in-ground NSL atmosphere having attended games. However, as defined earlier, general perceptions of the NSL were largely impacted by negative media coverage, which created an image of ethnically based violence.[51] This point was highlighted by subject 15, who was put off watching the NSL due to 'the ethnic backgrounds and the violence you traditionally got'. It was illuminating that subject 15 had attended one NSL game in its duration, that being the grand final of its final season in 2004. The almost textbook perception of the NSL from a non-fan further supports Hughson's argument regarding the negative role of the media on Australian football. It was also evident from some Sydney FC members that they reneged on supporting the NSL purely through a lack of awareness, as subject 6, an Australian male, divulged: 'to be perfectly honest I just didn't know about it. I knew it was there but it wasn't sort of one of those things that was advertised greatly.' The comments regarding the media show that not only was there a media-developed perception of ethnic violence, but a lack of positive publicity and marketing to develop awareness of the NSL.

Attempts to develop clubs without ethnicity led to a proliferation of 'Australian' football clubs during the 1990s. These served an obvious purpose of providing 'Australians' with football clubs to support. Notable examples of these clubs in Sydney include Northern Spirit and Parramatta Power. Both attempted to engage a mainstream audience. Some fans that engaged in brief support of Northern Spirit in particular found the presence of ethnicity from other clubs to be a deterrent. For example, Subject 3 noted:

> We didn't stop supporting them [Northern Spirit], I stopped going to games because
> there was a lot of ethnic stuff going on, not so much with Northern Spirit, but we went

to see games with Sydney United, I think and others and there was lots of stuff like the kind of singing and things that went on.

The ideal of 'Australian' football clubs did at times develop notable interest in the NSL.[52] However, subject 3's allusion to the ongoing presence of ethnicity from rival clubs provides an insight into why supporter numbers in these clubs may have dropped off (with the exception of Perth Glory, which sustained supporter numbers).

Responses from individuals who hadn't supported the NSL consistently outlined the core weaknesses of the NSL from an outsider's perspective. Some viewed it as ethnically exclusive, whilst others merely articulated that they couldn't identify with the competition, choosing to pursue support of the Socceroos and European-based clubs instead. Perceptions of ethnically based violence were also evident, although drawn from a dualist perspective of those that had attended games in the NSL and those that had developed an idea of the league from media sources. To contrast and elaborate upon current understanding of the NSL, fans of the previous competition are addressed below.

**NSL fans**

Fans of the NSL in the sample group were drawn from a plethora of clubs includ-ing: APIA, Sydney Olympic, Northern Spirit, Hakoah/Sydney City, Marconi and Parramatta Power. Respondents who had followed the NSL closely provided inter-esting, if sometimes contrasting, reports regarding the milieu of the old competition. The process of ethnic affiliation and identification, as widely discussed,[53] was a clear theme of fan involvement in the NSL. Subject 18, a first generation Australian with Greek heritage, described the role of cultural affiliation in his support of Sydney Olympic: 'I was a supporter of Sydney Olympic. Again because of my background, being Greek, European background you usually identify back then with a group or a team that was from an ethnic base.' This was commonplace amongst supporters of the ethnically based clubs listed. However, the process of identifica-tion based on nationalism was also evident in so-called 'Australian' clubs. Fans of Northern Spirit in the sample group were drawn from predominantly Anglo-Saxon backgrounds. This group of fans used support of Northern Spirit to fill the football void that was created post-migration to the antipodes.

Perceptions of the NSL developed through long-term support of the competition varied between fans. Subject 12, an Australian with Spanish heritage, had been intro-duced to support of South Melbourne through Greek friends. As he stated: 'I was one of those rare ones who used to go to watch South Melbourne because I love the game, not because I was Greek.' Subject 12 represented an interesting case as he did not identify culturally with South Melbourne. His support was derived from a support of football in a broader sense. Despite supporting South Melbourne, subject 12 felt disconnected from the NSL: 'the whole thing that it was a very Greek club it turned me off, I didn't support the idea of the old league, I didn't like how the clubs were just for Greeks or just for Croatians'. This argument is based on the premise that football clubs, in subject 12's opinion, should appeal to broader populations. As subject 12 did not culturally identify with South Melbourne, his support of an ethnically based club was an anomaly in the respondent group.

For some NSL fans, ethnic exclusivity was a noticeable issue, which provided an interesting finding. While the ethnicity of most interview subjects made progression into NSL clubs straightforward, some experienced problems. For example, subject 18 found identifying with a different NSL club difficult after the relegation of APIA Leichhardt from the NSL. His cultural contraction[54] and affiliation to Southern Italy made identification with other NSL clubs difficult. The other Sydney-based Italian NSL club, Marconi Stallions, was identified with Northern Italian culture. As he stated: 'You couldn't go for Sydney United unless you were Croatian, you couldn't go for Sydney Olympic unless you were Greek and you couldn't really go for those teams because it was based on ethnic backgrounds.' That NSL fans experienced issues with clubs being exclusive is interesting. It also aligns closely with Hughson's research into the closeness and embedded Croatian nationality at Sydney United Football Club which, it was argued, created a less accessible support environment than a club such as Marconi.[55] Furthermore, the expressive nature of nationalism[56] in some football clubs conceivably created unwelcoming atmospheres, even for hardened fans of the competition.

Nationalistic expressionism was highlighted by non-fans of NSL when alluding to perceived fears regarding safety after attending NSL games. Fans of the NSL provided contrasting opinions on this topic. When asked if the perceived hooligan problem in Australian football was a media construction, subject 11 retorted:

> Well I don't think it was a media construction half of the time, I think it was a media construction 100% of the time because, well as I say, from 1959 (the NSL started in 1977) through to well to the last NSL grand final, I regularly attended games and over that period of um, well more than 40 years I can remember genuine violent incidents at about maybe 2 or 3 games.

Subject 11's comments provide an interesting insight into a long-term fan's experience, although his views were contrasted by subjects 7 and 9, who both alluded to violence associated with ethnic rivalries. Such experiences drove subject 7 to cease attendance at Sydney Olympic games following 'one of the nastier games where there was a riot essentially … it left a bit of a bad taste in the mouth so we stopped [going]'. Subject 9, an Australian born in Greece, attributed such incidents to the 'passion' ethnic groups had for soccer. Despite some fans alluding to the inflammatory media constructions in this group, there was also support for the notion that at times the NSL's inextricable ties with expressive ethnicity led to unfortunate in-ground incidents.

Perspectives provided by fans of the NSL articulated sometimes contrasting images of the competition; however, little information was provided to separate clubs from an ethnically derived environment. Furthermore, the majority of NSL fans would have continued to support the competition if change had not occurred. As subject 18 outlined, 'I didn't see that there was any problem with it. I was just enjoying the games. But of course now I look back on it and it could have been so much better.' Considering this perspective, the following section combines both groups in order to address the extent to which respondents perceive the A-League to represent a departure from the previous context.

### Bringing the two groups together – into the A-League

The *raison d'être* of the A-League was to 'unite the tribes' which had served to marginalize the NSL and draw football's supporter base into the mainstream.[57] In order to achieve this, the FFA needed to provide a league that appealed to both football's 'silent majority'[58] of non-NSL fans, and established fans of the previous domestic competition. To achieve this, a considerable departure and process of change from the previous league culture was undertaken following the recommendations of *The Report of the NSL Task-Force*. The respondent group highlighted three major differences between the NSL and the A-League.

Firstly, fans alluded to the level of professionalism visible in the A-League. As outlined earlier in the study, the FFA implemented an extension of the recommendations of the NSL Task-Force, developing a one-team-per-city model. Despite some bad press about the smallness of the competition, Sydney FC members generally viewed the step positively, as subject 7 stated: 'the one city mentality was a good thing and one of the main reasons we decided to get membership and we could really get behind it quite quickly'. The decision to include eight teams was a clear step to protect against the problems the NSL experienced with insolvency. Subject 18, who gravitated to support the A-League from NSL club Sydney Olympic stated: 'I really liked the idea that there was going to be one Sydney team that everybody could follow. Some people were sceptical about the fact that there was only going to be 8 teams, but I thought that was good. Let's get the 8 teams being quality sides first.'

The stringent business model devised by the FFA attempted to add a level of corporate stability and professionalism to the A-League not seen in the NSL. Hallinan, Hughson and Burke found that fans of Melbourne Victory perceived the A-League as more professional.[59] Respondents from Sydney FC articulated a similar perspective on the A-League, which marked a notable shift from the NSL. Subject 5 said of the NSL, 'It just didn't seem very well organised, unfortunately'. In contrast subject 18 stated 'the A League is just total professionalism, obviously its just starting and can go so much further, but I attend games with my dad and with my mate and absolutely everything is so much better [than the NSL]'. Themes including the development of league-wide merchandising (through Reebok), TV advertisements and general media exposure were all seen as significant positives. In essence fans seemed content with the progress of the year old competition: 'Yeah look I just like the whole set up, it's very professional. You go to the games and everything is in its place' (subject 17). Such comments provide support for the findings of Hallinan, Hughson and Burke regarding the professionalism of the A-League.[60] It also articulated a clear separation from the maladministration that plagued the NSL.

Secondly, the Sydney FC members interviewed regarded the A-League as being removed from football's socio-cultural ethnic ties. As subject 1 tersely stated of the difference between NSL and A-League 'there's less ethnic'. For some non-NSL fans, an accessible competition, without ethnic ties, was important. Subject 20, an Australian with Hungarian heritage, explained:

> For me Sydney FC was a new possibility, a new way of going forward, it was a non-ethnic concept. The whole concept of ethnicity has always been a real pain. I've always tried to support clubs that haven't had an ethnic background and Sydney FC fitted the bill. It holds so much promise for the future and for football in Australia.

In effect, by removing ethnicity completely (with the exception of Queensland Roar's Dutch linkages[61]), the FFA created an avenue for anyone to support A-League teams, therefore reforming the domestic league from ethnically based clubs to culturally pluralist organizations. Hallinan, Hughson and Burke found that Melbourne Victory represented a clear departure from previous ethnic cultures.[62] The findings of this study would concur. As subject 10 explained: 'Everybody goes along to Sydney FC "united". You get all backgrounds of people ... There are people from all ethnic backgrounds. I mean I sit with guys that are in their late 70s and 80s that are Hungarian and everybody seems to be supporting Sydney.' All respondents concurred that through their own experiences, Sydney FC was more inclusive than the NSL. In effect there were no cultural barriers to supporting the club, therefore providing a professional organization that provided an avenue for football enthusiasts to support the club.

Thirdly, a tentative argument was presented by respondents regarding the perceived nationality of Sydney FC fans. When looking to address motivations for supporting the A-League, these arguments become especially pertinent. Subject 9 stated:

> I think at the end of the day, a couple of things have come out of this. The so called ethnics who don't want to progress in the marketplace and follow Sydney FC have been lost and those 2,000 fans who follow Sydney Olympic or Sydney Croatia or whoever they are they've been lost. We don't care to be honest with you, because we've picked up another 10–20,000 of the mainstream public and those people consider themselves as Australians irrespective of what their cultural background is and that's the key situation here.

Subject 9 alluded to the issue of perceived nationality in his comments. Subjects in this study were drawn from across the globe, but there was one consistent theme. Each respondent identified themselves as Australian and supported the Socceroos, regardless of where they were born, or other cultural affiliation. This is by no means a suggestion that all Sydney's supporters identify as Australian, however, it provides an interesting finding from the interviews conducted. The construct of support for country is discussed further in the following paragraphs, although it seems there is a notable research opportunity in this area: namely, to assess whether there is some cultural theme to those that support the A-League versus those that maintain their support of ethnically based state league clubs. As Hallinan, Hughson and Burke found, Springvale White Eagles maintained a distinct social function within the Serbian community.[63] It would be truly interesting to examine whether this is the result of primary cultural identification, or whether support of these clubs serves an ulterior social function in the current milieu.

## Motivation to support

Through the previous two sections, it is clear that the A-League is perceived as being fundamentally different to the NSL by both old and new fans of Australia's domestic football league. In this section the discussion addresses which factors Sydney FC members deemed salient[64] or important in their decision to become fans of the club. Responses to the question, 'What attracted you to become a member of Sydney FC?' regardless of previous support indicated that the members interviewed shared similar motivations for joining the club. It is also notable that in this study there were distinct similarities between fans that had and had not supported the NSL. All fans were motivated to support Sydney FC through an initial interest in football. As subject 8, a naturalized Australian from the UK asserted, his interest in Sydney FC emerged 'on a level of just wanting to see some football'. This perspective was not uncommon. Furthermore it is understandable given that some Sydney

FC members had waited most of their lives for an Australian domestic football club that they could identify with, while NSL fans had endured an 18-month hiatus following the disbanding of the competition. Each fan interviewed supported the Socceroos (Australia's national football team) regardless of their cultural origins or affiliations.

Hay's assertion that Melbourne Victory's crowd was driven by the interest of the existing population underlies an interesting point.[65] Although not clarifying the specific aspect of 'interest', Hay's comments espoused that 'Australian' interest, not migration patterns, had categorized Melbourne Victory's support base. The importance of developing a competition with ethnically neutral, city-based clubs was a prominent factor in the diversification and engagement of Australia's 'existing population'. Research conducted by Lock, Taylor and Darcy outlined support of football as the salient motive in the attendance of Sydney FC's members.[66] The qualitative inquiry in this study provided some elaboration to complement these quantitatively derived findings. Results in this study suggest that the motivation 'support for football' was the most salient motive of the Sydney FC members interviewed. Sydney FC members identified their decision to become members of Sydney FC as a conscious move to support the success of football through the A-League. As subject 9 commented: 'Irrespective of who comes, we don't care whether you're Italian, Greek, Croatian, dinky di Aussie, Scottish, Jewish or Lebanese we're all Australians and we should be going there to support our team, in this case Sydney FC, to support the game of football.' This highlights that in essence Sydney FC is part of something larger, while also alluding to the theme of Australianness. Specifically, members saw support of Sydney FC as a vehicle to progress football in Australia. The reasons for progression included some fans wanting a domestic league that could rival or emulate European leagues. Subject 14, a naturalized Australian from the UK stated:

> Being a football fanatic, I want football to go forward and I think it's vitally important that I get behind it. Um, I was like on my membership I was like number 70. I was one of the first ones to get it and I just wanted it! I knew that this was it, the last chance to be what it is in Europe, where you can get 20–30,000 people at a game ... I just wanted to show my passion for football by getting behind it, supporting it.

There was a noticeable theme of 'investment' that emerged from interview responses. Comments alluding to 'getting behind it' and 'supporting the game of football' were frequent in the data. Subject 17 identified with what the FFA were trying to achieve: 'seeing what the FFA was trying to set up in Australia and I strongly believed in it and I wanted to support the game and I think it was very important for me being a soccer fan to actually get behind it and give it my full support'. This process of social identification with Sydney FC is far removed from the culture that permeated itself in the NSL.

In addition to supporting the success of football, subject 15 was more specific. While it was imperative to subject 15 that the A-League was successful, it represented a longer-term means to improve the national team. Subject 15 commented:

> The basic reason to get behind the A-League was that I was an Australian supporter, I went to all the Australian games and I thought that if you're going to support Australia you have to support it from the ground route ... We thought we wanted to be involved in the ground level and if Australia is going to progress in the world we have to have a strong national competition, so that's why we and some friends decided ok, we're going to become founding members.

This finding elaborated upon other statements regarding personal motivations to support; however, the general level of consensus linking the support group to the success of football in Australia was notable.

Although the broader applications of these finding require further testing, it seems apparent that fans are motivated in a different manner to support the A-League. National league football clubs are no longer institutions for the development of nationalistic identity, acculturation and status, in the way that ethnically based NSL clubs acted.[67] It appears that Sydney FC's members are motivated to support the club on the grounds of support for the game of football. This finding in fans of Sydney FC marks a notable shift in culture from the NSL.

## Conclusion

The findings of this study suggest that the A-League represents a noticeable shift in support culture in Sydney, when compared with the previous NSL milieu. Through providing insight into the NSL from a non-fan's perspective this study has attempted to provide some understanding of the 'silent majority' that fell outside of the prior league's attraction. Incorporating such arguments is useful in developing a clearer picture of why changes occurred to Australia's national football competition post-2003, and how this market was disenfranchised. The predominant difference between Sydney FC members that had supported the NSL, and those that had not, was cultural affiliation. Fans that were represented culturally by the NSL seemed to socially identify with it. Those that fell outside of the cultural affiliations of clubs, or felt threatened by them (in the case of Northern Spirit fans) were generally alienated from supporting the NSL. This argument highlights the fundamental issue with the ethnic heritage of the NSL. To many migrants, football clubs across Australia served a vital purpose in the acculturation, happiness and social wellbeing processes. From this perspective the arguments presented in the literature on football in Australia are noteworthy. However, to the football fans that fell outside of the cultural affiliation of NSL clubs, the previous culture developed a sometimes unwelcoming and inaccessible environment, which harmed the NSL's popularity.

The A-League appears to have developed an environment that caters for both fans of the NSL, who carried ethnic affiliations, and the 'silent majority' that felt disengaged from the previous competition. It has provided a place where football supporters – regardless of cultural heritage – are able to form in support of football. From this perspective it seems that in its infancy the A-League has been a success, engaging a trend of football support generated by 'the interest of its existing population'. However the degree to which the A-League engages mainstream Australian society is unclear. It seems from the findings of this study, and other studies conducted in Melbourne, that A-League fan bases are diverse and amorphously formed from city-wide populations. Engaging the ambiguous and elusive 'mainstream Australian' market will be an ongoing task for the FFA. However, it is notable that since the restructure the A-League is attracting 'football fans' regardless of their cultural orientation.

## Notes
1. Mosely, 'Soccer'.
2. Hughson, 'Australian Soccer'.

3. Bradley, *Australian Soccer Federation*.
4. M. Cockerill, 'Lowy Targets Young, Welcomes Old'. *Sydney Morning Herald*, August 9, 2005, 35.
5. Crawford, *Report of the Independent Soccer Review Committee*.
6. Kemeny, *Report of the NSL Task-Force*.
7. Ibid.
8. Adair and Vamplew, *Sport in Australian History*; Hay, 'British Football'; Mosely, 'A Social History of Soccer'; Mosely, *Ethnic Involvement in Australian Soccer*; Vamplew, 'Violence in Australian Soccer'.
9. Mosely, 'A Social History of Soccer'.
10. Hay, 'British Football'; Kallinikios, *Soccer Boom*; Mosely, 'A Social History of Soccer'; Mosely, *Ethnic Involvement in Australian Soccer*.
11. Hay, 'British Football'.
12. Hughson, 'The Croatian Community'.
13. Mosely, *Ethnic Involvement in Australian Soccer*, 21.
14. Ibid.
15. Hughson, 'The Croatian Community'.
16. Mosely, *Ethnic Involvement in Australian Soccer*.
17. Ibid., 21.
18. Hughson, 'Australian Soccer'.
19. Hughson, '"The Wogs Are at It Again"'.
20. P. Kent, 'Dress for Distress: Hooligans with Flare'. *Daily Telegraph*, April 20, 2005, 28.
21. Hughson, '"The Wogs Are at It Again"'.
22. Ibid.
23. Ibid., 53.
24. Hughson, 'Australian Soccer's "Ethnic" Tribes'; Mosely, *Ethnic Involvement in Australian Soccer*; Vamplew, 'Violence in Australian Soccer'.
25. Mosely, 'Soccer'.
26. Ibid.
27. Vamplew, 'Violence in Australian Soccer'.
28. B. Cubby, 'Tribes Unite to Kick Off a League of their Own'. *Sydney Morning Herald*, August 27, 2005, 7.
29. J. Huxley, 'Football's New Kick-start'. *Sydney Morning Herald*, August 26, 2006, 28.
30. Hay, 'Fan Culture in Australian Football'; Hay, '"Our Wicked Foreign Game"'.
31. Lock, Taylor and Darcy, *Sport Fan Identity*; Lock, Taylor and Darcy, 'Fan Identity Formation'.
32. Hallinan, Hughson and Burke, 'Supporting the "World Game" in Australia'.
33. Hay, 'Fan Culture in Australian Football', 101.
34. Bradley, *Australian Soccer Federation*.
35. Kemeny, *Report of the NSL Task-Force*.
36. Lock, Taylor and Darcy, 'Fan Identity Formation'.
37. Burns, *Introduction to Research Methods*.
38. Hallinan, Hughson and Burke, 'Supporting the "World Game" in Australia', 18–19.
39. Hay, 'British Football'; Hughson, 'A Feel for the Game'; Hughson, 'A Tale of Two Tribes'; Mosely, *Ethnic Involvement in Australian Soccer*; Vamplew, 'Violence in Australian Soccer'.
40. Tajfel and Turner, 'An Integrative Theory of Intergroup Conflict'.
41. Tajfel, 'Experiments in a Vacuum', 31.
42. Hughson, 'The Boys Are Back in Town'.
43. Lock, 'The Development of Social Identity'.
44. Silverman, *Doing Qualitative Research*.
45. Armstrong, *Football Hooligans*.
46. Hay, 'British Football'; Hughson, 'A Feel for the Game'; Mosely, *Ethnic Involvement in Australian Soccer*; Vamplew, 'Violence in Australian Soccer'.
47. Bradley, *Australian Soccer Federation*.
48. Hughson, 'The Croatian Community'.
49. Ibid.
50. Mosely, *Ethnic Involvement in Australian Soccer*.
51. Hughson, '"The Wogs Are at It Again"'.
52. Hughson, 'A Tale of Two Tribes'.

53. Hay, 'British Football'; Hughson, 'A Feel for the Game'; Hughson, 'The Croatian Community'; Vamplew, 'Violence in Australian Soccer'.
54. Giulianotti, 'Supporters, Followers, Fans, and Flaneurs'.
55. Hughson, 'The Croatian Community'.
56. Hughson, 'Australian Soccer's "Ethnic" Tribes'.
57. Cubby, Hughson and Burke, 'Tribes Unite to Kick Off a League of Their Own'.
58. Cockerill, 'Lowy Targets Young, Welcomes Old'.
59. Hallinan, Hughson and Burke, 'Supporting the "World Game" in Australia'.
60. Ibid.
61. Hay, '"Our Wicked Foreign Game"'
62. Hallinan, Hughson and Burke, 'Supporting the "World Game" in Australia'.
63. Ibid.
64. Tajfel and Turner, 'An Integrative Theory of Intergroup Conflict'.
65. Hay, 'Fan Culture in Australian Football'.
66. Lock, Taylor and Darcy, 'Fan Identity Formation'.
67. Mosely, *Ethnic Involvement in Australian Soccer*.

## References

Adair, D., and W. Vamplew. *Sport in Australian History*. Melbourne: Oxford University Press, 1997.

Armstrong, G. *Football Hooligans: Knowing the Score*. Oxford: Berg, 1998.

Bradley, G. *Australian Soccer Federation: Final Report*. Sydney: Australian Soccer Federation, 1990.

Burns, R. *Introduction to Research Methods*. London: Sage Publications, 2000.

Crawford, D. *Report of the Independent Soccer Review Committee: Into the Structure, Governance and Management of Soccer in Australia,* ed. Independent Soccer Review. Belconnen: Australian Sports Commission, April 2003.

Giulianotti, R. 'Supporters, Followers, Fans, and Flaneurs: A Taxonomy of Spectator Identities in Football'. *Journal of Sport and Social Issues* 26, no. 1 (2002): 25–46.

Hallinan, C.J. 'Supporting the "World Game" in Australia: A Case Study of Fandom at National and Club Level'. *Soccer & Society* 8, no. 2 (2007): 283–97.

Hay, R. 'British Football, Wogball or the World Game? Towards a Social History of Victorian Soccer'. *Australian Society for Sports History: Studies in Sports History* 10 (1994): 44–79.

Hay, R. 'Fan Culture in Australian Football (Soccer): From Ethnic to Mainstream?' In *Football Fever: Moving the Goalposts,* ed. M. Nicholson, B. Stewart, and R. Hess, 91–105. Sydney: Maribyrnong Press, 2006.

Hay, R. '"Our Wicked Foreign Game": Why has Association Football (Soccer) not become the Main Code of Football in Australia?' *Soccer and Society* 7, no. 2–3 (2006): 165–86.

Hughson, J. 'Australian Soccer: "Ethnic" or "Aussie"? The Search for an Image'. *Current Affairs Bulletin* 68, no. 10 (1992): 12–16.

Hughson, J. 'A Feel for the Game: An Ethnographic Study of Soccer Support and Social Identity'. PhD diss. UNSW, 1996.

Hughson, J. 'The Croatian Community'. In *Sporting Immigrants,* ed. P. Mosely, R. Cashman, J. O'Hara, and H. Weatherburn, 50–62. Sydney: Walla Walla Press, 1997.

Hughson, J. 'The Boys are Back in Town: Soccer Support and the Social Reproduction of Masculinity'. *Journal of Sport and Social Issues* 24, no. 1 (2000): 8–23.

Hughson, J. 'A Tale of Two Tribes: Expressive Fandom in Australian Soccer's A-League'. In *Football Culture: Local Contests, Global Visions,* ed. G. Finn, and R. Giulianotti, 10–30. London: Frank Cass, 2000.

Hughson, J. '"The Wogs are at it again': The Media Reportage of Australian Soccer "riots"'. *Football Studies* 4, no. 1 (2001): 40–55.

Hughson, J. 'Australian Soccer's "Ethnic" Tribes: A New Case for the Carnivalesque'. In *Fighting Fans: Football Hooliganism as a World Phenomenon,* ed. E. Dunning, P. Murphy, I. Waddington, and A.E. Astrinakis, 37–48. Dublin: University College of Dublin Press, 2002.

Kallinikios, J. *Soccer Boom: The Transformation of Victorian Soccer Culture 1945–1963*. Sydney: Walla Walla Press, 2007.

Kemeny, A. *Report of the NSL Task-Force: Into the Structure of a New National League Soccer Competition.* Sydney: Australian Soccer Association, 2003.

Lock, D. 'The Development of Social Identity in Fans of a New Sports Team: Sydney FC, a Case Study'. Sydney: University of Technology, unpublished Ph.D. thesis.

Lock, D., T. Taylor, and S. Darcy. 'Sport Fan Identity and The New Kid on the Block'. In *European Academy of Sports Management.* Cyprus, 2006.

Lock, D. 'Fan Identity Formation in a New Football Club and a Revamped League: The A-League'. *Sport Marketing Europe,* no. 1 (2007): 30–5.

Mosely, P. 'A Social History of Soccer in New South Wales 1880–1957'. PhD diss. University of Sydney, 1987.

Mosely, P. *Ethnic Involvement in Australian Soccer: A History 1950–1990,* ed. Australian Sports Commission. Canberra: Applied Sports Research Program and National Sports Research Centre (Australia): National Sports Research Centre, 1995.

Mosely, P. 'Soccer'. In *Sporting Immigrants: Sport and Ethnicity in Australia,* ed. P. Mosely, R. Cashman, J. O'Hara, and H. Weatherburn, 155–73. Sydney: Walla Walla Press, 1997.

Silverman, D. *Doing Qualitative Research: A Practical Handbook.* London: Sage Publications, 2000.

Tajfel, H. 'Experiments in a Vacuum'. In *The Context of Social Psychology; a Critical Assessment,* ed. J. Israel, and H. Tajfel, 33–47. London: published in cooperation with the European Association of Experimental Psychology by Academic Press, 1972.

Tajfel, H., and J. Turner. 'An Integrative Theory of Intergroup Conflict'. In *The Social Psychology of Intergroup Relations,* ed. W. Austin, and S. Worchel. Monterey, CA: Brooks/Cole Publishing, 1979.

Vamplew, W. 'Violence in Australian Soccer: The Ethnic Contribution'. *ASSH Studies in Sports History* 10 (1994): 1–15.

# 'Fencing them in': the A-League, policing and the dilemma of public order

Ian Warren and Roy Hay

*School of History Heritage and Society, Deakin University, Victoria, Australia*

## Disorder and (r)evolution in Australian soccer

The desire for maintaining public order, safety and the development of appropriate, workable policing guidelines to manage soccer crowds in Australia and internationally has encouraged much research into the interactions between police and sports fans in recent decades. However, uncertainty remains over the fundamental causes of crowd misbehaviour, the types of behaviour warranting police intervention, and the ideal roles of police, in-house or contracted security personnel, venue managers and other relevant stakeholders in ensuring optimum crowd management. While soccer is by no means the only sport open to public scrutiny in Australia for its crowd disorder and dangerous patron behaviour,[1] the unprecedented popularity of the world game since the formation of the elite national Hyundai A-League competition in 2005 makes it highly necessary to develop a more sophisticated and reflective understanding of the dynamics of spectator behaviour at elite and sub-elite levels. It is also vital for senior police to develop clear and agreed public order protocols in collaboration with local governments, national and state soccer authorities, clubs, venue managers, in-house and contracted security personnel, and the fans themselves.

Much available international research and popular discussion of soccer 'hooliganism' focuses on the violent, disrespectful and innately disorderly tendencies of young male football supporters which compromise public safety. Consequently, definitions of hooligan behaviour can be extremely broad and fluid, ranging from the possession of offensive weapons to the direct use of violence against opposition fans, police or security personnel. According to a recent study by Frosdick and Newton,[2] available British statistics on reported incidents of football hooliganism suggest most unlawful activities do not involve overt acts of violence or assaults, but do involve dangerous, threatening and risky activities such as the possession of weapons or the discharge of missiles (usually bottles) within the venue environment. A hooligan incident is likely to occur at one match in 20 or two of the 46 senior matches held in England per week. These findings come after the 'hooligan problem' was supposed to have been solved by the introduction of specific, far-reaching and punitive anti-hooligan legislation, the introduction of all-seater stadia, substantial price and membership increases, and the widespread use of Closed Circuit Television surveillance systems. Since the introduction of these initiatives, most people accept that much hooligan behaviour has been displaced from English football venues, with up to 50% of incidents recorded by Frosdick and Newton occurring on the way to or from football venues. However, these results cannot be generalized to other countries.

Despite wide variances in the classification of hooligan incidents by official agencies, available Australian and international statistical data provides limited evidence to suggest soccer is characterized by the kinds of systematic violence which leads to widespread harm to other patrons or property in and around the venue environment. The systemic and institutionalized violence that characterized English soccer between the 1970s and early 1990s has now ceased and has never characterized Australian soccer. The English experience was the product of a series of highly negative, public and politicized interactions between organized cohorts of male football fans and the authorities, which saw the progressive escalation and institutionalization of violence in and around football venues over time.[3] However, popular understandings of the causes of this phenomenon, which place sole responsibility for the violence on the innately violent tendencies of soccer fans, continue to generate public fears and a 'moral panic' which equates soccer fandom with hooliganism. Nevertheless, most offences detected and officially processed by police at soccer and other major sports events do not have an organized or violent component, and generally involve public drunkenness, offensive language, the discharge of missiles and minor property offences.[4]

Soccer in Australia has been characterized as a sport plagued by spectator hooliganism, partly due to overseas experience and partly because of its post-war development as a popular spectator sport. Yet levels of disorder at elite or sub-elite levels are probably similar to or lower than those experienced at other Australian sports such as cricket, Australian Rules football, the rugby codes or auto racing. Soccer in Australia is tarnished partially by the sport's international reputation as a site for organized violent disorder, much of which stems from the 'hooligan disease' characterizing English football between the 1970s and mid-1990s,[5] and partially by its attraction to Southern European migrants as the primary sport of choice since the post-Second World War immigration boom.[6] The occurrence of a few sporadic and highly localized conflicts between rival Greek and Macedonian, or Serb and Croatian, football fans has generated a popular misconception that 'un-Australian' ethnic conflicts go hand-in-hand with soccer fandom. However, while some incidents might be attributable to long-standing and at times highly provocative ethnic rivalries,[7] much available research suggests pre-existing social, political or cultural tensions between rival ethnic groups generally have little direct relationship to the support of soccer or any other major participatory sport in Australia.[8] Despite the importance of other causal variables, ethnic conflict and the innate pathologies of soccer fans who engage in low level violence or public disorder remain embedded in popular discourse as the dominant explanations for why the behaviour of soccer supporters is different from, and more dangerous than, that of those who follow other sports.

A recent report by an Independent Soccer Inquiry into an incident in the New South Wales Premier League, a level below the elite national A-League competition, between fans of the Sydney United Football Club (SUFC), a team with predominantly Croatian support, and the Bonnyrigg White Eagles Sports Club (BWESC), comprising mainly Serb fans, highlights the problems associated with narrow cause and effect explanations of violence associated with ethnicity, individual pathology and soccer. Most supporting these clubs are the children and grandchildren of Croatian and Serbian migrants who settled in Australia during the post-Second World War immigration boom. Fears of ethnic rivalries were understandable, and press reports indicated the first match between these two clubs in 22 years warranted classification by police and League authorities as a 'high-risk fixture'. These concerns were realized when:

> The riots erupted about 3pm (AEDT), shortly before the start of the NSW Premier League match at the stadium in Edensor Park. Flares and other projectiles were thrown at the height of the incident and two police officers were injured while trying to calm the estimated 50 fans involved in the violence. Five people were arrested and were expected to be charged with a number of offences including assault[ing] police and affray, a police spokeswoman said.[9]

The Board of Directors of the sport's governing body in New South Wales (Soccer NSW) promptly launched an independent investigation into the incident which was released a month later. The first of the Inquiry's Terms of Reference directed the Panel to '[i]nvestigate and establish the cause of the crowd disturbance, with reference to any contributing political, cultural or social factors'.[10] Not surprisingly, the report found that long-standing racial tensions were the dominant causes of the violence which ensued.

> It is clear from the unsworn evidence placed before the Panel of Inquiry that the violent incidents were primarily caused by historic hostilities between SUFC supporters, predominantly of Croatian background, and BWESC supporters, largely of Serbian background. These rivalries are due to historical enmities and to some extent tensions dating back to the Second World War and revived by the recent wars and massacres in the Balkans. It is therefore of concern to the Inquiry that such enmity finds expression through soccer in Australia in 2005.[11]

Several recommendations were made by the Panel, including the imposition of 'punitive sanctions' against both clubs, and the possible expulsion of Sydney United from Soccer NSW if they became involved in any similar incidents in future. More broadly, the Panel recommended more sweeping legislative reforms to be applied to all sports, based on English legislation which criminalized football hooliganism in 1991 and 2000. The new laws would sit alongside tighter bans and enforcement procedures targeting violence and the display of inflammatory national or political flags, to be implemented by Soccer NSW at all venues, and with legislation to introduce enhanced police search and confiscation powers in and around sports venues, along with mandatory 12-month exclusion orders and potential lifetime bans for patrons found guilty of any of the following 'hooligan type behaviour':

- Drink related offences
- Disorderly behaviour
- Threatening behaviour
- Affray
- Violent disorder
- Assault
- Throwing missiles
- Breach of the peace
- Running on the pitch
- Racial/indecent chanting
- Drug offences
- Possession of weapon
- Criminal damage
- Indecent behaviour.[12]

Ironically, the report not only ignores the concerns of many scholars about the problems associated with enforcing these laws in and around English soccer venues,[13] but also downplays significant failures during the pre-event planning phase involving representatives from Soccer NSW, the clubs involved, a sub-contracted security firm working at the venue and the Local Area Commander of Police. Such findings contribute to, and perpetuate, false public perceptions of the roots of disorder within soccer venues, while creating misleading expectations about what are desirable, sustainable and effective crowd management procedures to be adopted at 'high-risk fixtures'. For those involved in violent activity, ethnic identity is more likely a convenient 'trigger-point' or excuse to legitimate a pre-existing willingness to engage in public disorder. But analysts must not gloss over the underlying motivations for violent activity including social identity,[14] youth, masculinity,[15] or even the desire to have some fun.[16] More importantly, by prioritizing the causes of violence at the scene of the event and developing punitive sanctions aimed at punishing detected offenders and deterring future instances of the same behaviour, official reports such as this relegate more meaningful notions of situational harm minimization, inter-agency communication and risk prevention central to safe event management, to the periphery.

The formation of the fully-professional Hyundai A-League competition in 2005 has significantly challenged the commonly accepted link between minority ethnic affiliation and Australian soccer fandom. The immense popularity of A-League as a spectator sport rivalling many of the more established Australian professional codes requires the prevention of disorderly conduct and associated harm in large closed venues. The scale of the A-League's popularity as a sports spectacle is unprecedented in Australia's soccer history, with average attendances at A-League games during the 2006–07 season of 12,166, which rivals crowds in the South Korean K-League, USA Major League Soccer, the Scottish Premier League and the Argentinian Premier League.[17] As Hay and McDonald point out, many fixtures during the same season involving the Melbourne Victory, which plays most home games at a 55,000 seater venue with a retractable roof designed mainly for Australian Rules football, exceeded 30,000 spectators.[18] Commensurate with this scale is the ethnic and social diversity of the new generation of A-League supporters. Research into support patterns at Melbourne Victory matches suggests the A-League fan base may be similar to that of any elite-level Australian Rules or Rugby League club.[19] A multi-ethnic support base now characterizes most Australian sport as migration patterns have shifted along with the behavioural norms and social identities of the second and third generation children of the original Southern European settlers. When disorder does occur, it is most likely to remain confined to sporadic conflicts at the sub-elite level where ethnic identity works in tandem with other situational dynamics fuelling interpersonal conflict.[20] This means conventional explanations linking ethnicity, Australian soccer and violence are overplayed in the popular imagination, and are misleading for their tendency to overlook the complexity of the evolving fan demographic, the emergence of discrete supporter groups or the intricate norms and rituals of soccer fandom.[21]

The rapidity of this shift at elite level Australian soccer has presented numerous challenges for police and allied agencies to ensure good order is maintained in soccer venues. There have been some instances of disorder reported at A-League venues which warrant particular attention. Three men were arrested and a further 15 patrons were evicted at a sell-out match between Adelaide United and Melbourne Victory at Hindmarsh Stadium in Adelaide in December 2006 after rival fans 'threw bottles at each other and players' and 'there were several fights and general disorderly behaviour issues including the throwing of flares during the match'.[22] Several flares were discharged during the 2006–07 A-League Grand Final between Melbourne Victory and Adelaide United, which the Victory won 6-0, despite strict warnings and heavy fines which apply in and around Melbourne's Telstra Dome venue.[23] In November 2007 '(p)olice used capsicum spray to control fans in wild clashes' between Melbourne Victory and Sydney FC fans at Telstra Dome. Eight people were evicted during the 0-0 draw, one was arrested for possessing a flare, and police maintained a cordon between a city bar and the venue to separate rival supporters.[24] Similar incidents have also been reported at friendly games between A-League and sub-elite teams during the off-season.[25] While these incidents warrant further empirical research into the emerging dynamics of Australian soccer support, there is also a parallel concern as to how police and other relevant stakeholders in the sport's administration can develop and enforce appropriate codes of patron conduct within an emerging crime prevention framework without eroding positive norms of fan expression which promote a carnival atmosphere at elite-level fixtures.

## The context of Australian policing

Different sporting events attract and produce extremely distinct crowd dynamics and cultures of fandom, and there have been several detailed studies into the role of police in maintaining good order in a diverse range of event settings.[26] Such work combines observations of crowd and policing dynamics, brief interviews with patrons when violence is actually occurring, extended interviews with police managers and operational personnel and observations of, or direct participation in, pre-event crowd management planning, post-event de-briefings and evaluation procedures. The findings are relatively consistent regardless of the jurisdictional focus, the theoretical foundations of the study, or the nature of the event and the environment in which it is held. Working within a social identity framework, the following quote from Stott and Hoggett aptly summarizes the dilemmas facing police and spectators in the management of collective disorder:

> where police used coercive force (e.g. baton charges) against those in the crowd who saw themselves as posing very little, if any, threat to public order there would be corresponding increases in the number of people in the crowd who perceived the police as an

illegitimate force. Such experiences among crowd members would then lead to a change in the crowd's social identity (their shared sense of 'us' and 'them') along two critically important dimensions. On the one hand, increasing numbers of people within the crowd would see conflict against the police as acceptable. On the other, it would create a redefined sense of unity in the crowd against the police that subsequently empowered those seeking confrontation. In other words, the development of widespread rioting was not simply a product of the presence of violent groups. Rather it *emerged* as the outcome of particular patterns of group interactions that occurred during the events themselves.[27]

Effective risk management at any event involves understanding patterns of group interaction and undertaking 'continuous threat assessments' to accurately target and deploy operational personnel when problems emerge. This means police must be sensitive in developing tactical measures which accommodate the 'lawful behaviours and intentions' of soccer fans, founded on 'positive interpersonal interaction' and the 'pro-active' identification of problem incidents within a 'community policing' framework. Such a framework emphasizes intelligence-based evidence gathering, low-key conflict management when incidents do occur,[28] and a strong knowledge of the dynamics of behaviour built on an informed understanding of the culture of the event. The ultimate challenge for police relates to how these tactics are developed, operationalized and administered in light of the specific event dynamics. In this respect, it is generally agreed that a multi-agency approach involving meaningful contributions from, and the development of sustained partnerships with, football authorities, local governments, venue managers, security personnel, club administrators and fan groups is crucial to the policing role at both the pre-event planning and operational stages.[29]

As a product of Australia's federal structure, each state jurisdiction has a separate criminal law, policing agency and law enforcement culture. This means each agency's organizational structure and operational practices are distinct, and trends in how risk management principles are developed, implemented and sustained are subject to variation. In addition the planning and operational imperatives vary for each event, as do its administration, the character of security networks and associated harm prevention arrangements. Nevertheless, Australian police services have already incorporated many of the procedures identified by Stott and Hoggett as part of their general law enforcement mandate. Three broad, interrelated, yet at times conflicting, trends have emerged in crime prevention discourse in Australian policing since the mid-1990s and provide the managerial and operational framework for its implementation in both elite and sub-elite soccer.

First, all Australian police services face increased internal and external demands to develop systematic, informed and evidence-based methods to target and reduce different forms of crime. Historically, much conventional policing activity involved reactive investigations into crimes after their commission and bringing offenders to justice through the criminal courts. However, public anxiety over crimes of violence, large scale crimes such as terrorism and the impact of minor street crimes and vagrancy in certain communities has pressured public police forces to coordinate a range of crime prevention initiatives founded on knowledge-based problem-solving principles.[30]

Crime prevention works in tandem with community policing. As a consequence, police must develop strategic and knowledge-driven approaches in identifying problems of concern in their communities, prioritizing these issues in light of the level of community concern, the harm the behaviour is generating, and available policing resources, and develop targeted responses, often with the assistance of a range of government, non-government and citizen groups.[31] Crime prevention strategies must therefore be 'context specific' and adaptable to meet the ongoing and changing demands arising from a particular community or crime problem.[32] In addition, the focus on crime prevention leads to heightened reciprocal cooperation between police and their communities through principles of 'responsibilisation'.[33] This encourages individuals or groups within a community to take a more proactive role in looking after their own interests, either by informing the police of their concerns about crime and wrongdoing in order to enhance police intelligence and knowledge-building, or by engaging in legitimate 'self-help' activities which minimize the enforcement burden facing police when crime occurs. Simple situational crime prevention measures involve the installation of locks or alarms to protect private property, but more elaborate measures could involve the employment of private security guards to patrol crime-prone regions. The overall aim of responsibilisation is to develop appropriate targeted preventative responses which simultaneously educate the community about crime, empower the community by delineating various low level crime control functions, while providing police with an informed knowledge-base upon which to generate and coordinate proactive initiatives commensurate with their formal enforcement expertise.[34]

Secondly, the knowledge-based foundations of crime prevention and community policing have infiltrated the internal management of police organizations. The demands of the new managerialism in Australian policing mean senior police need to be more cognizant of the importance of business principles in allocating resources, identifying and managing risks to operational members and the community more generally, and accounting for the costs of policing functions as well as the conduct of operational personnel throughout the internal hierarchical chain.[35] This is particularly crucial in large scale or complex operations such as mass demonstrations, which have the tendency to divert resources from routine community duties, while simultaneously raising public concerns and potential civil claims over police malpractice where force is deployed.[36] The realistic prospect that routine police conduct may trigger collective disorder in disadvantaged or hostile communities[37] is also crucial in driving police managers towards a new 'integrity-based' internal accountability framework which is preventative in focus, resource efficient and sensitive to community needs.[38] Therefore, external and internal factors work in tandem to produce a more accountable and responsive policing service, driven by more sophisticated managerial priorities at the top of the hierarchical chain, which ideally filter through the various levels of the organization and in turn into the public domain by way of responsive, resource efficient, ethical and accountable operational practices.

The third influence on contemporary policing stems logically from each of the previous developments and provides the means for senior police to reconfigure and implement their mandate within a preventative, community-based and resource-sensitive paradigm. Effective crime prevention and resource allocation require increased levels of inter-agency cooperation to accurately identify clear risk priorities and sustainable preventative responses. This means police must routinely work alongside other relevant stakeholders and develop ongoing, meaningful and sustainable relationships with a range of agencies which otherwise might appear to have little do to with issues of crime and its prevention. This process accepts that police do not possess a monopoly over the control and prevention of crime in contemporary society, but play a crucial role in raising community awareness of the limits of police responsibility over crime and promoting clear role identification and tasking amongst disparate government and non-government agencies.[39] This *brokerage* role[40] situates the public police at the centre of a hub of otherwise disparate individuals and agencies, to promote inter-agency communication, collaboration, knowledge-sharing and sustainable relationship building. Through this process the targets, methods, procedures and responsibilities for crime prevention can be delineated and shared through an informed and evolving knowledge-base.

While this form of nodal or networked governance is considered an important means of empowering communities affected by crime,[41] this collaborative inter-agency blueprint presents many new challenges for senior and operational police. For instance, there is no clear or consistent instruction manual on how to establish and maintain ongoing dialogues about crime and its control in diverse settings or amongst agencies and individuals with conflicting mandates or views. Viable communication under this framework is incremental and knowledge-driven. Operationalizing nodal governance requires patience, time and the development of agreed, consensual crime prevention options. In addition, the line between consensual and responsive relationship building and imposing a desired outcome is a very thin one. The recent history of policing and nodal governance in Australia highlights this as the core problem in making inter-agency cooperation a truly collaborative endeavour. According to Cherney,[42] the decision of the Victoria Police to develop a rival inter-agency programme when the state government-mandated *Safer Cities and Shires* partnership model did not conform to a preferred policing agenda, highlights how police may be unwilling to contribute meaningfully to the development of genuine, receptive and sustainable community-based links. The net result of this example allowed the police to revert to a more comfortable methodology which enabled them to steer or impose their views in setting regional crime control agendas, rather than act as a filter and conduit for inter-agency relationship-building, knowledge-gathering and problem-solving. Finally, the challenges of dealing with community development issues which underpin much crime and disorder are often proved to be beyond the scope of many community crime prevention strategies, which tend to generate quick fix solutions to overt, small-scale problems.[43] This raises the philosophical question of whether policing as a concept is equipped to deal with the root causes of crime which are generally the purview of other government, social welfare or charitable organizations.

Such problems are certainly no surprise given the largely autonomous history and reactive nature of many policing functions. Invariably, police managers are learning their inter-agency crime prevention craft as they proceed. At one level, this craft is predicated on the need for strong coordination which is sensitive to, and invokes, a complex web of internal and external community demands. At another level, the cultures of policing have always experienced difficulty grappling with the competing tensions associated with notions of authority and compassion which are embedded in the policing role.[44] For Chan,[45] the diverse array of external structural conditions which shape the environments in which police must interact, which are often very difficult to comprehend or control, have a very real tendency to reinforce an inward, non-reflective, self-justifying and self-marginalizing culture which distances them from their communities. As Stott and his associates have long pointed out,[46] these are the very conditions which necessitate the adoption of consensual, knowledge-based community policing principles, especially given the enormous damage which can ensue to soccer fans and innocent bystanders when disorder occurs, is managed badly and its dynamic and fluid characteristics are poorly understood, misinterpreted, or countered thorough rigid and confrontational tactics.

**The challenges of policing Australian soccer**

The major challenges facing police in the current environment of Australian soccer and are indicative of the different concerns over fan behaviour and changing support patterns which are emerging at each level of the sport. However, despite the qualitative differences in the levels and nature of support characterizing soccer at elite and sub-elite levels, the imperative to adopt a collaborative approach to the prevention of disorder and maintenance of patron safety involves a similar process of inter-agency collaboration. Police play a key role in coordinating this process given their mandate to act in the public interest to prevent and investigate crime when it does occur. However, as the foregoing clearly indicates, any efforts to implement a viable crime prevention blueprint must be adaptable and responsive to the different dynamics of support at each level of the game, while creating the opportunity for a diverse number of stakeholders with first-hand experience of terrace culture to play an active role not only in building the knowledge upon which public order can be maintained, but also in directly facilitating order maintenance in and around soccer venues on match days.

The rapid growth in support for the Hyundai A-League has surprised football authorities, other sporting codes and police.[47] Australia does have several other national sporting codes, but the ebb-and-flow of popular support, the rules and rituals observable on match days, the inter-club rivalries and intra-club factions and the internal and external politics and identities promoted by the sport are very distinctive. For those who have been born and bred with exposure to Australia's dominant football codes, developing a true appreciation of each of these dynamics is extremely challenging. Each of these issues warrants further empirical examination in their own right in light of Australia's robust sports culture.[48] However, such knowledge can also help with other facets of A-League development. For example, the maintenance of public order is crucial in marketing elite soccer in Australia as a desirable sporting choice for patrons who have previously had no direct exposure to the world game. Therefore, the rapidly growing interest in A-League soccer provides a unique opportunity to develop a series of knowledge-based research collaborations given the sport's high level of mass appeal, the desire to sustain this appeal within a competitive sporting market place and the obvious need to develop and maintain strategic and collaborative approaches to public order maintenance.

Most reported instances of disorder in Australian soccer are relatively minor in nature and do not involve systematic or institutionalized forms of violence prevalent in many overseas jurisdictions in recent times. The focus on ethnic conflict as the primary cause of disturbances in sub-elite soccer should not be allowed to obscure the emerging dynamic of soccer support at elite level, nor should the focus simply be on the violent tendencies of football hooligans. Tightening of criminal laws and associated penalties across the board may be counterproductive for all agencies charged with order maintenance in and around sports venues, as it does little to modify or improve the nature of pre-event planning, problem identification and collaborative, targeted crime prevention initiatives which are crucial in developing and implementing appropriate order maintenance strategies. This form of policy transfer is widely criticized in criminological literature as ill-founded and ineffective in dealing with the localized dynamics of crime and disorder.[49] Ultimately, the 'blame-game', which is a common feature of media reportage on football hooliganism[50] and filters into official public discourse and inquiries into soccer disorder, shifts the focus of responsibility away from those in the best position to implement meaningful preventative relationships, while planting the seeds of resentment amongst patrons affected by tighter restrictions on their conduct and those involved in operational order maintenance functions at future events.[51]

The fusion of discourses surrounding the causes of disorder at sub-elite and elite levels is of particular concern. The popular image of soccer in Australia is invariably tarnished by its history and developments which have emerged overseas. While there is some evidence to suggest fan culture amongst certain A-League clubs is mimicking patterns of sub-cultural support in European soccer,[52] more research is required to understand the similarities and distinctions between support trends in different cultures given the unique dynamics emerging in the Australian context. In addition, analogies between sub-elite and elite support trends are misleading and potentially counterproductive. This is particularly so given the changing dynamic of soccer patronage at sub-elite level, where the explanatory power of traditional ethnic rivalries has less weight as older generations of supporters die out and new generations of Australians take their place.[53] Other causal variables such as youth and masculinity do have some relevance in understanding the causes of disorderly behaviour when it emerges. However, the development of meaningful preventative relationships, which recognizes that fan behaviour is only part of the public order equation and is contingent on the social context of the crowd management function particular to each event setting, is crucial.

The Report of the Independent Panel of Inquiry identified several limitations in the order maintenance functions despite the extent of pre-event planning for this 'high-risk fixture'. Both clubs were clearly aware of concerns expressed by police and administrators of Soccer NSW surrounding pre-match venue security and were instructed to help with the implementation of the following initiatives:

- Spectators of the competing clubs will not be segregated, due to lack of facilities in the Northern end of the ground.
- Security supervision of the Sydney United Sports Centre will take place twenty-four hours prior to the match kick-off.
- Security will carry out searches and bag searches at the main gate prior to spectator entry with the assistance of metal detectors.
- The sale and consumption of alcohol will be confined to the two designated areas. Alcohol is not to be consumed at random all around the ground. SUFC officials are to supervise these alcohol areas.
- No signs, banners or flags will be permitted into the ground. Any found inside the facility are to be removed from the ground.[54]

Despite these measures the disorder leading to the Inquiry ensued and the formal investigation into its causes focused exclusively on expanded criminal law powers aimed at stamping out hooliganism from football venues. Most regrettably, the breakdown of the extensive network of pre-event planning arrangements is given little attention in the Inquiry or its recommendations, at the expense of a tighter legal regime which has little evidence to support effectiveness in reducing disorder in the United Kingdom since its introduction.[55] If this approach to articulating the causes of disorder is translated into other soccer environments, regardless of whether or how effective such measures might seem, the misplaced focus could have highly damaging effects on the game, its supporters and those entrusted with law enforcement and order maintenance functions.

Comparisons between A-League fan behaviours and those evident in sub-elite soccer, other Australian football codes, or in light of global trends in football support must therefore be done cautiously and should be sensitive to gaining appropriate knowledge of the variations in fan dynamics and the environmental settings of each event. The same dilemma applies to the importation of policing and crowd management trends which might have a bearing on the law enforcement function. As the literature on public order policing demonstrates, preventing crowd disorder is contingent on adapting policing techniques to accommodate each distinct environment, and the development of appropriate knowledge of event dynamics through a continuous dialogue with relevant stakeholders. Even though standards of good practice in community crime prevention might have some level of general applicability across different environments, at the immediate level what is proven to work in one setting may be counterproductive or inappropriate in another.[56] The very nature of nodal governance is designed to accommodate different types of problem solving relationships to deal with different classes of crime in different environmental settings. While unified philosophies might drive these initiatives behind the scenes, their successful operationalization in any given community or crime prevention context is subject to immense variation and warrants more credence in formal investigations when disorder occurs to hone their effectiveness within a crime prevention rubric.

For police to fully embrace a collaborative, knowledge-based function, an important starting point might be to accept that certain elements of soccer fan culture cannot be fully understood or controlled in the desired way without producing some collateral damage, at least in the short term. It is better for police to understand what they can control and to exercise these functions well, while building the appropriate knowledge of fan culture over time, rather than grappling with the unfamiliarity of an emerging and intricate culture from the outset using the wrong foundations, languages, methodologies or processes. By recognizing that certain cultural forces cannot be fully understood, and therefore governed, controlled or disciplined within one's own frame of reference, a culture of 'accommodation' can be developed which, over time, can lead to the required mutual understanding, acceptance and trust between parties with divergent interests or ways of viewing the world. This is an incremental process which is essential to informed and agreed knowledge building. Over time, as relationships strengthen, languages become shared between the parties, raising the prospect of more concrete, sustainable and effective preventative arrangements. This does not necessarily mean disorder in the sports environment will be completely eliminated. Rather, each agency will have clearer role delineation in line with the public interest as coordinated and overseen by senior police driving the networked order maintenance agenda from the centre. In turn, as new problems, causal explanations or stakeholders emerge into the framework, the relationships driven by police need to be flexible to accommodate these changes.

Organizations which are crucial in this process at elite-level include the sport's national governing body, the Football Federation Australia, the clubs in each region, local governments, venue managers, in-house and sub-contracted security managers, local councils where venues are located and, importantly, fan groups. At sub-elite level state and local league administrators fill the place of the national governing body, but other relevant stakeholders remain largely the same. The differences rest mainly with the different concerns, bodies of knowledge and collaborative responses which much be driven by the immediate context of each event. The role of each of these organizations is to provide guidance on their respective concerns, capacities and roles in assisting with the development and implementation of collaborative harm prevention strategies. This in turn clarifies the optimum roles of managerial and operational police, based on their respective mandates and obligations within and beyond the venue environment. In addition, each stakeholder has an important role in gathering information relevant to ongoing risk assessment and profiling for law enforcement purposes, which in turn assists police in developing knowledge-based and targeted responses to overt criminal behaviour where it is identified as being a major issue of concern amongst stakeholder groups.

It is conceivable that each organization might have a conflicting view as to the actual and optimum role of police in and around the football venue, or how such roles should be operationalized in any given case. In addition, if certain order maintenance or prevention functions are delegated to other agencies such as clubs or security personnel, it is important for police to exercise appropriate oversight to facilitate compliance amongst each agency throughout the pre-event planning phase and during the event itself. However, the track record of Australian police in developing proactive crime prevention relationships with the private sector at major events is patchy. Research conducted at the Melbourne Cricket Ground in the early 1990s identified the need for meaningful collaborative partnerships to enhance public safety at major sporting events as a priority area, particularly given the rapid emergence of in-house and contracted security in these environments.[57] A more recent study has reinforced these concerns,[58] indicating the promotion of meaningful inter-agency cooperation across a larger number of agencies is an ongoing problem not confined to routine sporting events[59] and requires a more proactive brokerage, role-delineation and oversight function to be coordinated by senior police. This role is being conducted successfully at some major sporting events. For example, security personnel working at the Melbourne Cricket Ground are regularly audited and assessed for their capacity to quell disorderly incidents at 'pressure-point' locations within the venue. Efforts by police to coordinate enforcement strategies at the Sydney Football Stadium receive praise from fans for their inclusive and collaborative approach. The Victoria Police also conducted a large public forum in May 2007 examining the causes of public disorder, drawing on the expertise of various local and interstate panel members from the academic, youth and enforcement sectors. Such initiatives are part of an emerging commitment by senior police to take their brokerage function seriously and harness the existing expertise, networks and capacities of a diverse range of stakeholders to build a more sophisticated knowledge-base on certain problems of concern to the community more generally.

Interestingly, while the Independent Panel of Inquiry identified several security breaches which contributed to the disorder,[60] most of which were attributed to the lax security arrangements adopted by the Sydney United Football Club, the final report was largely silent on how police can encourage other agencies to comply with clear harm prevention directives either before or during the event. A detailed reading of the report indicates senior police involved with the event's management did little to directly oversee or promote compliance by other stakeholders in the 24 hours leading to the event. This confers a great deal of trust in the capacity and willingness of other bodies to fulfil their assigned tasks in the desired manner, ultimately to the detriment of good order in this particular case. Regardless of the potential causes of this lack of oversight, it would seem desirable for senior police to delegate such a function to an appropriate operational member, rather than simply being a reactive presence at the event after the trouble has emerged. This would ensure any roles involving other agencies which are delegated or brokered in the pre-event planning process would be enforced with direct oversight, thereby conforming to the appropriate preventative standards. This also indicates that the police brokerage function extends beyond the identification and coordination of appropriate functions by senior managers, but filters throughout the organization by involving operational personnel in meaningful oversight and coordination functions commensurate with their expertise in the event environment. This is also a profound redefinition of conventional operational policing functions, but is crucial in ensuring increasingly complex interagency harm prevention arrangements are implemented in practice, while providing a further avenue for knowledge-gathering and transfer from within the organization to further enhance the senior management coordination role.

This process differs little from the inter-agency coordination approach adopted in other Australian and international settings as a 'best-practice' crime prevention blueprint. This blueprint is designed to develop sustainable, informed and participatory relationships between diverse stakeholders, which are sensitive to their specific concerns in the environment in question.[61] Arguably, the most difficult group to engage within this planning framework are the fans themselves. Available research into Australian soccer support indicates the A-League is revolutionizing the conventional view of soccer fandom in Australia.[62] This is where police might have to rely on secondary networks involving clubs or willing supporter groups to develop the short-term knowledge of behaviours soccer patrons believe to be of concern in and around event venues and appropriate measures of meeting these concerns to accommodate rather than marginalize certain supporter factions. The recent incidents of disorder at A-League fixtures are relatively minor, but are also problematic for all stakeholders interested in the welfare of the world game in Australia. Police may already be marginalized amongst some supporter groups aggrieved at the use of capsicum spray in closed venues, as the You Tube postings of the routine 'ripping' of flares in and around the Telstradome venue in defiance of clear directives to the contrary attests. It might be more feasible for senior police to realign their focus with other youth agencies with a direct mandate in public order maintenance[63] and thereby concede that their task in harnessing the direct trust, mutual respect and meaningful involvement of certain supporter groups requires more ongoing development. Indeed, Australian police have often had difficulty understanding and dealing with the behaviour of young people in a range of environments[64] and the emerging tendency for large-scale alcohol-fuelled disorder,[65] 'swarming',[66] and sustained rioting in disadvantaged suburbs directly targeting the police[67] ideally warrants the development of independent nodes of police knowledge-building through which a more detailed understanding of the dynamics of certain forms of soccer support can be forged.

These challenges facing Australian police are by no means insurmountable. What is required is an understanding of the evolving nature of the police brokerage function and a commitment to realigning conventional managerial and operational priorities in ways which place the notion of knowledge-based crime prevention at the forefront. When disorder does emerge, however minor it might be, rather than focusing on the problems of fan behaviour, the emphasis should be more inward and reflective, pinpointing elements of the brokerage function which require further modification and adapting the roles and responsibilities of each stakeholder accordingly. What remains clear is that the level of interagency cooperation and knowledge building also extends to conducting further and ongoing research into the various dimensions of fan culture at Australian soccer at both elite and sub-elite levels, independently of the nature, frequency or severity of disorder reported in these environments. By drawing together the expertise of a range of disparate agencies, through a variety of governance nodes, police will be well-situated to meet the challenges of their evolving role in what has conventionally been considered a hostile public order environment.

## Notes

1. In January 2007 the Melbourne print media devoted extensive coverage to a 'riot' between Serbian and Croatian fans at the annual Australian Open tennis tournament. The incident sparked comparisons with soccer fans given the ethnic affiliations of those involved: see J. Halloran, 'Why Tennis? There Was No Soccer On'. *Sydney Morning Herald*, January 16, 2007. http://www.smh.com.au/news/tennis/why-tennis-there-was-no-soccer-on/2007/01/15/1168709679361.html?page=fullpage#contentSwap1; H. Lloyd-McDonald, and M. Schulz, 'Race Row Rocks Open'. *Herald Sun*, January 15, 2007. http://www.news.com.au/heraldsun/story/0,21985,21060876-661,00.html; Australian Associated Press (AAP), 'Police Underestimated Tennis Risk: Nixon'. *The Age*, January 23, 2007. http://www.theage.com.au/news/national/police-underestimated-tennis-risk-nixon/2007/01/23/1169518693498.html. The following month attempts to ban the Mexican Wave, a common ritual at Australian one-day cricket fixtures, proved unsuccessful even though police and event organizers held legitimate concerns regarding the dangers of fans throwing projectiles: see Australian Associated Press (AAP), 'Mexican Wavers Ejected from MCG'. *The Age*, February 5, 2007. http://www.theage.com.au/news/national/mexican-wavers-ejected-from-mcg/2007/02/05/1170523986508.html; D. Buttler, 'MCG Hit By Waves of Protest'. *Herald Sun*, February 5, 2007. http://www.news.com.au/heraldsun/story/0,21985,21170834-661,00.html. At the time of writing a second incident at the Australian Open Tennis was widely reported in the Australian media. A police officer was forced to publicly defend his decision to use capsicum spray against a group of Greek tennis fans allegedly led by a 'serial pest' who had previously been banned from attending Victorian State League soccer matches for 10 years by the South Melbourne Soccer Club. See 'Policeman Defends Australian Open Spray'. *Herald Sun*, January 17, 2008. http://www.news.com.au/heraldsun/story/0,21985,23064340-661,00.html; B. Doherty, J. Medew, and A. Petrie, 'Greek Fans Threaten Legal Action Over Spray'. *The Age*, January 17, 2008. http://www.theage.com.au/news/national/greek-fans-threaten-legal-action-over-spray/2008/01/16/1200419885255.html.
2. Frosdick and Newton, 'The Nature and Extent of Football Hooliganism'.
3. See generally Warren, *Football, Crowds and Cultures*.
4. Trivizaz, 'Offences and Offenders'; Warren, *Football, Crowds and Cultures*, 48–50 and 87–94.
5. Taylor, *The Hillsborough Stadium Disaster*.
6. Hay, 'Croatia'; Hay, '"Those Bloody Croatians"'; Hay, '"Our Wicked Foreign Game"'; Warren, 'Soccer Subcultures in Australia'.
7. Independent Soccer Inquiry NSW, *Report of the Independent Panel of Inquiry*, 14.
8. Hughson, 'The Boys in Blue'; Poynting, 'Bulldog Whistling'.
9. Australian Associated Press (AAP), 'Five Arrested After Riot at Sydney Soccer Match'. *Sydney Morning Herald*, March 13, 2005. http://www.smh.com.au/news/National/Five-arrested-after-riot-at-Sydney-soccer-match/2005/03/13/1110649053161.html. See also Independent Soccer Inquiry NSW, *Report of the Independent Panel of Inquiry*, 10–12.
10. Independent Soccer Inquiry NSW, *Report of the Independent Panel of Inquiry*, 7.
11. Ibid., 14.
12. Ibid., 29.
13. Greenfield and Osborn, 'After the Act?'; Greenfield and Osborn, 'When the Writ Hits the Fan'; Warren, *Football, Crowds and Cultures*, Chapters 4 and 8.
14. Stott, Hutchison and Drury, '"Hooligans" Abroad?'.
15. Connell, *Masculinities*.
16. Katz, *Seductions of Crime*.
17. Hay and McDonald, '"A Victory for the Fans?"', 307.
18. Ibid., 312.
19. Hay, 'Fan Culture in Australian Football'; Hay and McDonald, '"A Victory for the Fans?"'; Hallinan, Hughson and Burke, 'Supporting the World Game in Australia'.

20. Hallinan, Hughson and Burke, 'Supporting the World Game in Australia'.
21. Hay, 'Fan Culture in Australian Football'; Hay and McDonald, '"A Victory for the Fans?"'; Hay and Warren, 'Who supports Melbourne Victory?'.
22. D. Nankervis, 'Violence Mars Soccer'. *Adelaide Now*, December 3, 2006. http://www. news.com.au/adelaidenow/story/0,22606,20860637-2682,00.html.
23. Video footage of flares being discharged during and after this match can be found on You Tube. See 'Melbourne Victory supporters rip flare after the Grand final'. *You Tube* at http:// /www.youtube.com/watch?v=3BOHe4otFZA; 'Melbourne victory fans @ spenser st before A league final'. *You Tube* at http://www.youtube.com/watch?v=MdbphEC7Rwc& feature=related.
24. 'Cops Spray Melbourne Victory Soccer Fans'. *Sunday Herald Sun*, November 11, 2007. http://www.news.com.au/heraldsun/story/0,21985,22739174-2862,00.html; J. Massoud, T. Smithies and P. Desira, 'Soccer Chiefs Vow to Clean Up Violence'. *Herald Sun*, November 13, 2007. http://www.news.com.au/heraldsun/story/0,21985,22749470-2883,00.html; M. Draper, 'Capsicum Spray Used on A-League Fans', November 11, 2007. *News.com.au* at http://www.news. au/story/0,23599,22739024-29277,00.html.
25. 'Victory Match Marred by Crowd Violence'. *ABC News*, June 21, 2007. http:// www.abc.net.au/news/stories/2007/06/21/1957447.htm.
26. See generally Cunneen *et al.*, *Dynamics of Collective Conflict*; Warren, *Football, Crowds and Cultures*, Chaps 1 and 2.
27. Stott and Hoggett, *An Analysis of the Policing of Domestic Football*, 3–4, emphasis in original, references omitted.
28. Ibid., 1–2.
29. Ibid., 2. This point was examined in Independent Soccer Inquiry NSW, *Report of the Independent Panel of Inquiry*, but the recommendations focused primarily on the adoption of zero tolerance strategies directly aimed at creating expanded law enforcement powers and more punitive sanctions against errant soccer fans.
30. Cherney, 'Problem Solving for Crime Prevention'; Shaftoe, *Crime Prevention*.
31. Homel, 'The Whole of Government Approach'.
32. Cherney, 'Problem Solving for Crime Prevention'; Lee and Herborn, 'The Role of Place Management'.
33. Palmer and Whelan, 'Policing in the "Communal Spaces"'.
34. Ratcliffe, 'Intelligence-led Policing'.
35. Etter and Palmer, *Police Leadership in Australasia*.
36. Ombudsman, *Investigation of Police Action*; M. Harvey, P. Anderson and M. Buttler, 'Pollies Praise Police'. *Herald Sun*, November 20, 2006. http://www.news.com.au/herald-sun/story/0,21985,20786398-5010461,00.html; M. Buttler, 'Police G20 Riot Probe'. *Herald Sun*, January 30, 2007. http://www.news.com.au/heraldsun/story/0,21985,21139026-661,00.html; B. Doherty, J. Medew and A. Petrie, 'Greek Fans Threaten Legal Action Over Spray'. *The Age*, January 17, 2008. http://www.theage.com.au/news/national/greek-fans-threaten-legal-action-over-spray/2008/01/16/1200419885255.html.
37. Findlay, 'Globalisation and Urban Crime'; Lee, 'Public Dissent and Governmental Neglect'; Owen, 'Moral Indignation'; Weatherburn, 'Riots, Policing and Social Disadvantage'.
38. Goldsmith, 'The Pursuit of Police Integrity'.
39. Walters, 'Cops and Consultation'.
40. de Lint, 'Keeping Open Windows'; Ericson and Haggerty, *Policing the Risk Society*.
41. Shearing and Wood, 'Nodal Governance'.
42. Cherney, 'Crime Prevention/Community Safety Partnerships'.
43. Lane and Henry, 'Beyond Symptoms'.
44. Coady *et al.*, *Violence and Police Culture*.
45. Chan, *Changing Police Culture*.
46. Stott and Reicher, 'Crowd Action as Intergroup Process'; Stott, Hutchison and Drury, '"Hooligans" Abroad?'; Stott, 'Police Expectations'; Reicher *et al.*, 'An Integrated Approach to Crowd Psychology'; Stott and Hoggett, *An Analysis of the Policing of Domestic Football*.
47. 'Transcript: Melbourne Victory in the A-League grand final this weekend'. *Stateline Victoria*, February 16, 2007. http://www.abc.net.au/stateline/vic/content/2006/s1849901.htm.
48. Hay and McDonald, '"A Victory for the Fans?"'; Hay and Warren, 'Who supports Melbourne Victory?'; Hallinan, Hughson and Burke, 'Supporting the World Game in Australia'.

49. Newburn and Jones 'Symbolising Crime Control'.
50. Poulton, '"Fantasy Football Hooliganism"'.
51. Cunneen *et al.*, *Dynamics of Collective Conflict*; Warren, *Football, Crowds and Cultures*; Greenfield and Osborn, 'When the Writ Hits the Fan'; Stott and Hoggett, *An Analysis of the Policing of Domestic Football*; Stott, 'Police Expectations'.
52. Hay, 'Fan Culture in Australian Football'; Hay and Warren, 'Who supports Melbourne Victory?'.
53. Hallinan, Hughson and Burke, 'Supporting the World Game in Australia'; Hay, 'Croatia'; Hay, '"Those Bloody Croatians"'.
54. Independent Soccer Inquiry NSW, *Report of the Independent Panel of Inquiry*, 9.
55. Stott and Hoggett, *An Analysis of the Policing of Domestic Football*. This report indicates, despite tighter and more far-reaching police powers, that the values underpinning how they are enforced are more viable measures of their effectiveness.
56. Commonwealth Attorney-General's Department, *The National Research Project*; Stott and Hoggett, *An Analysis of the Policing of Domestic Football*.
57. Warren, *Football, Crowds and Cultures*; Warren, 'Patron Cultures, Policing and Security'.
58. Whelan, *The Restructuring of Policing*.
59. Australian National Audit Office (ANAO), *Commonwealth Agencies' Security Preparations*; Warren, *Football, Crowds and Cultures*, 157–60.
60. Independent Soccer Inquiry NSW, *Report of the Independent Panel of Inquiry*, 17.
61. Commonwealth Attorney-General's Department, *The National Research Project*.
62. Hay and McDonald, '"A Victory for the Fans?"'; Hay and Warren, 'Who supports Melbourne Victory?'; Hallinan, Hughson and Burke, 'Supporting the World Game in Australia'.
63. Youth Affairs Council of Victoria (YACVic), *YACVic's Response*.
64. White and Alder, *The Police and Young People*.
65. Australian Associated Press (AAP), 'Police Pelted with Bottles at Wild Party'. *The Age*, January 13, 2008. http://www.theage.com.au/studys/2008/01/13/1200159256384.html. This study is one of many in recent years where police have been directly attacked by under-age party-goers after complaints filed by members of the community annoyed at their behaviour. In this particular incident the police air wing and dog squad were commissioned to quell the behaviour of up to 500 teenagers who attended a house party organized while the host's parents were interstate.
66. White, 'Swarming'.
67. Findlay, 'Globalisation and Urban Crime'; Lee, 'Public Dissent and Governmental Neglect'; Owen, 'Moral Indignation'; Weatherburn, 'Riots, Policing and Social Disadvantage'.

## References

Australian National Audit Office (ANAO). *Commonwealth Agencies' Security Preparations for the Sydney 2000 Olympic Games: Performance Audit.* Canberra: Commonwealth of Australia, 1998.
Chan, J. *Changing Police Culture: Policing in a Multicultural Society.* Cambridge: Cambridge University Press, 1997.
Cherney, A. 'Crime Prevention/Community Safety Partnerships in Action: Victorian Experience'. *Current Issues in Criminal Justice* 15, no. 3 (2004): 237–52.
Cherney, A. 'Problem Solving for Crime Prevention'. *Trends and Issues in Crime and Criminal Justice* (Australian Institute of Criminology), 314 (2006).
Coady, A., S. James, S. Miller, and S. O'Keefe, eds. *Violence and Police Culture.* Melbourne: Melbourne University Press, 2000.
Commonwealth Attorney-General's Department. *The National Research Project into Good Practice in Community Crime Prevention.* Barton, ACT: Commonwealth Attorney-General's Department, 2003.
Connell, R.W. *Masculinities.* St Leonards, NSW: Allen and Unwin, 1995.
Cunneen, C., M. Findlay, M. Lynch, and V. Tupper. *Dynamics of Collective Conflict: Riots at the Bathurst 'Bike Races.* Sydney: Law Book Company, 1989.
de Lint, W. 'Keeping Open Windows. Police as Access Brokers'. *British Journal of Criminology* 43, no. 2 (2003): 379–97.

Ericson, R.V., and K.D. Haggerty. *Policing the Risk Society.* Toronto: University of Toronto Press, 1997.

Etter, B., and M. Palmer, eds. *Police Leadership in Australasia.* Leichhardt, NSW: Federation Press, 1995.

Findlay, M. 'Globalisation and Urban Crime: Mean Streets or Lost Suburbs'. *Current Issues in Criminal Justice* 17, no. 2 (2005): 291–304.

Frosdick, S., and R. Newton. 'The Nature and Extent of Football Hooliganism in England and Wales'. *Soccer and Society* 7, no. 4 (2006): 403–22.

Goldsmith, A. 'The Pursuit of Police Integrity: Leadership and Governance Dimensions'. *Current Issues in Criminal Justice* 13, no. 2 (2001): 185–202.

Greenfield, S., and G. Osborn. 'After the Act? The (Re)construction and Regulation of Football Fandom'. *Journal of Civil Liberties* 1, no. 1 (1996): 7–28.

Greenfield, S. 'When the Writ Hits the Fan: Panic Law and Football Fandom'. In *Fanatics! Power, Identity and Fandom in Football,* ed. Adam Brown, 235–49. London: Routledge, 1998.

Hallinan, C., J. Hughson, and M. Burke. 'Supporting the World Game in Australia: A Case Study of Fandom at National and Club Level'. *Soccer and Society* 8, no. 2 (2007): 283–97.

Hay, R. 'Croatia: Community, Conflict and Culture: The Role of Soccer Clubs in Migrant Identity'. *Journal of Immigrants and Minorities* 17, no. 1 (1998): 49–66.

Hay, R. '"Those Bloody Croatians": Croatian Soccer Teams, Ethnicity and Violence in Australia, 1950–1999'. In *Fear and Loathing in World Football,* ed. Gary Armstrong and Richard Giulianotti, 77–90. Oxford: Berg, 2001.

Hay, R. '"Our Wicked Foreign Game": Why Has Association Football (Soccer) Not Become the Main Code of Football in Australia?' *Soccer and Society* 7, no. 2/3 (2006): 165–86.

Hay, R. 'Fan Culture in Australian Football (Soccer): From Ethnic to Mainstream?' In *Football Fever: Moving the Goalposts,* ed. Matthew Nicholson, Bob Stewart and Rob Hess. Melbourne: Maribyrnong Press, 2006.

Hay, R., and H. McDonald. '"A Victory for the Fans?" Melbourne's New Football Club in Historical Perspective'. *Soccer and Society* 8, no. 2/3 (2007): 298–315.

Hay, R., and I. Warren. 'Who Supports Melbourne Victory? A Preliminary Inquiry into Crowd Make-up and Dynamics in the New A-League'. In *Behind the Play: Football in Australia,* ed. Peter Burke and June Senyard, 239–60. Melbourne: Maribyrnong Press, 2008 (forthcoming).

Homel, P. 'The Whole of Government Approach to Crime Prevention'. *Trends and Issues in Crime and Criminal Justice* (Australian Institute of Criminology), 287 (2004).

Hughson, J. 'The Boys in Blue and the Bad Blue Boys: A Case Study of Interactive Relations Between the Police and Ethnic Youth in Western Sydney'. *Australian Journal of Social Issues* 34, no. 2 (1999): 167–82.

Independent Soccer Inquiry NSW. *Report of the Independent Panel of Inquiry into the Crowd Disturbances at the Sydney United Sports Centre on Sunday 13 March 2005.* Sydney: Independent Soccer Inquiry, 2005.

Katz, J. *Seductions of Crime: Moral and Sensual Attractions in Doing Evil.* New York: Basic Books, 1988.

Lane, M., and K. Henry. 'Beyond Symptoms: Crime Prevention and Community Development'. *Australian Journal of Social Issues* 39, no. 1 (2004): 201–13.

Laycock, G. 'Research for Police: Who Needs It?'. *Trends and Issues in Crime and Criminal Justice* (Australian Institute of Criminology), 211 (2001).

Lee, M. 'Public Dissent and Governmental Neglect: Isolating and Excluding Macquarie Fields'. *Current Issues in Criminal Justice* 18, no. 1 (2006): 32–50.

Lee, M., and P. Herborn. 'The Role of Place Management in Crime Prevention: Some Reflections on Governmentality and Government Strategies'. *Current Issues in Criminal Justice* 15, no. 1 (2003): 26–39.

Newburn, T., and T. Jones. 'Symbolising Crime Control: Reflections on Zero Tolerance'. *Theoretical Criminology* 11, no. 2 (2007): 221–44.

Owen, J.R. 'Moral Indignation, Criminality, and the Rioting Crowd in Macquarie Fields'. *Current Issues in Criminal Justice* 18, no. 1 (2006): 5–19.

Palmer, D., and C. Whelan. 'Policing in the "Communal Spaces" of Major Event Venues'. *Police Practice and Research* 8, no. 5 (2007): 401–14.

Poulton, E. '"Fantasy Football Hooliganism" in Popular Media'. *Media, Culture and Society* 29, no. 1 (2006): 151–64.

Poynting, S., 'Bulldog Whistling: Criminalization of Young Lebanese-Australian Rugby League Fans'. *Internet Journal of Criminology* (2005). www.internetjournalofcriminology.com.

Ratcliffe, J.H. 'Intelligence-led Policing'. *Trends and Issues in Crime and Criminal Justice* (Australian Institute of Criminology), 248 (2003).

Reicher, S., C. Stott, P. Cronin, and O. Adang. 'An Integrated Approach to Crowd Psychology and Public Order Policing'. *Policing: An International Journal of Police Strategies and Management* 27, no. 4 (2004): 558–72.

Shaftoe, H. *Crime Prevention, Facts, Fallacies and the Future.* London: Palgrave Macmillan, 2004.

Shearing, C., and J. Wood. 'Nodal Governance, Democracy, and the New "Denizens"'. *Journal of Law and Society* 20, no. 3 (2003): 400–19.

Stott, C. 'Police Expectations and the Control of English Soccer Fans at "Euro 2000"'. *Policing: An International Journal of Police Strategies and Management* 26, no. 4 (2003): 640–55.

Stott, C., and J. Hoggett. *An Analysis of the Policing of Domestic Football in England and Wales: Operational Practice and Crowd Dynamics.* Liverpool: Henri Tajfel Laboratory, School of Psychology, University of Liverpool (2006). www.liv.ac.uk/psychology/staff/CStott/PolicingFootballPhaseOneReport.pdf.

Stott, C., and S. Reicher. 'Crowd Action as Intergroup Process: Introducing the Police Perspective'. *European Journal of Social Psychology* 28, no. 4 (1998): 509–29.

Stott, C., P. Hutchison, and P. Drury. '"Hooligans" Abroad? Inter-group Dynamics, Social Identity and Participation in Collective "Disorder" at the 1998 World Cup Finals'. *British Journal of Social Psychology* 40, no. 3 (2001): 359–84.

The Ombudsman (Victoria). *Investigation of Police Action at the World Economic Forum Demonstrations, September 2000.* Melbourne: The Ombudsman (Victoria), 2001.

Taylor, L.J. *The Hillsborough Stadium Disaster, Final Report.* London: Home Office, 1990.

Trivizas, E. 'Offences and Offenders in Football Crowd Disorders' *British Journal of Criminology* 20, no. 3 (1980): 276–88.

Walters, M. 'Cops and Consultation: Police Accountability and Community Teams in New South Wales'. *Alternative Law Journal* 30, no. 3 (2005): 112–15, 148.

Warren, I. 'Soccer Subcultures in Australia'. In *Ethnic Minority Youth in Australia: Challenges and Myths,* ed. Carmel Guerra and Rob White, 121–31. Hobart: National Clearinghouse for Youth Studies, 1995.

Warren, I. 'Patron Cultures, Policing and Security: Trends from Two Australian Sports Sites'. *Security Journal* 10, no. 2/3 (1998): 111–19.

Warren, I. *Football, Crowds and Cultures: Comparing English and Australian Law and Enforcement Trends.* Campbelltown, NSW: ASSH Studies in Sports History No. 13, 2003.

Weatherburn, D. 'Riots, Policing and Social Disadvantage: Learning from the Riots in Macquarie Fields and Redfern'. *Current Issues in Criminal Justice* 18, no. 1 (2006): 20–31.

Whelan, C. 'The Restructuring of Policing: The Public-Private Interface at major Event Venues in Victoria? A Research Thesis'. BA diss., Deakin University, Waurn Ponds, Victoria, 2004.

White, R. 'Swarming and the Social Dynamics of Group Violence'. *Trends and Issues in Crime and Criminal Justice* (Australian Institute of Criminology), 326 (2006).

White, R., and C. Alder, eds. *The Police and Young People in Australia.* Melbourne: Cambridge University Press, 1994.

Youth Affairs Council of Victoria (YACVic). *YACVic's Response: 'A Good Night For All' Options For Improving Safety and Amenity in Inner City Entertainment Precincts.* Melbourne: YACVic, 2005.

# INDEX

References to end notes are indicated by 'n.' plus note number, e.g. 37 n.1

For Product Safety Concerns and Information please contact our EU
representative  GPSR@taylorandfrancis.com
Taylor & Francis Verlag GmbH, Kaufingerstraße 24, 80331 München, Germany

www.ingramcontent.com/pod-product-compliance
Lightning Source LLC
Chambersburg PA
CBHW081435270326
41932CB00019B/3218

9 781138 880580